FORMATTING & SUBMITTING YOUR Manuscript

edition 2

Cynthia Laufenberg

and the editors of Writer's Digest Books

WRITER'S DIGEST BOOKS
CINCINNATI, OHIO
www.writersdigest.com

ABOUT THE AUTHOR

Cynthia Laufenberg is a writer and editor living in Narberth, Pennsylvania. She is former managing editor of *Writer's Digest Books* and has contributed articles to *Writer's Market, Novel & Short Story Writer's Market,* and *Songwriter's Market.* She has also written for *HealthyPet* and *Vitality Digest* magazines.

Formatting & Submitting Your Manuscript 2nd Edition. Copyright © 2004 by Writer's Digest Books. Manufactured in the United States of America. All rights reserved. No part of this book may be reproduced in any form or by any electronic or mechanical means including information storage and retrieval systems without permission in writing from the publisher, except by a reviewer, who may quote brief passages in a review. Published by Writer's Digest Books, an imprint of F + -W Publications, Inc., 4700 East Galbraith Road, Cincinnati, Ohio 45236. (800) 289-0963. Second edition.

Visit our Web site at www.writersdigest.com for information on more resources for writers.

To receive a free weekly e-mail newsletter delivering tips and updates about writing and about Writer's Digest products, register directly at our Web site at http://writersdigest.com.

10   09   08   07   06   6   5   4   3   2

Library of Congress Cataloging-in-Publication Data
Formatting & submitting your manuscript / by Cynthia Laufenberg and the editors of Writer's Digest
  Books.—2nd ed.
    p.   cm.
  Includes index.
  ISBN-13: 978-1-58297-290-9 (pbk.: alk. paper)
  ISBN-10: 1-58297-290-7 (pbk.: alk. paper)
    1. Manuscript preparation (Authorship). 2. Authorship—Marketing. I. Laufenberg, Cynthia.
PN160.N44   2004
808'.02—dc22   2004040697
                                              CIP

Edited by Michelle Ruberg
Designed by Sandy Conopeotis Kent
Cover designed by Beckmeyer Design

Introduction

Welcome to the second edition of *Formatting and Submitting Your Manuscript*! Everything in this book has been updated, with new chapters added for children's writing, specific fiction genres (mystery, romance, horror, science fiction), and personal essays as well as expanded information on submitting your work electronically. We've also included more samples of good (and bad!) submissions to not only show you how it's done right but also to illustrate the common mistakes that many writers make when submitting their work so you can avoid making those same mistakes, too.

Why is proper formatting so important when sending a submission? It's the content that counts, right? Well, yes, the content is the most important thing—a perfect presentation won't help sell inferior material. But proper formatting helps you to distinguish yourself as a professional and get your point across clearly. Beyond that, perfect margins and ideal spacing won't prevail over dull, poorly written work in the mind of an editor. On the other hand, editors have been known to forgive a few formatting glitches when a great story or concept shines clearly through the clutter.

So what is the point of this book, you might ask?

This book is simply a tool to keep you from sweating the details. With a complete set of manuscript formats in hand, you can confidently set about the real work of writing without having to worry if your header is in the right place or your indentation is correct. You shouldn't let formatting worries stand in the way of creativity, or let sloppy formatting stand in the way of great work. Beginning writers, especially, often get caught in a trap—either letting the minutiae of manuscript formats bog down and frustrate their creativity, or throwing all caution to the wind and submitting work so poorly organized that editor's can't follow it or summarily reject it. Each mistake is the mark of an amateur.

Beyond the mechanics of page formatting, this book also takes you through the finer points of how to structure your submissions, from query letters to books and screenplays. This information is more important than the look of a page because it addresses the fundamental issues of how your work is organized. The organization has a tremendous impact on whether your work captures the attention of readers, starting with the most important one—the editor.

Keep in mind that the examples presented here are only models and are not set in stone. They are meant only as starting points that give you the confidence to go forward with your own projects. You will find, over time, variations that work better for you and your editor. You will also find that different editors and applications require variations. There are a few guidelines, however, that *are* set in stone: Always address your submission to a specific editor. Don't misspell the editor's name. Don't misspell the name of the publication. And don't submit via e-mail unless specifically requested by an editor or if a publication's guidelines state that it is acceptable.

Ultimately, do what works for you. Don't mangle your work in order to fit it into some set format you find in a book. Especially avoid trying to copy the style of the examples you see here. Besides disliking poorly organized, sloppy submissions, most editors also grow tired of formulaic writing once they've encountered the same formula dozens of times. You'll find that editors value freshness, creativity, and insight above slavish adherence to a formula. Even in highly formulaic genres, your ability to bring a fresh approach within the confines of the grenre is highly prized.

At the end of the book we've included some forms meant to help you organize your work and your submissions. Look at these as suggested solutions, not burdensome mandates. These are only offered to make your life easier. Depending on your computer setup, these forms may not even be useful to you. By no means feel that you have somehow violated some tenet of an imaginary writer's code if you don't religiously use these forms. Do what works best to keep you organized.

In the increasingly competitive world of publishing, professionalism counts. If you present your work in a professional manner, you present yourself as a professional as well. Use this book to help guide your work into the hands of those who can get it published. We wish you the best of luck!

NONFICTION

CHAPTER ONE

ARTICLES

What You Need to Submit

Submitting articles is a sequential process that starts with sending a query to an editor, continues through getting acceptance to do the article, and ends with submitting the article. Barring some bumps along the way, the process is that simple.

Before you write an article, you should sell it. You can submit finished articles, but this is usually a recipe for disappointment. Most editors want queries before assigning articles. And even if the editor likes the article, he's likely to want to provide some guidance before it's written. Working on spec is usually an unprofitable habit for freelancers.

The query letter is the time-honored traditional method for selling an article. Articles do get sold with telephone pitches, but that's usually only after the writer has developed a relationship with an editor. Just as you don't like to be interrupted at dinner with unsolicited telemarketing pitches for replacement windows or Florida time-share condominiums, editors don't like to be interrupted from their work with pitches for stories.

The Query Letter
SUBMISSION TIPS

The query should serve several primary purposes:
- Sell your idea through a brief, catchy description.
- Tell the editor how you would handle the lead and develop the article.
- Show that you're familiar with the publication and how your article would fit with it.
- Indicate why you're qualified to write this article.

When applicable—and when possible within space constraints—the query should also:
- State the availability of photography or other artwork. (If this is a key selling point, you should definitely include such information. If it's not, these details can be discussed when the editor contacts you about an assignment.)
- Provide a working title that succinctly and enticingly sums up your idea for the editor.
- Estimate an article length. (The article should be as long as you think is necessary to cover the topic, keeping in mind the typical length of pieces in the publication. Remember: the editor may think otherwise.)

- Outline possible sidebars.
- Summarize the supporting material, such as anecdotes, interviews, statistics, etc.
- State when the article will be available.
- Indicate if you're submitting this idea simultaneously to other publications.

A side benefit for the writer is that preparing the query helps define the project and develop a lead and a strategy for completing the assignment well before you actually have to do it. The down side is that a query letter can take longer to write, word-for-word, than the article itself.

Query letters are something of a genre unto themselves. Writing them successfully requires considerable attention to detail and tight editing to fit the one-page standard—a widely observed rule for article queries.

FORMATTING SPECS

- Use a standard font or typeface (avoid bold, script or italics, except for publication titles).
- Your name, address, phone number, e-mail, and fax should appear in the top right corner or on your letterhead.
- Use a 1″ margin on all sides.
- Address the query to a specific editor, preferably the editor assigned to handle freelance submissions or the section you're writing for. (Call to get the appropriate name and gender.)
- Keep it to one page. If necessary, use a resume or list of credits attached separately to provide additional information.
- Include an SASE or postcard for reply, and state in the letter you have done so, either in the body of the letter or in a listing of enclosures. (The postcard is cheaper and easier for everyone involved. You can have them printed in bulk.)
- Use block format (no indentations, extra space between paragraphs).
- Single-space the body of the letter and double-space between paragraphs.
- Mention that you can send the manuscript on disk or via e-mail.
- Thank the editor for considering your proposal.

OTHER DOS AND DON'TS

- Do mention previous publishing credits that pertain to the article you're proposing.
- Don't take up half a page listing credits of little interest to the editor. If you have extensive credits that pertain to the query, list them on an enclosed sheet.
- Do indicate familiarity with the publication. It's okay to make a positive comment, too, if it's sincere and appropriate. But don't get obsequious.
- Don't request writer's guidelines or a sample copy in your letter. This clearly indicates you're not familiar enough to query. You should request guidelines before you send a query (see the Request for Guidelines letter on p. 22).
- Don't overpromise. If you can't deliver, it will soon become obvious to the editor.
- Don't tell the editor the idea already has been rejected by another publication. Such full disclosure does you no good and isn't necessary.

- Do enclose clippings, especially when they're applicable to the idea you're proposing. No more than three are necessary, or even desirable.
- Do send copies, not originals, of your clippings. They can always get lost, even if you include an SASE. Photocopied clips are assumed to be disposable; if you want them back, say so in your letter, and make sure you include an SASE with sufficient postage.
- Don't discuss payment terms. It's premature.

A good query letter outlines the specific proposal, with definitive subject matter, sources, and applicable expertise. Are you well versed enough on your subject matter to write knowledgeably about it? It's your job in the query letter to convince the editor that you are the writer for the job. What captures my attention is clear, concise writing that showcases the writer's attention to detail. Standouts include well-documented research, interviews with well-known writers, and relevant essays.

—Nan Leslie, fiction editor, *The Green Hills Literary Lantern*

ARTICLE QUERY LETTER #1: NONFICTION

Jack Neff
555 W. Fourth St.
Cincinnati, OH 45200
(513) 555-9000
writer@email.com

One of many
letterhead styles
you can use.

December 10, 2004

1 line

Edward Fictitious
Managing Editor
Inc.
77 N. Washington St.
Boston, MA 02114

Always address a
specific editor.

Not necessary; easy
to remove if you
need an extra line
of space.

1 line

Dear Mr. Fictitious:

1 line

1 line

Custom Cleaner Inc.'s doom was sealed before the company's first
home dry cleaning kit reached stores. Procter & Gamble Co. already was preparing a competing product. And when P&G announced
its plans, retailers wouldn't stock Custom Cleaner.

1" margin

A two-paragraph
comparison con-
trast lead. Also
shows you have an-
ecdotes ready to
use.

1 line between
paragraphs

Clean Shower, another upstart cleaning product, seemed headed
for a similar fate. After a promising initial reception in the
market, the no-scrub daily shower cleaner inspired knockoffs
from such well-heeled rivals as Clorox Co. But Automation Inc.,
maker of Clean Shower, fought back successfully, increasing
sales by boosting advertising even as four competing brands hit
the market.

Estimated word
count.

In a 1,000-word article, I would like to use such case studies
to explore how entrepreneurs respond, and sometimes even prevail, when established competitors invade their turf. I believe
this would strongly appeal to *Inc.* readers who invest in new
products—and usually harbor deep fears of sudden ruin at the
hands of giant foes.

Explains how the
article would be
developed.

Shows familiarity
with publication
and its readers.

Use one or two
sentences to high-
light qualifications.

I am a freelance business writer who has published two books on
start-up businesses, and for eight years I've covered the consumer products industry for *Advertising Age* and other national
business publications. In this work, I've encountered numerous
start-up companies that have launched novel products only to
face potentially fatal competition.

Be polite.

Thanks for your time and consideration. I look forward to hearing from you.

Be positive without
being pushy.

Sincerely,

Signature

Jack Neff

Detail enclosures.
(If space is tight,
mention enclosures
in the body of the
letter.)

Encl.: Reply postcard
       Clippings

ARTICLE QUERY LETTER #2: NONFICTION

Beverly Goodnostrum
3212 Saw Palmetto Blvd.
Gardenia, CA 54311
(415) 555-1000
bevgood@email.com

It's perfectly acceptable to type your name in the top right corner, along with your address and phone number.

Date letters here or beneath your name and address.

January 6, 2004

1 line

Ellie Editor
Prevention
33 E. Minor St.
Emmaus, PA 18098

1 line

Dear Ms. Editor:

1 line

Factual statement of the problem your article will solve can work; however, it may not turn out to be the article lead.

Sales of vitamins and other dietary supplements have been doubling every four years, as consumer awareness of their health benefits grows. But the crush of publicity surrounding supplements obscures the growing confusion about proper dosages and formulations.

Shows familiarity with the magazine's focus and editorial direction.

1" margin

I have noted *Prevention*'s growing coverage of supplements and functional foods with interest. I believe many of your readers now are looking for a solidly researched guide to help them develop their vitamin and supplement regimens. The 2,000-word article I propose would be a primer on today's ten most popular supplements, including:

Single-spaced text

Word count

- How to know the right dosage
- How to evaluate quality, including understanding bioavailability and marker compounds
- How to find the best values

Explains exactly how the article will be developed.

Good to include information about possible sidebars.

I would include a 200-word sidebar on how to find similar information on any supplement.

1 line between paragraphs

I have been a health writer for ten years, writing for such publications as *Your Health*, *Vim and Vigor* and *Family Circle*. I am querying other health publications, but would tailor the article to the requirements of *Prevention* and turn around a manuscript within three weeks of notification. Enclosed are some of my clippings and a postpaid reply postcard.

Brief description of qualifications.

Details when article will be available.

If you're making simultaneous queries, say so matter-of-factly. It's good to indicate that you realize the same article won't fit everyone's format.

Polite. Positive.

Thanks for your time. I look forward to working with you.

If you're tight on space, you can skip mentioning enclosures below.

Respectfully,

Beverly Goodnostrum

Signature

ARTICLE QUERY LETTER: NONFICTION COLUMN

Jack Neff
555 W. Fourth St.
Cincinnati, OH 45200
(513) 555-9000
Fax: (513) 555-9091
writer@email.com

March 2, 2004

Peter Woodman
Better Homes and Gardens Wood
P.O. Box 1212
Des Moines, IA 55155-1212

Dear Mr. Woodman:

As you may remember from our interview last month, I am the author of the book *Make Your Woodworking Pay for Itself*. You mentioned that you might be interested in a column on ''The Business Side of Woodworking,'' so I'm writing to offer possible
topics. Here are three ideas I have for initial columns:

1. Getting free publicity for your work and your business. This
would cover the basics of getting free media attention, which actually can be more effective than advertising. I would cover
such basics as crafting press releases, developing relation-
ships with local media, and taking advantage of any promotional
opportunities.

2. Selling direct to consumers. This column would examine the
fine points both of making a sale (obviously more of an issue
with higher-ticket items) and dealing with the public (e.g., difficult and demanding customers). I would draw heavily on experience from woodworkers who are very good at this, including one
with a storefront business, one who makes a living selling very
high-ticket wood carvings to business executives, and a cabinet-
maker who does a lot of custom work.

3. Taxes for woodworkers. If you have a woodworking business,
particularly if you're a hobbyist/woodworker, many complex tax
issues arise. I'd highlight some of the key ones, such as the
hobby/business distinction and deducting expenses for home
workshops.

Thanks again for your interest. I look forward to hearing from
you.

Respectfully,

Jack Neff

Encl.: SASE

Margin notes:

If editor is already familiar with you, certainly note that.

An opportunity to make a call that isn't so cold.

Brief descriptions of several column ideas show you can deliver more than once.

1 line

1 line

1 line

1" margin

1 line between paragraphs

Single-spaced text

Signature

QUERY LETTER: MISTAKES TO AVOID

Joseph Getajob
555 Goingnowhere Lane
Misadventure, IA 60116

No phone number or e-mail address.

August 12, 2004

Colombia Journalism Review
1235 W. Fifty-fifth St.
New York, NY 10022

To whom it may concern:

Misspelling the magazine's name is a killer.

Shows he didn't even do the basic research to find an editor's name.

I am a formerly unemployed journalist interested in writing an exposé about one of the least credible news organizations in America—my former employer. This would also be an inspirational tale about my comeback as a successful writer of action-adventure novels.

Raises red flags of ax-grinding, potential libel suit.

No indication of how he would hook readers.

I would also provide anecdotes about how other journalists have overcome similar bad experiences and gone on to bounce back in other jobs or occupations.

Don't promise anecdotes or research you don't have. If you have them, briefly describe them.

Enclosed, please find a self-addressed stamped envelope for your writer's guidelines and $4 for a sample copy.

Never ask for the guidelines or sample copy in a query. One more sign of no research.

Please reply within fourteen days, or I will need to look else-where. I look forward to your reaction. **Probably not.**

Don't adopt an attitude.

Sincerely,

Joseph Getajob

Electronic Queries

SUBMISSION TIPS

The digital age has brought an air of informality to communications between editors and writers. Keep in mind, however, that the computer did not redefine manners. Communications with a new editor should still be formal and respectful whether you make contact by mail, fax, or e-mail. Once you've developed a relationship, you can afford to become less formal. Because the editor is familiar with your writing experience and ability to develop an article, you might pitch story ideas over the phone or in one- or two-sentence e-mails. But rarely will an editor make a judgment based on casual contact with a new writer.

Thus, the basic format and tone of an electronic query wouldn't be much different than a query on paper, but certain features of e-mail do dictate different strategies.

FORMATTING SPECS

- Include the same information you would in a paper query—your name, address, phone, fax, etc. The top right-hand corner or top center position is fine for this, in keeping with the paper tradition, though you can also include this information in a signature line at the end. It isn't necessary to include your e-mail address in the body of the e-mail, however, since the editor can reply with the click of a button and your e-mail address will be preserved along with the e-mail if he saves it for later response.
- Fill in the subject line of the e-mail with a description of your query. This gives you an extra selling line and can be a good place for the proposed title of your work.
- Follow the same format you would with a paper query, including the date, salutation and block paragraph format. Leaving out these formalities isn't unusual, but there's no good reason to do away with them just because it's an e-mail. The information could be useful to the editor, and it never hurts to be polite.

HOW TO INCLUDE CLIPS WITH E-MAILED QUERIES

When you send an e-mail query, you can provide clips five ways. There are no generally accepted standards for which is best, but the pros and cons of each method are described below:

1. Include a line telling the editor that clips are available on request. Then, mail, fax, or e-mail clips according to the editor's preference. This is a convenient solution for the writer, but not necessarily for the editor. The clips aren't available immediately, so you potentially slow the decision process by adding an additional step, and you lose any speed you've gained by e-mailing the query in the first place.

2. Include electronic versions of the clips in the body of the e-mail message. This can make for an awfully long e-mail, and it doesn't look as presentable as other alternatives, but it may be better than making the editor wait to download attachments or log on to a Web site.

3. Include electronic versions of the articles as attachments. The disadvantage here is the editor has to download the clips, which can take several minutes. Also, if there's a format disparity, the editor may not be able to read the attachment. The safest bet is to attach the documents as ".rtf" or ".txt" files, which should be readable with any word processing software, although you will lose formatting.

4. Send the clips as a separate e-mail message. This cuts the download time and eliminates software-related glitches, but it clutters the editor's e-mail box.

5. Set up a personal Web page and include your clips as hypertext links in or at the end of the e-mail (e.g., www.aolmembers.com/jackneff/smallbusinessclips). Setting up and maintaining the page takes a considerable amount of effort, but it may be the most convenient and reliable way for editors to access your clips electronically. Most Internet access providers provide personal Web page services, but you'll have to learn how to set up your own page. Don't bother with high-graphic bells and whistles. Editors who click on your clips don't want to wait for the graphics to download.

Most editors will accept your original, unedited manuscripts (unless you want to retype articles that have appeared in print). These provide a more accurate reading of what the editor can expect. Simply indicate the publication and issue date where they appeared.

When your clips are available online, you may be able to include a link directly to a clip at a publication's Web site or Web edition. Only do this, however, if you can provide a URL that will take the editor directly to your work. It's unreasonable to expect an editor to click and browse to find your clip.

OTHER DOS AND DON'TS

- Don't use all caps or exclamation points in the subject line. These are among the dreaded earmarks of spam and will cause some editors to summarily delete your e-mail.
- Don't submit an e-mail query unless you know it's welcome. Listings in *Writer's Market* or *Writer's Digest* will indicate whether electronic queries are accepted. If you can't find a listing, call the publication to check.
- Don't send an e-mail query to the editor's personal e-mail address unless expressly directed to do so. Many publications maintain separate e-mail addresses for queries.
- Don't insert clip art graphics or other images.
- Do attach or provide links to photos or graphics when you already have digital versions stored on your computer and their availability will help sell your article. They may take a long time to download, but the editor only needs to do it if she's interested.
- Do indicate how you'll make your clips and other supporting material available.

If you were wondering about the future of communications with editors, consider this: Americans sent more pieces of e-mail than regular first-class mail in 2002, according to Roberta Fusaro in the February 3, 2003, issue of *Computer World* magazine. Internet research firm eMarketer Inc. discovered that 3.4 trillion pieces of e-mail were sent in the U.S. during the year, compared to 107 billion first-class items.

E-MAIL QUERY

TO: editor@fastcompany.com
CC:
SUBJECT: Brain wedgies for bug spray marketers

You can use this space for your working title.

Jack Neff
555 W. Fourth St.
Cincinnati, OH 45200
(513) 555-9000
writer@email.com

March 17, 2004

Bill Businessman
Senior Editor
Fast Company
77 N. Washington St.
Boston, MA 02114-1927

Dear Mr. Businessman: 1 line

1 line

An attempt to hook a magazine that focuses largely on high-tech companies with a story about a low-tech one.

Despite toiling in such unglamorous businesses as bug spray and toilet bowl cleaners, S.C. Johnson & Son has had three of the top-ten new product concepts in the past two years, as rated by AcuPOLL, a Cincinnati market research firm.

How do they create fresh ideas for very old product categories? ''Brain wedgies.'' That's what Marc Marsan, president of Sawtooth Invention Company, calls tactics he uses to shock corporate clients out of creative complacency. Sample brain wedgies include having male executives walk around wearing sanitary napkins or masked marketing executives describe how they use toilet paper. Marsan also mixes into his sessions thinkers from other fields, such as former football coach Sam Wyche, inventor of the no-huddle offense.

Describe your special circumstances.

I've been invited to go through one of Marsan's product development sessions with S.C. Johnson—on the ground rules that I can't discuss specific product ideas before they go to market. Still, I believe the story of a seemingly staid company using shock tactics to spark creativity would fit with *Fast Company*'s focus on how smart companies work.

Always address qualifications.

I'm a Cincinnati-based freelance business writer who covers consumer goods for *Advertising Age* and other business publications. I know it's pushy to get demanding in a story pitch, but, because of the imminent approach of the session and S.C. Johnson's natural suspicion about reporters without firm assignments, I would like to hear from you by March 20. I can provide clips by e-mail or fax if you're interested.

In this case, if they don't like the concept, the clips aren't necessary.

Thanks for your time. I look forward to hearing from you soon.

Best wishes,

Jack Neff

1 line

This fits on one printed page, too. Don't abuse the formlessness of e-mail to become verbose.

1 line between paragraphs

Provides justification for a quick response.

You can save an electronic version of your signature in e-mail programs, but it's not vital.

E-MAIL QUERY: MISTAKES TO AVOID

TO: editor@entrepreneur.com

CC:

SUBJECT: ARTICLE FOR FAST COMPANY MAGAZINE

Dear Editor,

I'm interesting in writing for you magazine. I have been working on an article on business ethics that I think will work well for Fast Company.

I have submitted this article to seven other business magazines but they have all passed on it. I hope you are interested in it. I expect to be paid three dollars per word for this article.

Thank you for your time and consideration.

Amy Amateur

P.S. I'm attaching one of my published articles.

Don't type in all caps.

Typo. Be sure to read through your letter before you hit "send."

Never say that you have been rejected by other magazines.

Make sure your clip is actually attached—and in a format that's compatible with most computers.

This tells the editor nothing about your article.

Shows that simple research to find the editor's name wasn't done.

Tells the editor nothing about your article. E-mail queries should be just as detailed as mail queries.

Never mention payment. A query is used to gauge interest in an article.

Fax Queries

WHY NOT TO FAX QUERIES

It's relatively quick and easy to slip a query on the fax—but this is the least reliable and potentially most annoying way to pitch your article. Even if the publication accepts faxed queries, you'd be advised to try a letter or e-mail instead.

What's wrong with faxed queries?

- Faxes tend to get lost or misrouted within organizations more frequently than letters or e-mails.
- The fax machine is an extremely unreliable technology. At times faxes get jammed, shredded and stretched to the point of illegibility. They can easily fall prey to fax paper jams, get stuck in a fax machine's computer memory, or just thrown out along with scads of other unsolicited offers that clog the fax pile. Even when your fax machine or software indicates a fax has gone through, sometimes it hasn't.
- You'll frequently end up faxing your query to the wrong fax machine, increasing the likelihood that it won't even get to the editor's desk.
- If the editor's fax uses thermal paper, your query will end up on a curly, poorly reproduced sheet that may fade before the editor has had a chance to consider it.
- Reproduction quality of faxes can be very poor, making them hard to read.
- You can't enclose a self-addressed stamped envelope or postcard with a fax or provide the convenience of a quick e-mail response. Unless you include a toll-free number for response, you're making the customer bear the time and financial burden of response. Thus, editors are much less likely to respond.
- It's harder to attach clips with a fax than to either a mail or e-mail query. Once you've pushed all those clips through a fax machine, you've consumed a lot of your time and your editor's fax paper. People seldom appreciate twenty-page unsolicited faxes.

Before e-mail became widespread, faxed queries often made sense for time-sensitive topics. These days, however, editors expect you to have e-mail if you're pressed for time.

Only send faxed queries if you have permission from the publisher or if submission guidelines state it is acceptable.

FORMATTING TIPS

In those rare cases when a faxed query is called for, here are some tips for making them work as well as possible.

- Keep the format the same as a letter query, unless you're also faxing clips. If you're just faxing the letter, you don't need a cover sheet announcing the letter is coming.
- If you do fax a clip, fax only one, preferably of no more than three pages. Less is better.
- If you fax a clip, use a cover page to indicate the total page count of the transmission. Avoid Post-it-style fax notes that clutter the page.
- Try a sans serif font, which should make it easier to read on the other end.

Follow-Up and Update Letters

Occasionally lines get crossed, mail gets lost and plans change. And sometimes, editors are just plain rude. For whatever reason, your postcard or SASE is never returned, the article you submit never appears, or you don't get paid. You may need to follow up on a query, article submission, or payment. Here are some polite, gentle ways to go about it.

SUBMISSION TIPS

When you haven't heard back from a publication within a reasonable time, such as sixty days or the reporting period cited in *Writer's Market*, send a brief, businesslike inquiry.

FORMATTING SPECS

- As with queries, address it to the correct editor and use proper greetings and salutations.
- Enclose a reply postcard or SASE (except in a follow-up on a late payment), in case your original was lost.

OTHER DOS AND DON'TS

- Do be businesslike and polite.
- Do briefly explain the history behind your request (e.g., "I sent you a query with a prepaid reply postcard on . . .").
- Don't be emotional or accusatory or jump to conclusions about what happened.

For follow-up, postcards are good, especially if they have a touch of humor (being deadly serious is . . . well, deadly). E-mail is acceptable these days, too. Phone calls are still taboo—unless an editor has you on her speed dial and your picture on her desk.

—Mary Lou Carney, editor-in-chief, *Guideposts for Teens*

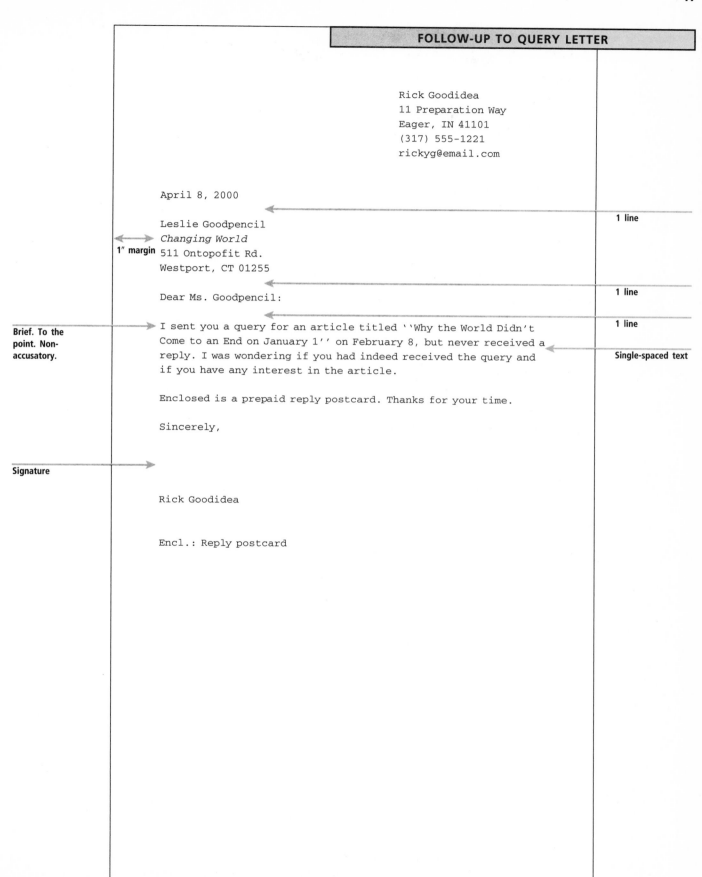

FOLLOW-UP TO QUERY LETTER

Rick Goodidea
11 Preparation Way
Eager, IN 41101
(317) 555-1221
rickyg@email.com

April 8, 2000

Leslie Goodpencil
Changing World
511 Ontopofit Rd.
Westport, CT 01255

Dear Ms. Goodpencil:

I sent you a query for an article titled ''Why the World Didn't
Come to an End on January 1'' on February 8, but never received a
reply. I was wondering if you had indeed received the query and
if you have any interest in the article.

Enclosed is a prepaid reply postcard. Thanks for your time.

Sincerely,

Rick Goodidea

Encl.: Reply postcard

1 line

1" margin

1 line

1 line

Single-spaced text

Brief. To the
point. Non-
accusatory.

Signature

FOLLOW-UP TO ARTICLE SUBMISSION

Rick Goodidea
11 Preparation Way
Gary, IN 41101
(317) 555-1221
rickyg@email.com

October 20, 2000

Leslie Goodpencil   1 line
Changing World
511 Ontopofit Rd.
Westport, CT 01255

Dear Ms. Goodpencil: 1 line

After discussing the assignment with you on April 20, I sent the   1 line
manuscript ''Why the World Didn't Come to an End on January 1''
on May 2.   Single-spaced text

1 line between paragraphs

Can you tell me when the article will be published? Enclosed is
an SASE.

Be polite, not demanding.

Thanks again for this chance to write for *Changing World*. I look
forward to hearing from you.

1″ margin

Sincerely,

                                                                     Signature

Rick Goodidea

Still good to enclose an SASE at this point.

Encl.: SASE

INQUIRY ABOUT LATE PAYMENT

Rick Goodidea
11 Preparation Way
Gary, IN 41101
(317) 555-1221
rickyg@email.com

December 31, 2000

1 line

Leslie Goodpencil
Changing World
511 Ontopofit Rd.
Westport, CT 01255

1 line

Dear Ms. Goodpencil:

1 line

1″ margin

My article, ''Why the World Didn't Come to an End on January 1,'' was published in the November issue of *Changing World*, which reached newsstands on October 27, and I sent an invoice November 1.

1 line between paragraphs

Be firm, but not hostile or accusatory.

Though your publication's policy is to pay upon publication, I still have not received payment. Could you check on the status of the payment for me? I've enclosed a second invoice, in case the first was lost.

Be polite as usual.

Thanks very much for your help.

Sincerely,

Signature

Rick Goodidea

No need for an SASE at this point. Do your creditors provide return postage?

Encl.: Invoice

Letter Offering Reprint Rights

SUBMISSION TIPS

Send a brief letter describing the article and where it ran. Since the article is enclosed, don't give it a glowing send-off—it should sell itself. If you can provide any follow-up information on the article's impact or how it was received in its original market, however, that could help you sell reprint rights. Also offer any ideas you might have on how the article could be adapted to the publication's needs.

FORMATTING SPECS

- Use similar format to query and follow-up and letters.
- Keep it short. Two or three brief paragraphs will do.
- Enclose a reply postcard.

Request for Guidelines Letter

SUBMISSION TIPS

Just send a brief letter stating that you want to receive the publication's writer's guidelines. Before you send the letter, use a search engine, such as www.google.com, to find whether the publication has a Web site and whether writer's guidelines are included on the site.

FORMATTING SPECS

- Address the letter to the correct editor. Check *Writer's Market* listings when available, or use the phone (you needn't ask for the editor—just get the name and address).
- Use block or semiblock format.
- Keep it simple. One paragraph will do.
- Include your name, address, phone number, and e-mail.
- Enclose an SASE.

OTHER DOS AND DON'TS

- Don't try to pitch yourself or a story at this point. This may not even be read by an editor, and all you need are the guidelines, anyway.
- Don't use "Dear Sir," "To whom it may concern" or other indications that you don't know who the editor is.

LETTER OFFERING REPRINT RIGHTS

Jason Secondcycle
333 Rapid Run Rd.
Spin City, NY 14011
(914) 555-1400
jason2@email.net

September 20, 2004

1 line

Richard Smartbuyer
The Daily Planet
P.O. Box 123
Planet, IA 51556

1 line

Dear Mr. Smartbuyer:

1 line

Single-spaced text

Enclosed is a copy of my article titled "The 10 Best Spelunking Destinations in America" as it appeared in the August issue of *Cavedweller* magazine.

1 line between paragraphs

Mention positive results in the initial publication when possible.

This article produced more positive mail than any other in the magazine's history. I believe it would also be of interest to readers of your Sunday travel section, few of whom subscribe to *Cavedweller*.

You still need to tell why the article would work for this publication.

1" margin

Please call or return the enclosed prepaid reply postcard if you're interested. Please also let me know if I can revise the article in any way to make it of more use to your readers.

It doesn't hurt to offer ways to add value by reslanting/ revising the article.

Sincerely,

Signature

Jason Secondcycle

Encl.: Reply postcard

REQUEST FOR GUIDELINES LETTER: NONFICTION

Rick Goodidea
11 Preparation Way
Gary, IN 41101
(317) 555-1221
rickyg@email.com

September 28, 2004

1 line

Leslie Goodpencil
Changing World
511 Ontopofit Rd.
Westport, CT 01255

1 line

Even here, it can pay to know the editor's name.

Dear Ms. Goodpencil:

1 line

I'm interested in writing for *Changing World* magazine, but first would like to see your writer's guidelines. Could you please send them to me in the enclosed SASE? I wasn't able to locate guidelines on your Web site, but if they are available electronically, please e-mail them to me at rickyg@email.com.

Single-spaced text

1″ margin

Thanks for your help.

Sincerely,

Signature

Rick Goodidea

Encl.: SASE

Reply Postcard

If you're a bit paranoid about whether your article actually makes it to the publication, you may send a reply postcard along. Having it signed by the editor (or someone on the staff) and sent back to you will alleviate any worries that the package didn't make it to its destination. Two caveats: (1) Not all editors are gracious enough to send your reply postcards back—but most do. (2) Just because you receive a postcard reply from a publication, you cannot assume your story has been read or will be read in the next few days or even weeks. Your reply postcard's only function is to let you know your submission has been received.

Your best bet to ensure an editor will return your reply postcard is to make it neat and simple to use. That means typing your postcard and not asking the editor to do anything other than note your submission has been received. Although it's okay to leave a small space for "Comments," keep the space very small and never expect it to be filled in—most editors simply don't have the time or a reason to write anything in it. You'll turn off an editor if you ask him to do too much.

Creating a suitable and functional reply postcard is easy. If you create a reply postcard similar to the one on the following page you'll be just fine. Above all, remember to keep things short and sweet—and, of course, always supply the postage for the card.

A SASE should always be included in a query letter, along with an e-mail address in case we need to contact with questions, etc. (if you don't have an e-mail address, get one). Writing history and a couple of clips are also good to send, but choose carefully. Only your mother cares about everything you've ever published!

—**Mary Lou Carney, editor-in-chief,** *Guidesposts for Teens*

REPLY POSTCARDS

Jack Neff
555 W. Fourth St.
Cincinnati, OH 45200

Front of card.

Your query was received on _____ .
We need more time to consider your query and will be in touch. ☐
Yes, we are interested in your idea. An editor will be in touch soon. ☐
No, we are not interested in your article at this time. ☐
Please send the following additional information (see below). ☐
Comments: _____
_____
_____

Back of card —
submitted.

Date _____
Yes, your article was received on _____
We need more time to consider you query and will be in touch. ☐
No, we are not interested in your article at this time. ☐
Please send the following additional information (see below). ☐
Comments: _____
_____
_____

Back of card —
follow-up.

I would like to reprint your article. Please call me. ☐
No, we are not interested in your article. ☐
Please send the following additional information (see below). ☐
Comments: _____
_____
_____
_____

Back of card —
letter offering
reprint rights.

The Article

WHAT YOU NEED TO SUBMIT

Compared to the query letter that leads up to the article, formatting the article itself is relatively easy. The style and approach of each article is different, of course, and beyond the scope of this book. However, the layout of the printed page and the information is relatively clear-cut. All you need is:

- A cover letter
- Your article

This section will guide you through the cover letter and the article itself, including information on e-mailing and faxing articles and the differences between magazine and newspaper-style articles.

Cover Letter

SUBMISSION TIPS

By the time you send the article, the editor should already know who you are and about the article. The cover letter accomplishes a few additional functions:

- It provides details that may be important in the editing and fact-checking process, including names, addresses, and phone numbers of sources.
- It informs the editor of the status of photographs and graphics that will accompany the article (whether they're enclosed or coming from another party).
- It provides information about how you can be reached for questions.

FORMATTING SPECS

- Use a standard font or typeface (avoid bold, script or italics, except for publication titles).
- Put your name, address, phone number, e-mail, and fax on the top right-hand corner or in your letterhead.
- Use 1″ margins on all sides.
- Address it to a specific editor (call and get the appropriate editor's name and gender).
- Use block letter format (no indentations, extra space between paragraphs).
- If you need more than a page, use it. The editor will need this information in handling your manuscript.
- Provide a word count.
- Provide contact names of sources if needed.
- Mention any details the editor should know in editing the manuscript, such as difficulty in reaching a particular source or conflicting data you received and how you resolved the conflict.
- Tell about the status of photography or other artwork when appropriate.
- Thank the editor for the assignment and express your interest in writing for the publication again.
- Only send your article via fax if you have permission from the publisher or if submission guidelines state it is acceptable.

Electronic Cover Letter

SUBMISSION TIPS

Once an editor is interested in seeing your article, he may ask you to send the article via e-mail. Don't send the article by itself—just because you're using e-mail doesn't mean you should forego a cover letter. The cover letter will provide the editor with valuable information regarding your article and should include the same information as one sent via mail.

FORMATTING SPECS

- Include the same information in your cover letter as you would in a paper cover letter—name, address, pone, fax, etc. It's not necessary to include your e-mail address in the body of the e-mail, since the editor can easily click "Reply" to respond.
- Use the subject line to introduce the title of your article.
- Follow the same format you would with a paper cover letter, including date, salutation, and block paragraph format.

OTHER DOS AND DON'TS

- Don't use all caps or exclamation points in the subject line.
- Don't insert clip art graphics or other images in your cover letter. Keep it simple.

A big mistake that writers make is not proofreading a cover letter or manuscript before hitting the send button. If there's a typo or a mistake in a cover letter or in the beginning of a nonfiction story, how do I know if any of the facts presented in the article or the cover letter can be trusted?

—Lisa Allmendinger, editor, *I Love Cats*

ARTICLE COVER LETTER: NONFICTION

Jack Neff
555 W. Fourth St.
Cincinnati, OH 45200
(513) 555-9000
Fax: (513) 555-9001
writer@email.com

January 5, 2004

1 line

Elizabeth Cook
Food Processing
333 Michigan Ave.
Chicago, IL 60612

1 line

Some informality is OK at this point.

Dear Libby:

1 line

Enclosed is ``Foods for (Shelf) Life'' (1,500 words) for the March issue.

1 line

Provide information about photography, if you have it.

Photos should have arrived from the National Sunflower Association and USDA. If you don't receive them by the end of the week, please let me know and I'll call to check on their status.

Single-spaced text

1 line between paragraphs

Tell how you can be reached for questions when necessary.

I'll be away on business from Jan. 7-10, but I will be checking voice mail daily. Feel free to leave any questions on my voice mail, and I'll answer them on yours if I can't return the call when you're in the office.

Here are the contact numbers for sources:

1" margin

Many publications require contact names and numbers. The cover letter is a good place for this.

Jeff Miller, agronomist with the U.S. Department of Agriculture, (716) 555-4322
Pamela J. White, professor of food science at Iowa State University, (515) 555-1224
Larry Kleingartner, executive director of the National Sunflower Association, Bismarck, ND, (716) 555-3400
Shin Hasegawa, a biochemist at the USDA's Agricultural Research Service in Albany, CA, (510) 555-6070

Thanks again for the assignment. I look forward to working with you again soon.

A subtle plea for future assignments is fine—but don't beg.

Best wishes,

Signature

Jack Neff

Encl.: Manuscript, ``Foods for (Shelf) Life''

Article Manuscript

SUBMISSION TIPS

Show you're a professional by submitting a clean, grammatically correct and properly spelled manuscript that hews as closely as possible to the style of the publication. For tips on submitting your article electronically, see page 36.

FORMATTING SPECS

- Use a 1″ margin on all sides.
- Don't number the first page.
- Include rights offered or negotiated and a word count in the top right corner of the first page.
- If you have one or more sidebars, indicate this in the top right corner of the first page, along with the word count for each sidebar.
- Include your name, address, phone number, fax, and e-mail in the top left corner of the first page.
- Put the working title in all caps or boldface and the subtitle underlined or in italic centered, about one-third of the way down the page from the top margin.
- Skip one line and write "by" in lowercase, then skip another line and put your name. (If using a pseudonym, put that name in all caps, and then on the next line put your real name in parentheses.)
- Drop four lines, indent, and begin the article.
- Double-space the entire text of the story.
- Put a slug, a one- to two-word name, at the top left corner of the header in the second and preceding pages.
- Put page numbers (2–the end of the article) in the top right-hand corner of the header.
- Keep type size 10–12 points.
- Optional: At the article's end, put a "–30–" or "–###–" notation. This is more of a relic in publishing than a necessity, but some writers feel insecure without it. It won't hurt to do it or leave it out.
- When sending an accepted article, be sure to send a copy of the article on disk or CD along with the hard copy. See page 36 for information on how to format your article on the disk or CD.

OTHER DOS AND DON'TS

- Do use paper clips in the top left corner of your manuscript (butterfly clips or paper clamps for articles of more than ten pages).
- Don't use staples.
- Don't clip, and especially don't staple, your cover letter to the manuscript.
- Don't use a separate cover page. It's pretentious for an article-length manuscript and wholly unnecessary.
- Don't justify text or align the right margin. Ragged right is fine.
- Don't insult the editor's intelligence or intentions by putting a copyright notice on the manuscript. It's copyrighted as soon as you write it.
- Don't use unusual fonts. A simple Times Roman will do fine.

- Do include suggested subheads in the body of your manuscript if the magazine's style is to use subheads; however, don't rely on subheads as a substitute for transitions. Subheads may need to be removed for layout/page composition purposes. Besides, they're an editor's prerogative. Don't count on them staying where you put them.
- Don't fax your article unless you have permission from the publisher or if submission guidelines state it is acceptable.

WINNING STYLE POINTS

Virtually all newspapers and many magazines use some variation of Associated Press style. Other magazines and most books use *The Chicago Manual of Style* from The University of Chicago Press. Thus, two books that should be on the shelves of freelancers include *The Associated Press Stylebook and Libel Manual* and *The Chicago Manual of Style*. The latter provides useful general guidance on grammar and usage issues in addition to style points.

The most common style questions concern such areas as numbers, localities, abbreviations and capitalization. Style manuals also cover such fine points as the difference in usage between *lawyer* and *attorney*. It's a good idea to at least skim through the style manuals to become familiar with the usage issues they cover, in addition to using them as references when unsure about a style issue.

Most publications have style rules of their own that deviate from whichever standard they use. Freelancers can't realistically be expected to know all the rules before first being published in a magazine, but try to be familiar with the publication's basic style standards.

> What really impresses me is someone who actually takes the time to search our archives and makes sure that we haven't written about their story idea before. If you're pitching a story on a rather familiar topic—for example, Google, or blogging, or e-mail viruses, or the wonders of Linux—you had better made extra-double-sure that we haven't run a piece on that very topic five years ago. The entire back catalogue of our magazine is online. Why are you taking all the time to put together a pitch if you can't take the time to do a two-minute search of our site?
>
> —Chris Baker, editorial assistant, *Wired Magazine*

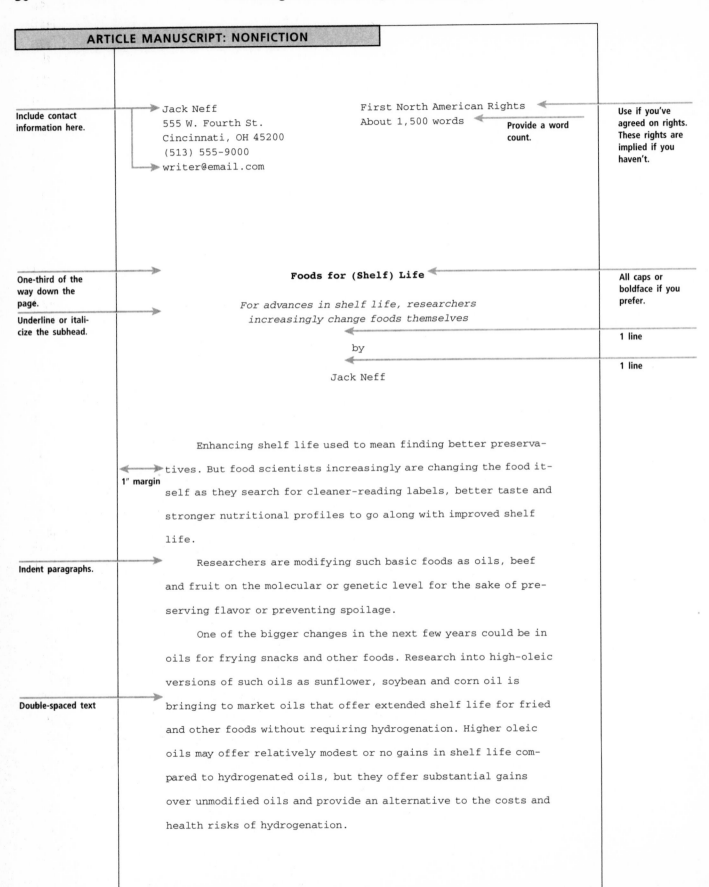

ARTICLE MANUSCRIPT: NONFICTION

Include contact information here.

Jack Neff
555 W. Fourth St.
Cincinnati, OH 45200
(513) 555-9000
writer@email.com

First North American Rights
About 1,500 words

Provide a word count.

Use if you've agreed on rights. These rights are implied if you haven't.

One-third of the way down the page.

Underline or italicize the subhead.

Foods for (Shelf) Life

*For advances in shelf life, researchers
increasingly change foods themselves*

by

Jack Neff

All caps or boldface if you prefer.

1 line

1 line

Enhancing shelf life used to mean finding better preserva-

tives. But food scientists increasingly are changing the food it-

self as they search for cleaner-reading labels, better taste and

stronger nutritional profiles to go along with improved shelf

life.

1" margin

Indent paragraphs.

Researchers are modifying such basic foods as oils, beef

and fruit on the molecular or genetic level for the sake of pre-

serving flavor or preventing spoilage.

One of the bigger changes in the next few years could be in

oils for frying snacks and other foods. Research into high-oleic

Double-spaced text

versions of such oils as sunflower, soybean and corn oil is

bringing to market oils that offer extended shelf life for fried

and other foods without requiring hydrogenation. Higher oleic

oils may offer relatively modest or no gains in shelf life com-

pared to hydrogenated oils, but they offer substantial gains

over unmodified oils and provide an alternative to the costs and

health risks of hydrogenation.

ARTICLE MANUSCRIPT, INSIDE/END PAGE: NONFICTION

Shelf Life   5

Slug line at the
top left.

Page number.

A side benefit of the enzyme may be prevention of tumor formation. Separate studies at Baylor University and the University
of Western Ontario found the enzyme inhibited oral cancer tumors
in hamsters and human breast cancer cells in mice.

Vitamin E as Beef Preservative

It's OK to include
subheads, but
make sure your
article will work
without them here.

Consumers also won't have to wait so long to see the benefits from the addition of megadoses of vitamin E to the diets of
beef cattle.

Food processors have long used vitamin E as a natural preservative in some foods. In recent years, agricultural research
in U.S. and England has found that adding vitamin E to the diets
of both forage and grain-fed cattle one hundred days before
slaughter can increase the shelf life of the beef.

In one study in Britain, among cattle given 1,500 international units of vitamin E a day, compared with a natural diet sup-
plying 30-40 international units, shelf life was improved by two
to three days. In the U.S., inclusion of vitamin E in animal feed
is becoming increasingly standard practice, as supermarket buyers begin to specify it. Use of vitamin E cuts waste in the meat
supply chain by thirty dollars per head of cattle at a cost of
only two to three dollars per head, according to the USDA.

''By changing the cattle's diet, we can extend shelf life
for retailers and potentially increase profit margins for grow-
ers and processors, too,'' says Richard Wilson, spokesman for
the USDA Agricultural Research Service. ''You don't find many
technologies so cheap and so effective.''

No need to mark the
end. Especially avoid
using "The End" in
nonfiction articles. Use
"—30—" or "—
###—" if you must.

Sidebars

SUBMISSION TIPS

For sidebars included with articles, start the sidebar on a new page immediately following the last page of the main bar. Don't include all the front page information you put at the beginning of the main bar. Simply use a header that says "Sidebar: (Same slug you used for the article)" in the top left corner and a word count in the top right corner.

FORMATTING SPECS

- With the exception just noted, follow the same formatting specs used with the article manuscript.
- Don't number the first page of the sidebar, but do number subsequent pages, if there are any.
- Use the sidebar slug in the header of the second and following pages, along with a page number, in the same format as a regular article.

OTHER DOS AND DON'TS

- Don't use staples to attach your sidebar page.
- Don't justify text or align the right margin.
- Do include suggested heads and subheads for your sidebar.

I recommend printing out a cover letter or a submission as hard copy and sleeping on it for a night. The next morning, reread it, and if it looks fine then go ahead and ship it out. What is sometimes caught in the new light of day can make the difference between a sale or a rejection.

—Lisa Allmendinger, editor, *I Love Cats* Magazine

ARTICLE MANUSCRIPT WITH SIDEBARS: NONFICTION

Jack Neff
555 W. Fourth St.
Cincinnati, OH 45200
(513) 555-9000
Fax: (513) 555-9001
writer@email.com

First North American Rights
About 1,500 words, plus sidebars of 225 and 150 words

Indicate the side-
bars separately
here as part of
the package.

One-third of the
way down the
page.

Timid Steps Toward Brave 'Nute' World

Boldface

1 line

*Major food players get feet wet
but produce few patents so far*

Italicized

1 line

by

1 line

Jack Neff

4 lines

Indent paragraphs.

Nutraceuticals may have captured the interest and imagination of major food companies. But at least based on patent activity, they don't appear to have captured many research and development dollars yet.

A *Food Processing* review of patents granted in the 1990s

1" margin

shows that major food companies have received fewer than sixty
patents for nutraceutical products. One company alone, Procter &
Gamble Co., accounts for more than half of those. Even P&G, however, denies it has a ''nutraceutical'' business.

That doesn't necessarily mean the food industry's R&D or pa-

Double-spaced

tent activity in nutraceuticals is slack. But it does show that
functional foods research has yet to produce the types of break-
throughs that can be easily patented. That could change quickly
as interest in the area grows.

ARTICLE SIDEBAR: NONFICTION

Sidebar: Nutraceuticals   About 225 words

Sidebar slug line on the first page.

Repeat the word count for the sidebar.

Patents From Major Food Companies

Here's how the major food companies rank by number of nutra-
ceutical-related patents, and a roundup of products for which
they hold patents.

1. Procter & Gamble Co.   37

1" margin

Psyllium and other cholesterol-lowering drinks and compounds, tea extracts, fortified drink mixes, enhanced bioavailability of nutrients and system for physiological feedback in administration of nutrients.

Double-spaced, just like manuscript text.

2. Kellogg Co.   7

Psyllium and other cholesterol-lowering foods, improved
iron fortification.

3. Unilever NV   4

Probiotic for treating irritable bowel syndrome, antioxidant tea extracts.

4. Quaker Oats Co.   2

Cholesterol lowering through beta-glucans.

5. Mars Co.   1

Antioxidant sports bar.

6. General Mills Inc.   1

Psyllium muffin mix.

7. Nabisco Foods Co.   1

High-oleic rice oil.

8. Suntory   1

Fermented tea products added to foods for prevention of
tooth decay and gum disease.

Slug line →

Sidebar: Nutraceuticals   2 ←

Paginate the
sidebar separately,
starting on the
second page.

9. Campbell Soup Co.   1

Marketing research system for measuring effectiveness of

diet programs.

10. PepsiCo   1

Hunger-suppressing food.

11. Wrigley Co.   1

Cavity- and gingivitis-fighting chewing gum.

Note: Counted as nutraceutical patents were foods manip-

ulated to provide some kind of positive health benefit, or di-

etary supplements designed for addition to foods and enhanced to

provide a health benefit. Not counted were foods or additives ma-

nipulated to decrease negative health effects, such as fat

replacers.

Source: U.S. Patent and Trademark Office, Food Processing

Research

Electronic Article Manuscripts

SUBMISSION TIPS

Submitting articles electronically isn't so much about what you do as what you *don't* do. Don't sweat the details of an electronic manuscript format, because all the details will likely be worked out in-house at the publication.

For the most part, preparing an electronic manuscript is a matter of unformatting what you've already got.

Of course, the key consideration is whether the publication takes electronic submissions, and if they do, whether they want them on disk, CD, or via e-mail.

FORMATTING SPECS

- Find out from the editor how she prefers to get files—in a particular word processing software format or as a generic file.
- The safest way to e-mail an article is as a text attachment. Saving the article as text strips out all the formatting and reduces the chances it will come out as gibberish on the other end.
- When in doubt, and when the editor doesn't specify, attach the article to the e-mail or save it to disk or CD two ways: in your native word processing software format and as a text file.
- Beyond these rules, formatting is mainly a matter of removing potential glitches from your copy. For instance, don't put two spaces after a sentence. Typesetters automatically handle the space, and your extra spaces may need to be removed by an editor.
- Likewise, don't double- or triple-space electronic files by using hard returns, as the spacing could also foul up production.
- For similar reasons, don't include headers, footers, or page numbers on the electronic file. They can only cause problems in editing and production.
- Otherwise, include the name, address, rights and word count information at the top of the article, as you would with a paper manuscript.
- Don't put any copyright information on the manuscript. It's copyrighted when you write it, and the editor knows this.
- Generally, put all the information you would normally include in the cover letter into your e-mail and attach the article as an e-mail attachment.
- If you mail a disk or CD, use the same kind of cover letter you would with a paper manuscript. Include a hard copy of the manuscript in the envelope, just as a point of reference if glitches appear in the electronic copy.

FILING NEWSPAPER AND NEWSMAGAZINE SUBMISSION TIPS

Standards for filing stories to newspapers and weekly newsmagazines may vary somewhat from those for longer-cycle publications. Since these publications are so time sensitive and their staff so pressed for time, electronic submissions are the norm. Thus, the manuscript chosen for this section will be a story filed for a weekly business newsmagazine (other than some of the preceding "de-formatting" steps, format your regular magazine articles the same as paper transmissions).

FORMATTING SPECS

- Put information you might normally include in a cover letter or e-mail body in a note on top of the file for newspaper or newsmagazine filings. This includes information about photos, unusual spellings and how you can be contacted with questions.
- Preferences vary widely among publications, but it's usually a good idea to note the editor who should see the file first. This can help avoid confusion.
- Generally, send only text files and make sure you've taken steps detailed earlier to remove formatting that could cause problems.

OTHER DOS AND DON'TS

- Do call after you've sent a file to make sure it can be received. Electronic transfers can be unreliable, and deadlines for news publications are tight.
- Do note at the top of the file where you can be reached if you're not going to be close to the phone, especially if your editor is working on a daily deadline.
- Don't use "–30–" or "–###–" to mark the end of your article. Only use the appropriate code here, if there is one.
- Do try to learn the style, especially with news publications. On tight deadlines, copy editors get very testy about having to make style changes.
- Do include a suggested headline. It isn't necessary, and it probably won't fit, but it could be a starting point for the editor.

> I absolutely prefer receiving a submission via e-mail. That way I can forward it around to several potential editors who may be interested.
>
> —Chris Baker, editorial assistant, *Wired Magazine*

ELECTRONIC MANUSCRIPT SUBMISSION

FROM: JACK NEFF, (513) 555-9000, Cell: (513) 555-2800
TO: JUDY POLLACK

Credit information.

Use a note at the top of the file to convey key information.

Suggested headline.

There is no reason to center elements in an electronic submission. Write it as it will appear in an article.

Text is flush left.

Single spaced

1 line between paragraphs

Art information.

How to get in touch.

Anticipate questions and confirm unusual spellings.

Note: I gave our Wichita stringer a contributor mention. For art, a bottle of Physique should arrive via FedEx on your desk this morning. I'll be out of the office this afternoon, but you can call me at the cell phone number above. Please leave any questions on my voice mail, so I can answer them on yours if you're not there when I call back. FYI, the line includes three kinds of conditioners, four shampoos, three gels, and four hair sprays.

P&G hair line touts style over stiffness

by Jack Neff

Procter & Gamble Co. is launching a test of Physique, a fourteen-item premium-priced hair care line for men and women positioned as offering styling benefits without causing ''stiff, sticky hair.''

P&G is hoping consumers' wallets won't be sticky, as either product retails for $7-$8 each in their Wichita, Kan., and Little Rock, Ark., test markets.

A marketing campaign from Saatchi & Saatchi, New York, including TV, print, sampling and in-store and local event promotion, breaks this week.

Ads with the tag line: ''Physique for phenomenal style'' will feature models Mark Vanderloo and Esther Candace and focus on the brand's combination of ''science and style,'' a P&G spokeswoman said.

Physique's sleek, silver packaging features a prominent sigma symbol and ellipse shape as a play on the application of physics to hair styling—and particularly on breaking the law that styled hair has to be stiff and sticky.

''Our consumer research found style-conscious people don't want to settle for hair care products that leave their hair stiff or sticky,'' said Lisa Napolione, director of Physique product development.

Physique incorporates two points P&G has used to position its Pantene brand in the past year—a simultaneous appeal to men and women and flexible-hold technology. That leaves the question of how Physique will set itself apart from P&G's top hair care brand.

''The product lines are really going after two different consumer needs,'' the spokeswoman said. Physique is aimed at ''the styling-driven consumer'' while Pantene targets consumers who just want ''healthy, shiny hair.''

But she acknowledges Physique's effect on sales of P&G's other hair care lines—particularly Pantene and Vidal Sassoon—will be among factors monitored in test markets.

Though a major mass-market brand priced on par with salon-only brands may be unprecedented, salon-only marketers haven't had much success keeping their products off mass-market shelves, undermining that point of difference, says Tom Vierhile, president of Marketing Intelligence Ltd., a Naples, N.Y., new product research firm.

Pantene's flexible-hold technology has had strong appeal to consumers, he said, but he doesn't see anything in the Physique packaging that differentiates the brand from dozens of others on the market.

''What they do with the advertising is really going to be key,'' Mr. Vierhile said.

The stakes for P&G are potentially huge. Hair care has been among P&G's fastest-growing global categories in recent years, but Salomon Smith Barney analyst Holly Becker characterizes the sector as ''strong but slowing'' in the U.S.

P&G's share of the $1.5 billion shampoo category slipped to 35.4% last year from 36.6% in 1996 and fell to 33.8% in the first quarter of 1998, according to Salomon Smith Barney.

P&G faces growing competition from Clairol, which, behind the performance of its Herbal Essences brand, has built its share from 4.1% in 1996 to 9.6% in the first quarter of 1998, and Unilever, with its recent $82 million launch of Thermasilk heat-activated shampoo.

In the $855 billion conditioner category, P&G's share slipped from 18.5% in 1996 to 16.6% in the first quarter of 1998.

For first-quarter numbers to be down is unusual, since P&G generally loads much of its promotional effort into the first quarter.

''P&G needs another Pantene,'' Ms. Becker said in a recent report, ''and one may be on the way.''

The outlook has never been better globally. Pantene, Pert Plus and Head & Shoulders have been among P&G's strongest international brands. Analysts and agency executives say P&G looks to Physique as the next global hair care brand.

Physique had been among key P&G new-business projects at Wells Rich Greene BDDP before the company fired the roster shop in January. Agency executives say two top staffers who worked on the project at Wells moved on to Saatchi, continuing their work there.

Responding to critics who said P&G had lost its edge, Chairman-CEO John Pepper has vowed to bring new brands and categories to market, and Physique is the latest example.

It's the third new brand P&G has launched into test in the past six months, following test launches of the Dryel home dry cleaning system and ThermaCare disposable heat pads.

In the same span, the company has rolled two brands from test to national distribution—its Olean fat replacer and Febreze fabric deodorizer.

P&G also is expected to relaunch the Eagle Snacks brand it purchased in 1996 from Anheuser-Busch into a test market soon.

Contributor lines for this publication. → Contributing: Judann Pollack, Laura Petrecca, Lauri O'Toole.

Submitting Photos and Graphics With Your Article

SUBMISSION TIPS

When submitting photos, graphics, and information graphic material for your article, it's important to give editors as much information as possible. Few things are as frustrating for an editor—or as common—as scrambling to find artwork or information about artwork at the last minute.

FORMATTING SPECS

- Provide suggested captions for photo(s) on a separate page at the end of your manuscript (or appended to the end of an electronic file).
- Captions should be brief, descriptive, action-oriented, and in the present tense. Ultimately, caption writing is an editor's job, but she probably won't mind your help.
- Attach a form to the back of prints with key information (see Photo and Graphic Identification Form, p. 41).
- Use tape to attach the form to prints (never use staples).
- Use a code on the margin of slides, put the slides in an envelope and attach the envelope to the necessary form(s) with tape or staples.
- Put each transparency in its own coded envelope with the code corresponding to the information form.
- If the photo needs to be returned, provide a preaddressed, stamped mailer with sufficient strength and postage to get it through the mail intact. Preferably, allow the publication to keep prints when possible.
- If you have more than one photo or slide, use a coding system to keep captions and identifications straight.
- The digital photograph and graphic does away with most of this paper shuffling. The digital photo can be e-mailed, attached to an e-mail that also includes your manuscript, and downloaded directly into the editorial graphic system by the techno-savvy graphics or design editor. If you take your own photographs or work with a photographer, use digital files whenever you can.

OTHER DOS AND DON'TS

- Do make sure digital images are high-resolution. The minimum requirement for most high-resolution images is 300 dpi, and the image should be at least 3″ × 3″ in size. The publisher's guidelines will indicate the resolution and size of the image required, as well as the preferred file format—follow these guidelines! Do not refer editors to a Web site and ask them to copy the images; the resolution of these photos will not be high enough to reproduce a high-quality image (unless a download is provided).
- Don't send extremely large files via e-mail. If you have many high-resolution images, put the files on a disk or CD (ask the editor which format is preferred) and mail it to the editor along with a copy of your article.

CAPTION LIST

Slug line for the article.

Use codes with more than one photo.

Captions: Nutraceuticals

Photo A:

Researchers at Procter & Gamble Co.'s Sharon Woods laboratory

display tea beverage.

Credit: Procter & Gamble Co.

Always include a credit, even when it's simply the company that provided the photo.

Photo B:

Double-spaced text

Bill Mayer, president and general manager of Kellogg Co.'s Func-

tional Foods Division, discusses strategies for capitalizing on

the company's recent Food and Drug Administration approval for

health claims on psyllium-based cereals.

1″ margin

Credit: Andy Goodshot, Associated Press

Graphic

Kellogg Co. wasted no time getting its health claims into adver-

tising copy, placing this ad in women's and health magazines

within two weeks of FDA approval.

Reproduction of an ad also needs a caption for context.

PHOTO AND GRAPHIC IDENTIFICATION FORM

Date: _____ Code: _____

Slug: _____

Subject (in artwork): _____

_____

Editor: _____

Date article submitted: _____

Credit: _____

Direct questions to: Please return after use ☐
Jack Neff   Keep this for your files ☐
555 W. Fourth St.
Cincinnati, OH 45200
(513) 555-9000
Fax: (513) 555-9001
E-mail: writer@email.com

Submitting Information Graphic Material With Your Article

SUBMISSION TIPS

Providing information graphics isn't part of your job as a writer, but providing the information that goes into those graphics is. Since *USA Today* debuted in 1982, information graphics—with or without articles attached—have become a staple of journalism.

If you and your publication have the know-how, one of the best ways to submit information graphic material is in the form of a spreadsheet. A variety of word processing and graphics programs can create simple graphics using spreadsheet information.

You can also submit your information in tabular form on a separate page appended to the end of your article (or attached at the end of the electronic text file).

Because of the hundreds of ways such information can be presented, you'll have to tackle each situation on a case-by-case basis. Here are a few simple formatting specs.

FORMATTING SPECS

- Use a slug atop the printed page that links the graphic information to the article, i.e., "Graphic Information: Storyslug."
- Always include a line citing the source, even if it's only your own research (usually cited in the name of the publication, i.e., "Source: Yourpublication Research").
- Take special care to double-check the numbers and make sure the columnar material is properly matched. A relatively simple miscue can render an informational graphic useless, ludicrous or embarrassing.

OTHER DOS AND DON'TS

- Do ask the editor if the publication has a preferred format for receiving information graphic material.
- Don't forget to cite the source of your information.
- Do put the story slug at the top of each page.

If you haven't grabbed me in the first paragraph of your query letter, I don't read any further. There are too many good writers and I receive too many wonderful submissions to spend time continuing to read something that doesn't do it for me from the start.

—Lisa Allmendinger, editor, *I Love Cats* magazine

INFORMATION GRAPHIC TEXT

Story slug line.

Graphic information: DTC-Direct

This could be used in a bar chart or a graph.

Table 1

New database and direct-response pharmaceutical drug marketing programs by year:

1999   108
2000   201
2001   258
2002   38 (through mid-February)

Source: John Cummings and Partners

Table 2

Top drug companies in database marketing:

1. GlaxoSmithKline
2. Merck
3. Pharmacia-Upjohn
4. Schering-Plough

Cite the source of the information.

Source: John Cummings and Partners

CHAPTER TWO

BOOKS

What You Need to Submit

Creating a book proposal is the first step in selling a nonfiction book. Typically, you will need to submit a query letter, a detailed proposal including an outline, and at least one sample chapter. This all must be complete and reviewed—usually over the course of several months, by agents, editors, and business managers of the publisher—before the book writing begins in earnest.

For the writer, the proposal process should begin with some solid market research, which can prevent a considerable waste of time and energy. From the agent's or editor's point of view, however, the process starts with the query. That's where this chapter will begin.

Query to Agent
SUBMISSION TIPS

Most authors published by major commercial publishers are represented by agents. Establishing a relationship with an agent is often the first step toward selling your first book. Though you can present a proposal to an agent without a query, it makes more sense to query first. Inability to interest agents in your proposal is a strong sign that you need to rework or scrap your idea.

A query letter to an agent should:
- Make a convincing case for a compelling book concept
- Show why you are the person to write the book
- Outline the market potential for the book, including who the readers will be and what the competition is like.

Sum up your concept in a single paragraph if possible. It may seem impossible, but if you can't do it now, your agent won't be able to do it later. This may be the same hook used by an editor to convince the committee that ultimately decides on your book. Later, it will be used by the publisher's sales rep to get your book into stores. Ultimately, it will be used on the jacket to convince readers to buy it, generating the royalties that make this all a paying venture. So spend considerable time refining this concept.

Equally vital to your query is a brief description of the market for this book, why it's better than the competition, and, essentially, why it will fly off the shelves.

The final leg of the tripod in this query is why you are the perfect person to write this book.

FORMATTING SPECS

- The basic setup for a query to agents is similar to an article query.
- Use a standard font or typeface.
- Use a 1″ margin.
- Single-space the body of the letter; double-space between paragraphs.
- Use letterhead or type your personal information in the top right corner.
- Be polite.
- Try to keep the query to one page, but it's acceptable to go as long as 1½ pages.
- As with an article query, it doesn't hurt to grab the reader's attention with a strong lead making the case for your book.

OTHER DOS AND DON'TS

- Do address an agent by name. Don't use "To whom it may concern" or other nondescript salutations of its ilk.
- Do the basic research to find out what kinds of books the agent handles.
- Do find out if the agent charges a reading fee. Agents who are members of The Association of Authors' Representatives (www.arr-online.org) are not permitted to charge fees.
- Do summarize any relevant experience you have, especially in publishing books. If you've published before, you're likely to already have an agent, so the query model assumes a first-time book author.
- Do keep your query brief. Agents don't necessarily hold you to the one-page standard, since this is, after all, an entire book you're pitching. But don't go over two pages, and keep it to one if you can. As noted earlier, your pitch rides on three basic paragraphs.
- Do ask if the agent would like you to submit a full proposal, and indicate whether the proposal is ready now.
- Don't ask for proposal guidelines. Some agents offer these, but express the confidence that you can handle a proposal on your own. After all, you bought this book.
- Don't talk terms of the arrangement at this point. It's premature.
- Don't fax your query unless you have permission from the agent.

> A thorough query letter should detail what the book is about, why it was written (or will be written), who will buy it, and how it fits into our publishing program. If there are other similar books already on the market, the letter should explain how the proposed book is unique and why people will buy it over what's already out there. Also, prospective authors should tell us (briefly) about themselves and what makes them qualified to write the book.
>
> —Joelle Herr, managing editor, Running Press

Electronic Query Letter to an Editor or Agent

SUBMISSION TIPS

Many publishers and agents now accept queries via e-mail. Before you send a query off to a publisher or agent electronically, however, you must either have permission to send it via e-mail or make sure that their guidelines indicate that it is acceptable.

Communicating with a publisher or agent via e-mail should be just as formal and respectful as if you were sending it through the mail. The basic tone and format of the electronic query shouldn't be much different from a query sent on paper.

FORMATTING SPECS

- Include the same information you would in a paper query, including your name, address, phone, and fax, etc. The top right-hand corner or top center position is fine for this, though you can also include this information in a signature line at the end. It isn't necessary to include your e-mail address in the body of the e-mail, however, since the editor can reply easily with the click of a button.
- Put a description of your book or its title in the subject line.
- Follow the same format you would with a paper query, including the date, salutation to a specific editor and block paragraph format. See the above tips for submitting a paper query; the same rules apply.

OTHER DOS AND DON'TS

- Don't use all caps or exclamation points in the subject line unless the exclamation point is part of your book's title.
- Don't submit an e-mail query unless specifically requested by the publisher or agent or if it is stated clearly in their guidelines that it is acceptable.
- Don't insert clip art graphics or other images into your query letter. Keep it simple!

> A great lead (the first paragraph or two of the query) captures my attention. This could be a question, an anecdote, a statistic showing how many people make up the book's potential market, even a joke—if appropriate. The lead should be creative and intriguing. It should make me want to read on. A great lead does double duty—it not only captures my attention, it suggests to me that the author knows how to write.
>
> **—Stephen Blake Mettee, founder/publisher, Quill Driver/Word Dancer Press**

QUERY LETTER TO AGENT: NONFICTION BOOK

Roger McCallister
445 W. Fifth St.
Denver, CO 30311
(313) 555-1234
rogerme@email.com

July 5, 2004

Sabrina Smith
Smith & Smith Literary Agency
222 Forty-ninth St.
New York, NY 10111

Dear Ms. Smith:

When was the last time you tried selling an idea? Probably it was the last time you had a conversation.

In today's economy, regardless of your career, selling ideas is what you really do. And you do it in more directions than ever. Companies sell to customers, but they also sell ideas to suppliers. Employees pitch ideas to their bosses, and vice versa. In the modern team-filled corporation, you may be selling your ideas simultaneously to a wide array of peers, bosses and subordinates. Until now, however, there was no definitive book on how to sell ideas.

That's about to change. I am preparing a book, *Selling Your Ideas: The Career Survival Strategy of the 21st Century*, to fill the void. Hundreds of highly successful books have addressed sales tactics for salespeople, and dozens of highly successful books address persuasion skills for everyone else. But, up to now, no one has addressed a book to cover the one sales job in which everyone in corporate America engages—selling ideas. Unlike other sales and persuasion books, *Selling Your Ideas* addresses everyone in business on a department-by-department, function-by-function basis. Because virtually anyone at any walk of corporate life will be reflected in this book, the appeal is considerably wider than any previous work of its kind.

Included will be dozens of real-life case studies drawn from my twenty years as a corporate executive, trainer, marketing consultant and columnist for management publications. I am also an adjunct professor in the business department of the University of Denver and a past president of and consultant for the Business Executives Council.

I would be interested in sharing my detailed proposal with you at your convenience.

Sincerely,

Roger McCallister

Encl.: SASE

Annotations:

- 1 line
- Always address a specific agent.
- 1 line
- 1 line
- The hook.
- 1 line between paragraphs.
- Single-spaced text
- 1" margin
- Differentiates this book from the competition.
- Explains why he should write this book.
- A polite offer.
- Always include an SASE.

QUERY LETTER TO AGENT: MISTAKES TO AVOID

93 Try Again Lane
Notgood, NE
KarenBad@email.com
March 3, 2004

Smith and Smith Literary Agency
222 Forty-ninth St.
New York, NY 10111

ALWAYS address your query to a specific agent.

To Whom It May Concern:

Do your homework—know what kinds of books an agent works with before sending a query.

I hope you are interested in nonfiction books about birds, because that is the type of book I have written. I would like to sell it to a publisher, which of course means that I need an agent.

Don't be obvious—an agent knows why writers need agents.

This tells the agent absolutely nothing about the book. Explain how your book differs from others currently on the market.

The subject of birds is a big one, but I know that my book stands out from all the others. People all over the country love to read interesting stories about these fascinating creatures, so the book will appeal to just about anyone who loves birds—they don't even have to be birdwatchers or nature enthusiasts. I've attached the first four chapters of my book and will send the rest at your request.

Don't send book chapters unless asked by the agent. This is just a query.

Keep all your information focused on the book itself; don't waste time with anecdotes that have nothing to do with the book.

I had such a good time writing about this, my favorite subject, over the past ten years. I am a bird enthusiast and even met my husband while on a birding expedition in the mountains of New England in 1999.

Don't point out your (and the book's) shortcomings. If it needs editorial help, get some before you send it to an agent.

This is my first attempt at writing a book, I have written many articles that were never published on the subject so I thought it would be a good idea to put them all together in one book. I think that with the right editor's expertise and input this book has the potential to be a huge bestseller.

Don't exaggerate. Be confident in your work, but don't overstate it.

Thanks,

Karen Badquery

Query to Book Editor

SUBMISSION TIPS

The goals and strategies for a query to a book editor are essentially the same as with an agent query. Both the agent and editor are looking for a marketable book.

The book editor may play a role in shepherding the book through production—or at least hear about it when there are problems—so he or she may place a somewhat higher priority on the author's writing ability and track record in completing projects. Agents certainly care whether their authors have writing ability, but they're willing to work with or help find ghostwriters for books that are clear winners.

It also pays to be familiar with the publishing house, its imprints, recent titles published and how successful they've been. When possible, link your idea to a past success without portraying your book as a knockoff of the title you're citing. This not only helps the book editor understand why your book will succeed, but also helps the editor sell the idea internally. Publishers love nothing more than a proven formula for success, frequently shaping new acquisitions along the lines of successful past ones.

If you take this approach, do your homework. Misfiring by making an unsupported comparison or painting as a success a book that really wasn't can hurt you badly. If you're not sure of your facts, you're better to forgo this tactic.

The easiest and most effective way to do the kind of research you need is by using the search engine of an online bookseller, such as Amazon.com (www.amazon.com). Not only do the search engines allow you to search by topic and publisher, but they also, in the case of Amazon.com, tell you where the title ranks against all others in sales for that particular bookseller.

Of course, agents are the ones most likely to have the current information on publishing trends and to know the hot buttons of individual book editors, publishing houses and imprints. But, if you think you can handle it on your own, here goes.

FORMATTING SPECS

- Basically, format your letter for a publishing house similar to that for an agent.
- Again, address your letter to a specific editor. Do the research in *Writer's Market* and/or call to find the appropriate editor for your query.
- Show you're familiar with the publisher, possibly by comparing your book with other successful titles from the imprint.
- As with the agent query, build your query on the tripod of a strong, succinct concept, market insight, and convincing reason why you're the right person to write the book. Ultimately, "the hook" could be any of those three, or a combination, but you need all three to build your case.

OTHER DOS AND DON'TS

- Do try to keep your letter to one page, but if you need another page to elaborate using some solid information, use a second page.
- Do avoid rambling and wordiness, regardless of length.
- Don't overreach. Build a case for your qualifications based on reality.
- Don't come off as pompous, even if you do know everything about your topic.
- Don't fax or e-mail your query unless you have permission from the publisher or if submission guidelines state it is acceptable.

| QUERY LETTER TO BOOK EDITOR: NONFICTION BOOK |

Roger McCallister
445 W. Fifth St.
Denver, CO 30311
(313) 555-1234
rogermc@email.com

September 28, 2004

Alison Lovesbooks   *1 line*
AMACOM Books
1601 Broadway
New York, NY 10019

Always address a specific editor.

Dear Ms. Lovesbooks: *1 line*

When was the last time you tried selling an idea? Probably it was the   *1 line*
last time you had a conversation.

In today's economy, regardless of your career, selling ideas is what   *1 line between*
you really do. And you do it in more directions than ever. Companies   *paragraphs.*
sell to customers. Employees pitch ideas to their bosses, and vice
versa. In the modern team-filled corporation, you may be selling your   *Single-spaced*
ideas simultaneously to a wide array of peers, bosses and subordinates. *paragraphs.*
Until now, however, there was no definitive book on how to sell ideas.

1" margin

That's about to change. I am preparing a book, *Selling Your Ideas: The
Career Survival Strategy of the 21st Century*, to fill the void. No one
has addressed a book to cover the one sales job in which everyone in corporate America engages—selling ideas. Unlike other sales and persuasion books, *Selling Your Ideas* addresses everyone in business on a department-by-department, function-by-function basis. Because virtually
anyone at any walk of corporate life will see their situations reflected in this book, the appeal is considerably wider than any previous work of its kind.

How his background will help him write *and* sell the book.

Included will be dozens of real-life case studies drawn from my twenty
years as a corporate executive, trainer, marketing consultant and columnist for management publications. I am also an adjunct professor in the
business department of the University of Denver and a past president of
and consultant for the Business Executives Council.

I believe *Selling Your Ideas* would build on the winning formulas of two
successful AMACOM titles from recent years.

Shows familiarity with the publisher and the publisher's titles.

Like *The 2000 Percent Solution*, it will take an often humorous, case
study-based approach to the challenging issues of making changes
within organizations. But rather than approaching change from an organizational standpoint, *Selling Your Ideas* looks at the more approachable
task of becoming a more effective individual agent for change.

Like *The Anatomy of Persuasion*, my book approaches persuasion as an important tool for everyone in business. But *Selling Your Ideas* goes beyond presentation tactics and communications issues to look at a broad
range of strategies for selling ideas. I also will analyze strategies
for persuading specific people in specific corporate functions, plus
look extensively at strategies for selling ideas within corporate
teams.

Upbeat and polite.

I would be interested in sharing my detailed proposal with you at your
earliest convenience.

Sincerely,   *Signature*

Roger McCallister

Encl.: Reply postcard

QUERY LETTER TO BOOK EDITOR: MISTAKES TO AVOID

This is set up like a memo, not a formal letter, and doesn't include any information on who the letter is from, who it is going to, or even the date.

To: AMACOM BOOKS
New York City

Dear Editor,

ALWAYS address your queries to a specific editor that works with the type of book you're submitting.

Boring! You need to capture the editor's interest. This is the time to sell your idea, not your book.

I have written a great book on how to get a job in today's tight employment market. I think you'll want to add this book to your list and will be very happy when it sells like gangbusters.

This is a rambling, run-on sentence that doesn't tell the editor needed information.

Options today abound for those looking for work, but many folks don't know where to start—the newspaper, the Internet, friends, family, cold calling, there are many ways to get a job that may seem confusing to most job seekers, they are not sure where to start and sometimes just give up before they really start and end up standing on the umemployment line and feel unfulfilled and un- happy and eventually those checks will run out, and where will they end up?

How will your book do this? Be specific!

My book will tell readers where to start to find a job and how to best find a job that will make them happy. My book has been read by my many friends and family and they all said, wow, I wish I had this book when I was looking for a job, it really would have helped and I'd be much happier than I am now.

Editors don't care what friends and family think. State why you are the most qualified person to write this book and how you plan to differentiate it from the competition.

More bragging, with no information to back up such an outrageous claim.

A book like this will hit the best-seller lists right away be- cause it's the only one that tells it like it really is and doesn't kiss up to big corporations.

If you will send me your e-mail address I can e-mail you an elec- tronic copy of the manuscript so you can see for yourself what a great book it is, and how we will be raking in the money on this one.

Don't offer to send your book via e-mail. If the editor is interested, she will ask for more.

Being confident in your work is one thing—being arrogant and obnoxious is quite another.

Thanks for your time, and I look forward to working with you!

Sincerely,

Be sure to include your address, phone, and e-mail address.

Nathan Needshelp
(212) 555-2393

Book Proposals

WHAT YOU NEED TO SUBMIT

Like the article query, the book proposal is something of a genre in its own right. The differences are that it takes much more time and can vary considerably in length.

A fully thought-out book proposal should include the following:
- Cover letter
- Cover page
- Overview
- Marketing information or business case
- Competitive analysis
- Author information
- Chapter outline
- Sample chapter(s)
- Attachments that support your case

SUBMISSION TIPS

What agents and editors cite as most frequently lacking in book proposals is the marketing information. Authors often don't have a firm vision of who the readers of the book will be and how to reach them, or they don't know what the competition is and how to differentiate their books from existing titles.

Strange that the marketing information is so often missing, because it's really where any author should start. Before you ever set out on the time-consuming, painstaking journey toward a book proposal, you've got to know there's a market for your book. If you can't build a convincing business case for your book, go back to the drawing board.

That's why, even if the marketing and competition information doesn't come first in the proposal lineup, you should prepare these sections first. In fact, you should do your homework on these sections before you query an agent or book editor to submit a proposal.

What follows is a piece-by-piece look at the elements of the proposal.

Electronic Book Proposals

SUBMISSION TIPS

Once you send a query and an editor is interested in seeing your proposal, he may ask you to send it via e-mail. The editor will indicate what format he prefers to receive files—be sure to follow his guidelines.

- Don't forget the cover letter—just because you're using e-mail doesn't mean you don't need to introduce your proposal.
- An electronic proposal should include the same components as a proposal sent via regular mail. Pages 57-71 will detail what each part of the proposal should contain.
- Your cover letter can be included in the body of the e-mail. The additional elements of the proposal, including the cover page and overview, marketing/competitive analysis, author information, chapter outline, and sample chapters,

should be sent as a file attachment unless otherwise requested from the editor. Check the publisher's guidelines to make sure your attachments are in a file format that the publisher accepts.

FORMATTING SPECS

- Use the subject line of the e-mail to introduce the title of your book. This is a good place to continue "selling" your ideas.
- Keep everything simple by keeping it all together. It's not necessary to create a separate file for the cover page, overview, marketing analysis, competitive analysis, author information, chapter outlines, and chapter samples unless the editor specifically request them as separate files.
- A book proposal should follow the same format as a paper proposal, including a proposal slug and page numbers on every page. This will make it easy for the editor to keep everything in order when it is printed.

OTHER DOS AND DONT'S

- Don't use all caps in your subject line.
- Don't submit a book proposal electronically unless the editor or publisher's guidelines specifically request it.
- Do ask for specific file format guidelines to make sure the editor can open your files.
- Don't insert clip art graphics or images.

I love to see proposals from authors who are already writing, speaking to groups, holding workshops, and writing for magazines on the topic of their books. Don't wait for your book to sell to pursue these types of opportunities! Authors that have an established "platform" are committed to and knowledgeable about their chosen topics. And when they *do* have a book published, they can use all these resources to promote and sell the book.

—Michelle Howry, editor, Perigee Books

Cover Letter

SUBMISSION TIPS

Because so much information is included in the rest of the proposal, and because you should have already queried the agent or editor, the cover letter can be fairly brief. Don't use more than one page. Follow the same guidelines for submission to agents or book editors.

If you are submitting an unsolicited proposal, the cover letter should incorporate elements of the query letters provided earlier in the chapter, as well as introduce the proposal. The cover letter for a solicited manuscript, which will be modeled on pages 55 and 56, simply serves to introduce a proposal and covers the following points:

- An introductory paragraph introducing the proposal
- An outline of the information included in the proposal
- A concluding paragraph politely seeking a response

FORMATTING SPECS

- Use a standard font or typeface for the body of the letter.
- Letterhead is fine, but not required. If you don't use letterhead, put your name, address, phone number, etc. in the top right corner.
- Use a 1″ margin on all sides.
- Address a specific editor.
- Keep it to one page.
- Use block or semiblock letter format.
- Include an SASE or postcard for reply only if the proposal is unsolicited.
- Single-space the body of the letter and double-space between paragraphs.

OTHER DOS AND DON'TS

- Don't start your pitch all over again in the cover letter if you've already queried. Assume if your query made enough of an impression to spark interest that the agent or editor remembers the book idea and who you are.
- Don't ask for advice or criticism regarding your proposal. You'll get it either way, and asking can appear unprofessional. Many agents will offer advice or guidelines for proposals when they ask you to submit one.
- Don't mention copyright information. What you've put down here is indeed copyrighted, and you don't need to imply the agent or editor is out to steal your idea.
- Don't discuss payment or terms. It's still premature.
- Don't staple your cover letter to anything. A butterfly or clamp-style paper clip can hold the proposal elements together, and the cover letter will stand alone in front.
- Don't feel you must have a table of contents for your proposal. It won't hurt to have one, but it's really overkill in a document that's already quite long.
- Don't fax or e-mail your proposal unless you have permission from the publisher or if submission guidelines state it is acceptable.

COVER LETTER TO AGENT: NONFICTION BOOK

Roger McCallister
445 W. Fifth St.
Denver, CO 30311
(313) 555-1234
rogerme@email.com

August 30, 2004

1 line

Address a specific agent.

Sabrina Smith
Smith & Smith Literary Agency
222 Forty-ninth St.
New York, NY 10111

1″ margin

Dear Ms. Smith:

1 line

1 line

Enclosed is the proposal you requested for *Selling Your Ideas: The Career Survival Strategy of the 21st Century*.

Single-spaced paragraphs

1 line between paragraphs

Included in the proposal are a detailed market and competitive analysis, my biographical information, a complete chapter outline and three sample chapters.

Brief preview.

I hope after you've had a chance to review the proposal that you'll understand why I believe this book has so much promise. Please let me know if I can make any revisions or add any information to make the proposal more salable.

Seeking help, offering help.

Thanks for your time. I look forward to hearing from you.

Sincerely,

Signature

Roger McCallister

Encl.: Proposal

COVER LETTER TO EDITOR: NONFICTION BOOK

Roger McCallister

445 W. Fifth St.

Denver, CO 30311

(313) 555-1234

rogerme@email.com

August 30, 2004

1 line

**Address to
specific editor.**

Alison Lovesbooks

AMACOM Books

1601 Broadway

New York, NY 10019

1 line

1″ margin   Dear Ms. Lovesbooks:

1 line

Single-spaced text

Enclosed is the proposal you requested for *Selling Your Ideas:
The Career Survival Strategy of the 21st Century*.

1 line between
paragraphs.

Included in the proposal are a detailed market and competitive
analysis, my biographical information, a complete chapter outline and three sample chapters.

**Slightly different
offer.**

I hope after you've had a chance to review the proposal that
you'll understand why I believe this book has so much promise.
Please let me know if I can provide any additional information
to help you make your decision.

Thanks for your time. I look forward to hearing from you.

Sincerely,

Signature

Roger McCallister

Encl.: Proposal

Electronic Cover Letter

SUBMISSION TIPS

If an editor asks you to send your book proposal via e-mail, don't forget the cover letter. It will introduce your proposal to the editor and provide additional information regarding your article. The cover letter sent via e-mail should include the same information as one sent via mail.

FORMATTING SPECS

- Follow the same specs as you would for a cover letter being sent via mail.
- Include the same information in your cover letter as you would in a paper cover letter—name, address, phone, fax, etc. It's not necessary to include your e-mail address in the body of the e-mail, since the editor can easily click "Reply" to respond.
- Use the subject line to introduce the title of your article.
- Follow the same format you would with a paper cover letter, including the date, salutation, and block paragraph format.

OTHER DOS AND DONT'S

- Don't e-mail a book proposal to an editor unless she specifically requests it.
- Don't use all caps or exclamation points in the subject line.
- Don't insert clip art graphics or other images in your cover letter. Keep it simple.

Cover Page

SUBMISSION TIPS

This is the same as the cover page you'll use with the ultimate manuscript. It includes the title, estimated word count, and either your contact information (if submitting directly to an editor) or your agent's contact information (if submitting through an agent).

FORMATTING SPECS

- Your contact information goes in the top left corner if you're submitting to a book editor. If you're using an agent, the agent's contact information goes in the bottom right corner, and you don't put your address on the cover.
- Put an estimated word count (for the entire book, not for the proposal) in the top right corner.
- Center the title, subtitle, and author's name in the middle of the page.
- Conventionally, the title is in all capital letters and the subtitle is up-and-down. If you want you can use boldface for the title and italics for the subtitle.

OTHER DOS AND DON'TS

- Don't include both your address and the agent's. Use one or the other.
- Don't use a header or number the title page.

> The biggest mistakes writers make are when they try and "oversell" themselves and tell me how much they're oing to do to promote their book, all of which is usually much ado about nothin'. I get turned off immediately.
>
> **—Harvey Klinger, agent, Harvey Klinger, Inc. Literary Representation**

COVER PAGE: NONFICTION BOOK PROPOSAL

About 100,000 words

Optional at this point, but could be helpful.

No author name and address on agented proposal.

SELLING YOUR IDEAS

1 line

The Career Survival Strategy of the 21st Century

1 line

by

1 line

Roger McCallister

Centered in the middle of the page.

Sabrina Smith
Smith & Smith Literary Agency
222 Forty-ninth St.
New York, NY 10111
(212) 555-1229
ssmith@ssla.com

Agent information goes here for agented manuscript.

Overview

SUBMISSION TIPS

The overview is the place for your thirty-second sound-bite pitch. It incorporates elements of the concept, marketing, and competitive analysis, and author information you're about to present and ties them together convincingly, forcefully, and coherently.

This is just an overview, so it's only a page. Even though it's a small element of the proposal, it's a powerful one. You may use the same approach you used in the query, but the overview should be even more focused. Try to boil the pitch down to a single sentence, then use a paragraph or two to describe the contents of your book.

Resist the urge to give a blow-by-blow description of the rest of the proposal. No one needs a preview of a proposal. The overview is simply, to borrow from the corporate buzzword lexicon, "the top-line analysis," "the big picture," "the view from ten thousand feet."

You get the picture.

FORMATTING SPECS

- Start numbering your proposal with this page, with numbers in the top right corner.
- Use a slug in the top left corner of the header in this and succeeding pages.
- The slug should read "Proposal: Your Book Title Here."
- Center your heading, "Overview" and underline it.
- Double-space with a 1″ margin from here on out.

OTHER DOS AND DON'TS

- Do make sure the overview conveys a convincing hook, even though it's a freestyle exercise. Think of this as the speech the agent will make to the editor, the editor to the people on the editorial committee, the sales rep to the buyer, the book jacket to the reader.
- Do write your entire proposal in third person.

> One of the biggest mistakes I see writers make is having unrealistic expectations. A lot of writers seem ambitious in terms of the number of potential buyers for their books or make comparisons to blockbuster books that have been out for several years. Frequently writers also jump the gun and list what they would like to receive as an advance or what they would expect from our publicity department—and frequently these expectations are also so unrealistic that it hurts their chances.
>
> —Donya Dickerson, associate editor, McGraw-Hill

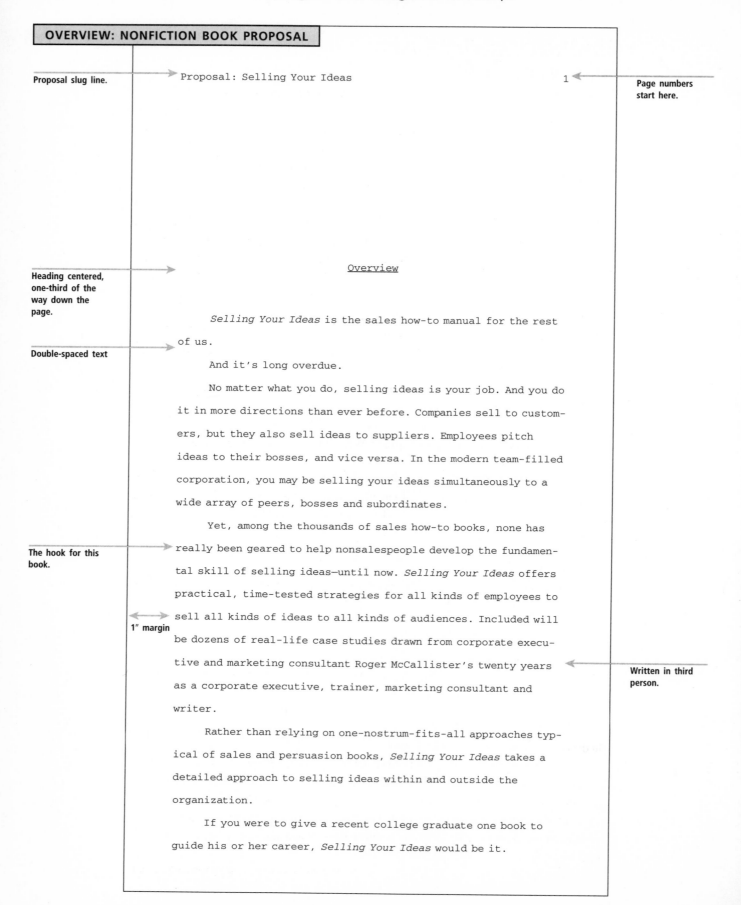

OVERVIEW: NONFICTION BOOK PROPOSAL

Proposal slug line.

Proposal: Selling Your Ideas   1

Page numbers start here.

Heading centered, one-third of the way down the page.

Overview

Double-spaced text

Selling Your Ideas is the sales how-to manual for the rest of us.

And it's long overdue.

No matter what you do, selling ideas is your job. And you do it in more directions than ever before. Companies sell to customers, but they also sell ideas to suppliers. Employees pitch ideas to their bosses, and vice versa. In the modern team-filled corporation, you may be selling your ideas simultaneously to a wide array of peers, bosses and subordinates.

The hook for this book.

Yet, among the thousands of sales how-to books, none has really been geared to help nonsalespeople develop the fundamental skill of selling ideas—until now. *Selling Your Ideas* offers practical, time-tested strategies for all kinds of employees to sell all kinds of ideas to all kinds of audiences. Included will

1" margin

be dozens of real-life case studies drawn from corporate executive and marketing consultant Roger McCallister's twenty years as a corporate executive, trainer, marketing consultant and writer.

Written in third person.

Rather than relying on one-nostrum-fits-all approaches typical of sales and persuasion books, *Selling Your Ideas* takes a detailed approach to selling ideas within and outside the organization.

If you were to give a recent college graduate one book to guide his or her career, *Selling Your Ideas* would be it.

Marketing Analysis
SUBMISSION TIPS

The marketing information section of your proposal answers that all-important question: Will this book sell? And it should answer the question in as much detail as possible. There are no limits on length here, beyond your ability to research and write. As with any part of your proposal, make this as tight and compelling as you can, and also offer any facts or figures you can find to prove your book will be a hit.

This section covers the product—your book—and the consumers—its readers. The areas to cover in this section include:

- Who is the audience? Describe them. How big is the potential readership base? Is it growing? What are some important facts about the readership base that a marketer would want to know? What kind of media do they like? What organizations do they belong to? Where do they shop?
- What trends could affect the book? Why would the audience be growing, buying more books or suddenly taking more interest in your book?
- Where, besides bookstores, could this book be sold?
- Are there special events, seasonal approaches or other special channels through which this book can be sold?
- What will the book be like, and how will that appeal to its readers?
- How will you approach the book? Will it have sidebars, callouts, interviews, pictures, charts, or other special features to hook the reader?
- What are the sources of information? What will the research be based on?

Closely linked to the marketing analysis is the competitive information that follows it. You may choose, in fact, to combine these into a single section. For the sake of breaking information down into the smallest manageable units, the subjects are handled separately here.

FORMATTING SPECS
Follow the same formatting guidelines as on p. 59-60. Formatting is similar to the rest of the inside of the book proposal.

OTHER DOS AND DON'TS
- Do write concisely and in third person.
- Don't be worried about the length. Take as long as you need to present all relevant marketing information.
- Do use charts, tables, and graphs here, if you have them.

On the market analysis section of a proposal:
I don't want to hear the market is two million people. Describe the reader. What kind of magazines do they read? What associations do they belong to? What conferences do they go to? What television shows do they watch? Draw a picture that connects the reader to other areas of the world so that a publisher can find coattails for promoting the book. The author needs to draw a picture of who her reader is and how that reader connects to other aspects of the world.

—Andrea Pedolsky, Altair Literary Agency, New York

MARKETING ANALYSIS: NONFICTION BOOK PROPOSAL

Slug line → Proposal—Selling Your Ideas   2 ← Page number

Heading centered, one-third of the way down the page.

<u>Marketing Analysis</u>

Potential readers of this book include anyone who works. ← Double-spaced text

But it will especially appeal to upwardly mobile middle and up-

per managers who have the difficult job of selling in many direc-

tions at once—including subordinates, bosses, other department

heads, vendors, customers, unions, etc. Because of the growing

acceptance of such management philosophies and tactics as ''em-

1" margin → powerment,'' cross-functional teams, consensus building, and

vendor-management quality efforts, these corporate soldiers

have seen their roles change dramatically in ways that force them

to sell their ideas more than ever before.

This is a market of more than 2.5 million people who are

heavy book buyers. According to a recent report by the American

Association of Middle Managers and the Business Executive Coun-

Full report in attachments. → cil (see attached report), middle managers buy an average of six

management and career-related titles annually—a higher average

than any other job classification in the survey.

Subheads may help clarify. → **Special Distribution Opportunities**

This book's special appeal opens additional distribution

channels beyond book stores. As a general-interest business

book with wide application to a variety of consumers, including

the small-office/home-office (SOHO) market, *Selling Your Ideas*

should have the power to win shelf space in end-aisle displays at

office superstores.

Competitive Analysis

SUBMISSION TIPS

This section details what books are similar to yours, how they have done in the marketplace, and how your book is different and better than they are.

There's no set format for handling this information, but it helps to begin with an overview of the genre or category into which your book fits, how that category is doing generally, and what the leading competitive titles are.

Then go into an analysis of no more than the top four or five leading competitors, looking at how those books have done and why yours is still needed. Even if the subject already has been covered, it may not have been covered for your audience, or the information may be hopelessly out of date because of changes in social mores or technology.

The traditional, seat-of-the-pants method for gathering this information is to visit a good-size bookstore, look for competing titles, and ask bookstore employees or owners how that title is selling. However, this haphazard approach is unlikely to impress editors.

At the very least, do some research in *Books in Print.* Find the CD-ROM or online version, which should be available through large municipal or university libraries.

An easier and potentially more effective desktop approach is to check the search engine at an online bookseller, such as Amazon.com (www.amazon.com). Searches here yield a wealth of information beyond the competing titles. You can also see where these titles rank in sales for Amazon.com, get commentaries from readers, and see what other books and authors are also popular buyers of the title. You can't get information on total number of books sold. But, combined with some inside sales information from other authors whose titles are listed at Amazon.com, you might be able to develop a ballpark estimate of how many copies a book has sold based on its Amazon ranking.

FORMATTING SPECS

- Formatting is similar to the rest of the inside of the book proposal.
- Limit the competitive titles you discuss to no more than four or five.
- Bulleted capsule treatment of competitive titles can work here, but isn't absolutely necessary. Do what works best for you.

OTHER DOS AND DON'TS

- Do use as much space as needed, but write concisely.
- Don't trash the competing titles. Point out what shortcomings they have that make room or create demand for your book.
- Don't contend that your book is so unique that it has no competition. Agents and editors will conclude either that you don't know, are fudging big time, or have offered an idea so bizarre or unappealing that no book should be published. You can always find a comparable book if you try hard enough.

> When, in the competitive titles section of a proposal, the author says something to the effect of, "there is no competition—my book is unlike anything published," that raises a red flag. That may be true (though it's unlikely!), but it doesn't help me to position the book for my editorial department, our sales department, and the rest of the publishing house. I really do look at the competitive titles section of the proposal, and if the author has done his or her homework, it shows.
>
> **—Michelle Howry, editor, Perigee Books**

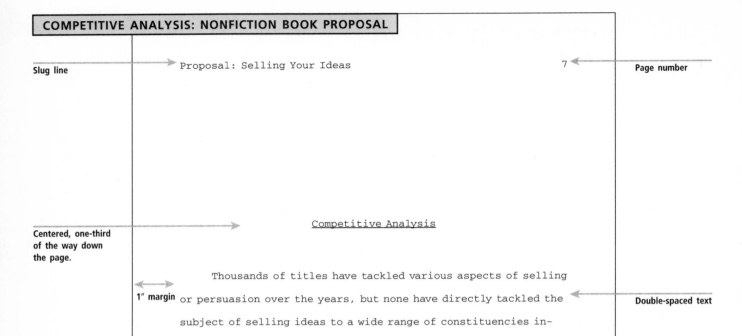

| COMPETITIVE ANALYSIS: NONFICTION BOOK PROPOSAL |

Slug line

Proposal: Selling Your Ideas   7

Page number

Centered, one-third of the way down the page.

Competitive Analysis

1″ margin

Thousands of titles have tackled various aspects of selling or persuasion over the years, but none have directly tackled the subject of selling ideas to a wide range of constituencies inside and outside the corporation.

Double-spaced text

Sales and persuasion titles are consistently strong performers. An analysis of titles listed by Amazon.com shows that more than fifty such titles have been published in the past year. They rank between 5 and 64,000 in sales for Amazon.com. In addition, analysis of older titles shows that the top 20 sales and persuasion books have a median ranking of 5,000, compared to 10,000 for the top 20 management theory books and 12,000 for the top 20 time-management books. Backlist sales potential in this category is substantial.

The four recent titles that come closest in subject to *Selling Your Ideas* have an average sales rank of 11,000. Two of those, however, focus narrowly on presentations, the broader books ranking 2,000 and 5,000, respectively.

Below is a detailed analysis of each title.

1) *The Anatomy of Persuasion: How to Persuade Others to Act on Your Ideas, Accept Your Proposals, Buy Your Products or Services, Hire You and Promote You.* This book covers ground similar to *Selling Your Ideas*, but without the department-by-department, case study-based approach. This is primarily a Dale Carnegie-style book that doesn't entirely reflect the forces at play in the modern organization.

Author Information

SUBMISSION TIPS

This section is about you, but only in the context of what makes you the perfect person to write this book. The section should also highlight any other information that makes you a salable author. This is not your life story; this is the story of how you will help the publisher sell books.

Good points to include in the author information are:

- Teaching credentials (professors can sell their books to students and other professors).
- Organizational affiliations, groups you head or any special audiences with whom you are connected and which could become channels for marketing the book.
- Previous publishing credits (including books, which show you can write one; articles, which show your expertise; and columns, which show a possible avenue of promotion).
- Any experience you have in other media (radio shows, TV shows, regular radio commentaries—anything that shows you could promote your book effectively in a variety of media).
- Compelling personal history that could help generate publicity and get you booked on talk shows.

This is not a résumé. It's a narrative description similar to what might appear on a book jacket.

Don't be crass or belabor the obvious. Editors know if you're founder and president of a group or a professor that you can use these positions to sell books. This section is a little more subtle than the rest. Try to come off as qualified and marketable without sounding like a jerk.

FORMATTING SPECS

- Place the slug in the top left corner. Page number goes in the top right corner. Double-space the text.
- Try to keep this to one page, regardless of how fascinating you are.
- Write this, like the rest of the proposal, in the third person.

OTHER DOS AND DON'TS

- Do write concisely.
- Don't overreach. State your history and qualifications accurately.
- Don't provide information that's irrelevant to the book's marketing, i.e., the story of your life ("He was born in a small log cabin just outside . . ."). Family and other details that may be appropriate in a jacket blurb aren't necessarily helpful here.

AUTHOR INFORMATION: NONFICTION BOOK PROPOSAL

Slug line

Proposal—Selling Your Ideas   12   **Page number**

Centered, one-third of the way down the page.

Author Information

He's qualified!

Roger McCallister has been selling ideas successfully both   **Double-spaced text**

inside and outside the corporation for more than twenty years.

He is a former senior vice president of sales and marketing for

Cyclops Steel Plating Corporation who now serves as a consultant

on customer service and marketing issues for more than two dozen

1" margin Fortune 500 corporations.

He is also adjunct professor of business administration at

He has a following—several really.

Denver University and former president of the Business Execu-

tive Council, a 300,000-member-strong educational and advocacy

group for middle managers. He continues to serve as a consultant

on sales and marketing issues for the BEC, and he is active in

Mentors International, a nationwide network of mentors and

protégés.

McCallister also writes a regular column on career plan-

Shows media-savvy and promotion skills.

ning for *Middle Manager* magazine and hosts a call-in radio show

on Denver public radio station WBZN-FM. He is also a frequent

speaker at business and trade organizations, having spoken at

fifteen events with a combined attendance of twenty-five thou-

sand over the past year.

Chapter Outline

SUBMISSION TIPS

The chapter outline provides an extended table of contents for your book. It includes a brief description of each chapter.

This need not, and probably should not, be in the classic outline format you learned in your high school composition class. Such an outline may help you actually write the book, but it's a little dry for the purposes of a proposal, which is meant to sell an editor on the merits of each chapter and show how it fits into the book.

FORMATTING SPECS

- You can put multiple chapters on each page of the outline, but it may be less confusing to describe one chapter per page.
- Number pages of the outline, continuing with the last number of the author information section.
- Use the same header you use with the rest of the proposal.
- If the book is divided into parts as well as chapters, first list the part and part heading, then the chapter and chapter heading.
- Indent paragraphs and otherwise follow the same format as the rest of the proposal.

OTHER DOS AND DON'TS

- Don't insert a new title page and start numbering all over again with the outline. The proposal is a single entity.
- Do describe how the chapter will unfold, including any sidebars, tables, charts, photos or other illustrations that will be included.
- Don't tell how many pages or photos you'll have in each chapter. Assuming you haven't actually written the book yet, it's impossible to know, and the information isn't likely to sway an editor.

On manuscript formatting:

"The best thing is to keep it really simple. You get a manuscript in the conventional printed form and edit on that, because it's easier to edit on that. Once all that's cleaned up, you have a hard-copy printout you turn over to a designer or typesetter. That person will style the heads. If the author has gone nuts with trying to style his or her own manuscript with a lot of italics or boldfacing or whatever, this creates a lot of extra work for the editor or typesetter. Keep it as simple as possible and as consistent as you can without trying to desktop publish the manuscript. The designer ultimately just clicks and undoes all that stuff."

—Peter Burford, publisher, Burford Books

CHAPTER OUTLINE: NONFICTION BOOK PROPOSAL

Slug line

Proposal—Selling Your Ideas   13   **Page number**

Centered, one-third of the way down the page.

Chapter Outline

"A" head for Part I.

Part I: Getting Ready   **Whatever format you use, be consistent.**

"B" head for Chapter.

Chapter 1
Overcoming Limitations

Double-spaced text

Every idea sold is sold by someone who has limitations. Those

who sell well are aware of them and overcome them. Dealing with

limitations is the best way of developing self-confidence. This

1" margin chapter explores strategies for self-assessment and overcoming

limitations.

- How to sort out and leverage your best qualities

- Identifying your limitations

- How to evaluate and sharpen your presentation skills

- How to evaluate and improve written presentations

- Why and how to be a continuous student

- Selecting and developing mentors

- Selecting and developing confidants

- How mentors and confidants can help

- How mentors and confidants can hurt

Sample Chapter(s)

SUBMISSION TIPS

Agents and editors almost always want to see at least one sample chapter, even from established authors. If you've already written a book in the same subject area, you might get by without a sample chapter. Even then, however, some editors insist.

The author's natural inclination is to send chapter one, but some agents recommend against this. If chapter one seems too complete, they argue, it might be hard to make a case for the rest of the book.

Ultimately, the number of sample chapters and which ones to send is your judgment call. Look at the chapter outline. Which chapters are most intriguing, most needed to make a case for the book, or most likely to make editors wonder if you can actually deliver on the promise made in the chapter outline? These are the chapters you should include.

FORMATTING SPECS

- Continue with the same slug and pagination as in the rest of the proposal.
- After the first page of the sample chapter, continue using the header and page number. You need not indicate the chapter number or title in subsequent pages.
- Use a 1″ margin on all sides.
- Double-space the text.
- Use a 10- or 12-point plain font such as Times New Roman, Arial, or Courier.

OTHER DOS AND DON'TS

- Do center chapter number and chapter title about one-third of the way down the page, leaving two lines in between.
- Don't assume you must submit chapter one. Submit the most compelling chapter or chapters.

I don't need to know about the author's hobbies, lifestyle, spouse, pets, or the like unless these things are somehow pertinent to the book. When authors ramble on about unimportant things in a book proposal, I figure they will do the same when writing the book.

—Stephen Blake Mettee, founder/publisher, Quill Driver/Word Dancer Press

SAMPLE CHAPTERS: NONFICTION BOOK PROPOSAL

Slug line for proposal, not chapter.

Maintain pagination.

Proposal—Selling Your Ideas   27

Centered, one-third of the way down the page.

Chapter 6

2 lines

Finding the Right Allies

4 lines

1" margin

Double-spaced text

You improve your chances of selling an idea significantly when you bring supportive constituencies on board early as advocates. Getting these early followers on board, however, can be difficult. Members of the group will carefully evaluate your idea and spot any weakness in your plan. Communication is the key to winning them over.

The best way to get any group within or outside the organization on board is by attaching your idea to their interests. If some element of your plan clearly works in the group's interest, you have a natural ally. But if nothing in your idea has any natural appeal to them, you need to find some way for the group to have ownership in your idea. Create a new piece of the plan or modify your idea based on input from the group. Good idea sellers, like good amoebas, stretch and absorb things from the environment around themselves, thereby creating a larger, stronger, healthier whole. As the process continues, initial groups of followers add to the idea and start to sell what is now becoming their idea. They will then bring other groups adjacent to themselves into the growing plan.

2 lines

Subheads help break up copy.

What You Must Know About the Group

Before you can approach the group with your idea, you need to understand some basic things about how it works. These include:

- Who are the leaders of the group, both the titular leaders and the actual ones?
- What are the incentives for the group?

Attachments

SUBMISSION TIPS

If you have supporting materials for your proposal, attach them at the end, preceded by a page that serves as a brief table of contents for them.

Articles from magazines or newspapers that support comments made in your proposal, and articles and columns you have published on the subject are good examples of the types of material that should be attached.

FORMATTING SPECS

- Use a single page with the heading "Attachments" or "Supporting Documents," followed by lines describing the documents.
- Number the Attachments introduction, but not the pages of the documents attached.

OTHER DOS AND DON'TS

- Do use endnotes if you have material from the sample chapter that needs to be referenced. For a discussion of endnotes, see page 87.
- Don't attach material just to make your proposal look more impressive. Size does not matter.

> What I need is enough information about the proposed project to make an informed decision. I need to know what the book is going to be about, who will buy it, how it differs from other books on the same subject, why the author is qualified to write it, what the author will help do to market it, a sample chapter or two, and number of other things.
>
> **—Stephen Blake Mettee, founder/publisher, Quill Driver/Word Dancer Press**

ATTACHMENTS: NONFICTION BOOK PROPOSAL

Slug line

Proposal—Selling Your Ideas   45

Maintain pagination on "Attachments" cover sheet, but leave the actual attached documents unnumbered.

Centered, one-third of the way down the page.

Attachments

Keep it brief.

Report from the American Association of Middle Managers and the

Double-spaced text

Flush left, no indent.

Business Executive Council, April 1999, ``The Middle Manager in

America: Growing Pressures on the Sandwich Generation.''

Column by Roger McCallister, ``Primacy of the Idea in Modern

Business Culture,'' *Middle Manager*, October, 1998.

Book Manuscript
SUBMISSION TIPS

The book manuscript is similar in most respects to the proposal format. This section begins with the basics of the body of the manuscript, then looks at the specific requirements for various elements of the front matter and back matter.

You may well end up submitting the manuscript in two or three stages to the publisher rather than in one installment, and you won't necessarily do this in sequential order. Regardless of that, maintain the same pagination system. Your word processing system will allow you to start with any page number you want in the header. Keep track of the first and last page numbers of each chapter to avoid confusion.

Books, like newspapers and magazines, have become increasingly varied in design in recent years. Sidebars, callout quotes, subheads and short pieces within chapters abound. No universal guidelines exist for handling these formats within books, so confer with your editor early on for guidelines.

FORMATTING SPECS

- Use a 1″ margin on all sides.
- Use a title page.
- Don't number the title page. Begin numbering with the first page of the text of the book, which usually will be the introduction or chapter one.
- Use a slug, either your last name or title of the book.
- Double-space the entire text of the book.
- Use a 10- or 12-point plain font such as Times New Roman, Arial or Courier.
- Generally, put sidebars, captions, and other elements that fall outside the flow of the main chapter at the end of the chapter rather than where you think they should fall. Design and space constraints will dictate their placement, and it's easier for editors and designers to have the elements in a single, easy-to-find location.
- When sending an accepted manuscript, send a disk or CD containing the manuscript along with the hard copy. See the section on Electronic Book Manuscripts below for tips on formatting your manuscript for disk or CD.

OTHER DOS AND DON'TS

- Don't staple anything.
- Don't punch holes in the pages or submit it in a three-ring binder.
- Do submit the manuscript loose-leaf in an envelope—that's why the slug and page numbers are there. If the editor wants to put it in a binder, he will do so.
- Do keep an original copy for yourself both on your computer hard drive and on a separate storage medium kept in a secure place, such as a fireproof safe.
- Don't justify text or align the right margin.
- Don't put any copyright information on the manuscript. It's copyrighted when you write it, and the editor knows this.

Electronic Book Manuscript

SUBMISSION TIPS

Some editors might ask you to submit your manuscript via e-mail or on a disk or CD. The editor can provide you with specific formatting guidelines indicating how she wants the manuscript sent and the type of files she prefers.

FORMATTING SPECS

- Before you send the manuscript, find out how the editor prefers to receive files.
- Use a 1″ margin on all sides.
- Use a title page.
- Remove any formatting that might cause potential glitches when the manuscript is typeset. For instance, don't put two spaces after a sentence, and don't double- or triple-space electronic files by using hard returns.
- Put sidebars, captions, and other elements at the end of each chapter.
- If the editor doesn't specify a particular file format, save the article as a text file. Most word processing programs can read basic text files.
- If you are sending the manuscript via e-mail, send it as an attachment to your e-mail unless the editor requests otherwise.

OTHER DOS AND DONT'S

- Don't use all caps in your subject line.
- Don't submit a manuscript electronically unless the editor specifically requests it.
- Do ask for specific file format guidelines to make sure the editor can open your files.
- Don't justify text or align the right margin.
- Don't put any copyright information on the manuscript. It's copyrighted when you write it, and the editor is aware of this.
- Do call after you've sent a file to make sure the editor has received it.

The biggest surprise I have had as an editor is that many authors, even well-published authors, turn in sloppy writing with the expectation that it is the editor's job to fix it before it gets into print. Today's editors don't have time to repair manuscripts. An editor may fix your problems once, but when you approach him a second time, don't be surprised if you find a cold reception.

—Stephen Blake Mettee, founder/publisher, Quill Driver/Word Dancer Press

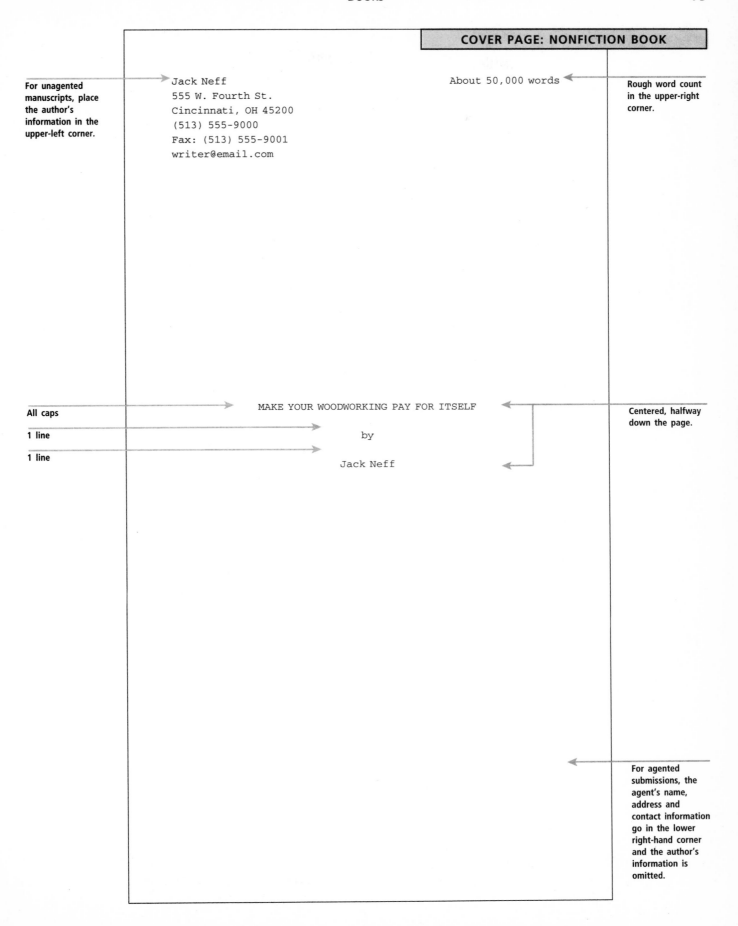

For unagented manuscripts, place the author's information in the upper-left corner.

Jack Neff
555 W. Fourth St.
Cincinnati, OH 45200
(513) 555-9000
Fax: (513) 555-9001
writer@email.com

About 50,000 words

COVER PAGE: NONFICTION BOOK

Rough word count in the upper-right corner.

All caps

MAKE YOUR WOODWORKING PAY FOR ITSELF

Centered, halfway down the page.

1 line

by

1 line

Jack Neff

For agented submissions, the agent's name, address and contact information go in the lower right-hand corner and the author's information is omitted.

MANUSCRIPT: NONFICTION BOOK

Slug line → Neff—Woodworking Pay   1 ← Page number

Centered, one-third of the way down the page. →

Chapter 1

← 2 lines

Develop a consistent hierarchy for these heads. →

Shop Smarts—Saving Money and Space

← 4 lines

Before you find ways to make money by selling woodworking

projects, it makes sense to study your workshop. Consider what

tools you really need, and create a plan for acquiring them.

Find ways to squeeze every penny you can out of the dollars you   ← Double-spaced text

1" margin spend on wood, tools and other supplies. The money you save by

shopping smart and cutting waste adds substantially to the money

you make. You don't have to pay tax on it, and it will make every-

thing you sell more profitable. And, waste hurts the environment

as much as your pocketbook.

← 2 lines

Equipment Basics—What You Really Need

Just which tools you need in your shop will depend on your

projects. Few tools are absolutely essential if you are inge-

nious in finding a way around them, but there are some items most

woodworkers would rather not do without.

Your Shop

How much room do you really need to set up shop? The answer

always depends on what you do. A woodcarver may be able to work

in the corner of a bedroom or basement. Some furniture makers

may feel the need for a 1000-square-foot workshop, plus addi-

tional room for milling and storing wood.

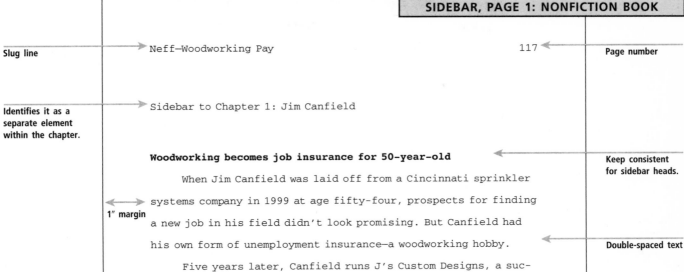

SIDEBAR, PAGE 1: NONFICTION BOOK

Slug line → Neff—Woodworking Pay   117 ← Page number

Identifies it as a
separate element → Sidebar to Chapter 1: Jim Canfield
within the chapter.

Woodworking becomes job insurance for 50-year-old ← Keep consistent
for sidebar heads.

When Jim Canfield was laid off from a Cincinnati sprinkler

1" margin → systems company in 1999 at age fifty-four, prospects for finding

a new job in his field didn't look promising. But Canfield had

his own form of unemployment insurance—a woodworking hobby. ← Double-spaced text

Five years later, Canfield runs J's Custom Designs, a suc-

cessful custom cabinetmaking business in Milford, Ohio. Having

overcome the hurdles of developing a reputation in a new busi-

ness, he now feels better off than when he lost his job.

''The majority of us working for the company had in the

back of our minds that we were going to retire there,'' Canfield

says. ''But I think you've got to get something to fall back on,

because I don't think there are any jobs you can call secure

today.''

Canfield already had some experience selling wood crafts

as a sideline occupation. He had made a potato bed for his wife

after she had threatened to pay thirty-five dollars for one if he

didn't do it. After he made the first one, he used it as a pat-

tern to make 250 more. He also made rocking dinosaurs, modeled

on rocking horses, for kids, and sold those through craft fairs.

But he hadn't thought too seriously about turning his side-

line into a new business. Years earlier, Canfield had considered

starting his own woodworking business but rejected the idea as

too risky at a time he had five children at home. Though he had

spent twenty-five years with his old employer, Canfield wasn't

planning to retire yet or embark on a new career. But when he was

laid off, he figured he had little to lose.

''When you're out of a job, you've got to do something,''

he says. ''I didn't want to relocate, and I didn't want to get

back into fire protection.''

SIDEBAR, PAGE 2: NONFICTION BOOK

Continue with the same slug line.

Neff—Woodworking Pay   118

Maintain pagination.

Canfield minimized the risk of his new venture several ways. He was able to rely on his wife's health insurance, removing one worry in starting his business. He started with the tools he already owned—a table saw, scroll saw, band saw, drill press, shaper, a few routers and assorted hand tools. His severance pay wasn't enough to buy more tools, and he didn't want risk going into debt.

He used some savings to rent a shop space in Blue Ash that helped him attract some walk-in customers. But he says the hardest part of the business for him initially was getting his name around.

''All of my contacts were in an entirely different field,'' he says. ''But the quality of my work helped get the name around. We tried other forms of advertising, but it really didn't work for what we do, which is custom furniture.''

J's Custom Designs now generates gross revenues of more than $100,000 a year. That's enough to allow Canfield to employ one of his sons. And it makes for a career Canfield prefers to his old one.

''It's enjoyable work. It's creative work. And every once in a while, you get a customer who pretty much gives you free hand in what you want to do—and that's even better.''

Captions

Keep with the element illustrated by photos—since the photos illustrate the sidebar text, they're placed here.

Photo A:
Jim Canfield sprays glue on a section of an entertainment center.

Photo B:
Jim Canfield tightens clamps on a section of an entertainment center.

Use codes if you have more than one.

Front Matter

SUBMISSION TIPS

The term "front matter" refers to a wide variety of items that fall between the cover and the body of the finished product. These include:

- Table of contents
- Dedication
- Epigraph or Inscription
- Foreword
- Preface
- Prologue
- Acknowledgments

As books have become increasingly graphic, publishers largely have done away with such genteel niceties as lists of illustrations, photos or tables, which could become books unto themselves and take up space without conveying much useful information.

Tables of contents, on the other hand, have grown to become more detailed and complex, as publishers push for more page breaks, sidebars, and other nontraditional points of entry to appease readers with increasingly short attention spans.

One thing all front matter has in common is that it is not numbered as part of your manuscript. In some cases, publishers number these elements separately with Roman numerals in the actual book. Generally, you don't need to worry about this unless you have a lot of front matter, or individual elements begin to span more than two pages. If your front matter is lengthy, number it using Roman numerals, or Arabic numerals and an altered slug that indicates the pages belong to the front matter.

FORMATTING SPECS

- Generally, front-matter pages are not numbered.
- Front-matter pages get slugs in the header.
- Heads for each element are centered.

OTHER DOS AND DON'TS

- Don't get carried away with most of these elements. Readers routinely skip over them, and they take up space that should be devoted to the text of the book. A book overladen with front matter is as annoying as a speaker who repeatedly clears his throat before speaking or opens with a long, pointless anecdote.
- Do have a good reason for including any of these elements. They are not requirements. You will not be penalized for skipping them, except for the table of contents and the acknowledgments.

In the front matter, people need to know how to spell the word *foreword*.
—Leslie Towle, president, Heritage Books Inc.

Table of Contents

SUBMISSION TIPS

This is what it's all about. Tables of contents are one of the first places a potential consumer goes to evaluate a nonfiction book. Somewhere along the line, publishers got wise to this fact. Now, editors look for the table of contents to be more complete, descriptive, and compelling than ever.

Nonfiction tables of contents are as varied as the books they describe, so prescribing a slapdash formula for them is pointless. Many remain bare bones, merely listing the chapter titles and page numbers. Increasingly, however, the table of contents for many books looks like the chapter outline in the book proposal—no-holds-barred hucksterism aimed at doing the same sales job on the reader as the author and/or agent did on the editor. So, keep that book proposal handy as you prepare the table of contents.

FORMATTING SPECS

- Center the heading "Table of Contents" or "Contents" one-third of the way down the page.
- Provide extra-wide margins, at least 1½".
- Don't number pages as part of the manuscript.
- Use a slug in the same place as the header in the rest of the manuscript.
- At the very least, include the chapter titles.
- Include such front-matter elements as prefaces, forewords, and prologues.
- Include back matter, such as the appendix or glossary.
- Don't include acknowledgments, dedications and other short bits of front matter.
- Page numbers are the numbers as they occur in your manuscript. The numbers in the book will be different, of course, and impossible for you to predict.

OTHER DOS AND DON'TS

- Do get a sense from the editor of what direction she wants from the table of contents. This should dictate how much you present and how you present it.

> We usually do the front matter ourselves because it's so changeable with the ultimate page count of the book. If you end up with a book that's 162 pages and you have to cut two pages to make it an even signature, you go to the front matter and figure out how to do that. Front matter is such a very minor editorial chore that I think the author should just (stick with the) obvious.
>
> —Peter Burford, publisher, Burford Books

TABLE OF CONTENTS: NONFICTION BOOK

Slug line → Neff—Woodworking Pay ← No number

Centered, one-third of the way down the page. →

Table of Contents

Dedications, Epigraphs, and Inscriptions

SUBMISSION TIPS

These short pieces are all handled similarly from a format standpoint. A dedication is a short statement dedicating the book to a person or persons, often in combination with some expression of affection. An epigraph or inscription is a quote that sums up, signifies or sets the tone for the book.

FORMATTING SPECS

- Dedications and epigraphs are centered about a third of the way down the page.
- Don't number the page.
- Use the slug in the header.
- Keep them to two or three lines.
- Don't put a heading above these to label them (e.g., "Dedication").

Foreword

SUBMISSION TIPS

A foreword is a commentary or review of the book written by an expert in the field or someone familiar with the story of the book's creation. If the name and the review do not add something to the appeal of the book, they serve no function.

FORMATTING SPECS

- Like the rest of the front matter, the foreword has a slug but no page numbers.
- Use a heading, starting about a third of the way down the first page.
- The name of the foreword's author goes flush right at the end of the text, followed by title and affiliation.
- Optional: Flush left after the text may go the city and year where and when the foreword was written.

OTHER DOS AND DON'TS

- Don't confuse the foreword with the preface or introduction. The foreword is written by someone other than the author.

> We provide authors with guidelines once they've signed a contract. Sometimes they don't follow these guidelines, which ultimately causes more work for me or for people in our production department. The biggest frustration is when the manuscript isn't organized logically or if the author tries to format it with a lot of bells and whistles. We have people who do design and formatting here so all that is taken out anyway. It saves time to not put extra formatting in there in the first place.
>
> —Donya Dickerson, associate editor, McGraw-Hill

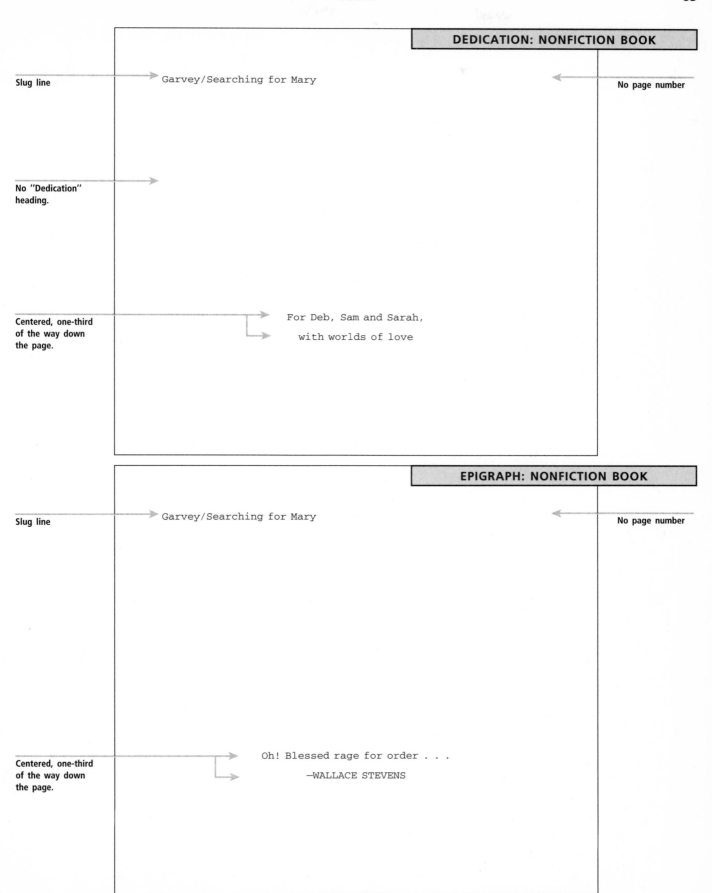

DEDICATION: NONFICTION BOOK

Slug line → Garvey/Searching for Mary ← No page number

No "Dedication" heading. →

Centered, one-third of the way down the page.
> For Deb, Sam and Sarah,
> with worlds of love

EPIGRAPH: NONFICTION BOOK

Slug line → Garvey/Searching for Mary ← No page number

Centered, one-third of the way down the page.
> Oh! Blessed rage for order . . .
> —WALLACE STEVENS

FOREWORD: NONFICTION BOOK

Foreword: Selling Your Ideas

One way to keep front matter organized is by providing a slug line for the section. Whatever information you include in your slug line, make sure it's consistent throughout the manuscript.

No page number

<u>Foreword</u>

Centered heading, one-third of the way down the page.

4 lines

I was there when Roger McCallister had his first big idea in business. He was a twenty-two-year-old sales representative for Cyclops Steel just out of college when he returned from a sales call very excited, clutching a handful of napkins covered with notes, scribbles, and diagrams. After he calmed down a bit, I soon discovered that he had landed on a concept that would radically change the steel industry forever.

Double-spaced text

1" margin

I never did quite understand how a sales rep fresh out of college came up with what would be known as the continuous casting process, but I quickly realized the power of his proposal. Unfortunately, the guys in engineering weren't used to taking cues from downy-faced salesmen just out of college. I knew we had a tough selling job ahead of us internally.

Good thing Roger already had an instinct for how to work the system. He had enlisted the help of his boss—me—and given me ownership of the idea at an early stage. Soon, I was using my contacts with junior-level executives in the engineering department to find out if this idea truly had legs. By the time we made a formal presentation to the engineering department, we already had the support of key people in that organization.

I watched Roger's career skyrocket after that day, and was witness to plenty more good ideas where the first came from. But more than just having good ideas, Roger learned quickly how to get other people to embrace them as their own.

When he came into my office twenty-three years later with the idea for this book, I knew he had a winner. If there was one person I would want selling my idea up and down the organization chart, Roger is the man. I know readers will come away armed with insights into how the system works and how ideas go from napkins to blueprints.

2 lines

Pittsburgh, 1999

Herman Oreschmelter
CEO, CycleX Corp.

Flush left.

Flush right.

Preface, Prologue, and Acknowledgments

SUBMISSION TIPS

Formatting for each of these front-matter elements is very similar, though each serves a different purpose. We've chosen to show you a sample acknowledgments page, but the same formatting applies to all front-matter elements discussed on this page.

A preface explains the story behind the book—the reason why it was written, the background, the unusual stories that were part of its creation. In other cases, a preface may serve as another pitch for the book, explaining why it's needed and how to use it—at least that's the theory. A preface sometimes gets muddled in with the purposes of an introduction or a prologue.

A prologue explains events or history that provide a context for the rest of the book. If you're writing a book that chronicles an event, for instance, the prologue might describe the events or forces that led up to that event.

Acknowledgments are the place where you thank the folks who helped you put the book together. Though the preface and prologue are purely optional, the acknowledgments are not. It's virtually impossible to write a nonfiction book without someone's help, and it's just plain impolite not to thank them. Though this is front matter, it's among the last things you'll write.

Publishers and editors generally consider the introduction part of the body of the book. But in some cases, the book's introduction is treated as front matter, too, and handled the same way as these other elements.

FORMATTING SPECS

- As with other front-matter elements, these are not numbered as part of the rest of the manuscript. They do, however, get slugs.
- If you have only one page for these elements, stick with the regular manuscript slug.
- If you have two or more pages in these elements, use a specialized slug for each element (e.g., Acknowledgments: Selling Your Idea), or use the regular manuscript slug and number the entire front-matter section separately using Roman numerals. It's really your call.
- For each element, drop about a third of the way down the page and use a centered heading.
- Then, drop an extra line, indent, and get started.

OTHER DOS AND DON'TS

- Do include these elements if they truly add something to the book.
- Don't include prefaces or prologues just to appear impressive. This is truly the mark of an amateur.
- Don't forget anyone who helped in preparation of the book when you write the acknowledgments, unless they don't want to be mentioned. It can pay to keep a running file of names and ways that people helped so you don't have to scramble for this information at the end.

ACKNOWLEDGMENTS: NONFICTION BOOK

Slug line

Neff—Insiders' Guide to Greater Cincinnati

No page number

Centered heading, one-third of the way down the page.

Acknowledgments

4 lines

Thanks to the many folks who provided tips and other assistance in the preparation of this book, particularly Gordon Baer

Double-spaced text

1" margin

for the back cover photo, Mary Anna DuSablon and Rita Heikenfeld for their insights on Cincinnati cuisine, and tipsters Julie Harrison, Michelle Howard, Bob Humble, Gail Paul, Irene Schaeffer, Joan Schaffield, Karen Tennant, Julie Whaley and Joel Williams.

Among the librarians and public relations people who went out of their way to help include Alliea Phipps, who must operate the fastest fax/modem this side of the Alleghenies, and Bea Rose for her assistance in procuring photos of Albert Sabin.

Thanks to coauthor Skip Tate for his help, not least of which was writing half the book. Also thanks to editor Molly Brewster and to Beth Storie and the rest of the crew at The Insiders' Guides for making this possible.

Special thanks go to my wife, Glenda, for general forebearance and for again taking everyone but the dogs away for the occasional cramming to meet deadlines.

Back Matter

SUBMISSION TIPS

It's a dirty job, but somebody has to do it—that would be you.

Back matter is that mostly unglamorous but necessary part of any nonfiction book that includes the endnotes, appendix, glossary, bibliography, epilogue, and index. Here's information on what they are and how to handle them:

- **Endnotes** are used mainly for scholarly manuscripts and business proposals but are sometimes included in other nonfiction books based on significant documentary research. They can be handy in eliminating the need to pepper the manuscript with attributions, allowing instead a quick reference to the endnote for anyone seeking the source of information. Endnotes may also be included in more scholarly articles. *The Chicago Manual of Style* is the definitive source on handling these and other back-matter issues.

- The **appendix** is used for material that supports information or arguments in the book but which is too lengthy to include or would hamper the natural flow of the book. It's similar to the attachments found on a book proposal.

- A **glossary** lists and defines special terminology used in the book, such as technical phrases, foreign words, and phrases, or any other specialized lexicon or jargon.

- The **bibliography** is a list of books cited in the manuscript, used in researching the manuscript or otherwise useful as further reading. A bibliography with a brief commentary or review of significant titles and why they're helpful adds some value to an otherwise fairly dry formality. The bibliography may also be called "Recommended Reading" or incorporated into a section on "Resources" that includes information on Web sites of interest, events or where to buy products related to the book's subject.

- The **epilogue** provides a final thought from the author, perhaps summing up the work's impact on the author or, in a revised edition, detailing changes that have occurred since or because of the book.

- The **index** is a more or less detailed listing of all the people, places, things, and concepts cited in the book. Generally, indexes are prepared by professional indexers who are paid a relatively nominal fee out of the author's royalties. Unless you have a special love for this kind of work, you're better off leaving it this way. This book won't cover how to do the index, but several specialized books are available if you're interested, such as the *Handbook of Indexing Techniques: A Guide for Beginning Indexers*, by Linda K. Fetters (Fetters Infomanagement Co.), and *Indexing Books*, by Nancy C. Mulvany (University of Chicago Press). There is also a chapter on indexing in *The Chicago Manual of Style*.

FORMATTING SPECS

- Unlike front matter, back matter is numbered as part of your manuscript.
- Back-matter pages take the same slug as the rest of the manuscript.
- All elements of the back matter start with a centered heading about a third of the way down the page and are double-spaced, like the rest of the manuscript.
- Because the details of these listings are far easier to grasp by seeing than reading about them, check the models that follow for additional details.
- The format for the appendix and epilogue are the same as for front-matter elements, except that they are numbered as part of the manuscript. See the front-matter section on page 79 for details.

OTHER DOS AND DON'TS

- Do only include these elements if you have a good reason. As with front matter, you don't get any extra credit for having a well-rounded assortment of back matter. Except for the index, and at times the bibliography, none of these elements are indispensable.

Check competitive books to see if your book needs an appendix, a glossary, a resource directory, a bibliography, or footnotes.

—Michael Larsen, agent and author, *How to Write a Book Proposal, 3rd Edition*

ENDNOTES: NONFICTION BOOK

Slug line

Simopoulos—The Omega Plan   332

Page number

Centered heading, one-third of the way down the page.

Comments and Endnotes

4 lines

1" margin

Chapter 1: Found: The Missing Ingredients for Optimal Health

2 lines

Indent each endnote.

    1. The chart has been adapted from a chart that appeared in reference 10 above. It compares the number of patients who were free from cardiac death and nonfatal heart attacks.

Double-spaced text

    2. De Longeril, M., P. Salen, and J. Delaye. ''Effect of a

Title

Authors

Mediterranean Type of Diet on the Rate of Cardiovascular Complications in Patients With Coronary Artery Disease.'' *J Amer Coll Cardiology*, 1996; 28(5):1103-8.

Journal title/year/ volume/number.

Page numbers

    3. Grady, D. ''Unusual Molecule Could Be Key to Cancer Patients' Weight Loss,'' in *The New York Times*. Jan. 4, 1996, p. B10.

BIBLIOGRAPHY: NONFICTION BOOK

Slug line

Garvey—Searching for Mary   235

Page number

Centered heading, one-third of the way down the page.

Bibliography

4 lines

Commentary adds value to the listings.

Literature available on the subject of Marian apparitions is copious and of wildly varying quality and credibility. Of works consulted in the course of my research, most of which are listed below, a few stand out as superior tools for readers interested in plumbing the subject to greater depths.

Double-spaced text

1″ margin

Sandra Zimdars-Swartz's *Encountering Mary* has set the standard for balanced, scholarly treatment of the phenomena of popularity among communities of believers. If you read only one more book on the subject, this should be the one.

No more succinct and helpful presentation of the Catholic Church's position in regard to claims of private revelation is to be found than in Benedict Groeschel's *A Still, Small Voice*.

Though only tangentially related to the subject of Marian apparitions, *The Physical Phenomena of Mysticism*, by Herbert Thurston, is a sublimely creepy compendium from the outer fringes of Roman Catholic lore—everything from stigmata to miraculous corpses. This book is out of print, but well worth searching for in the stacks of your local library—makes Stephen King read like A.A. Milne.

Flush left.

Ashton, Joan. *Mother of All Nations*. San Francisco: Harper and
    Row, 1989.
Christian, William A., Jr. *Apparitions in Late Medieval and Renaissance Spain*. Princeton, N.J.: Princeton University
    Press, 1981.

Indent second line of two-line listing.

GLOSSARY: NONFICTION BOOK

Slug line → Neff—Insider's Guide to Greater Cincinnati   405 ← Page number

Centered heading, one-third of the way down the page. →

Glossary

← 4 lines

Flush left. → Goetta: A mixture of oats and pork sausage developed by German ←

Indent the second line of a two-line definition. →   immigrants and peculiar to Cincinnati.   Double-spaced text

Please?: What many Cincinnatians say for ''Pardon me?'' or

''Come again?''

|← 1" margin →| Three-Way: Cincinnati Chili in its fundamental form, including,

from the bottom up, spaghetti, a runny meat-filled chili

seasoned with cocoa and cinnamon and grated cheddar

cheese. Note, there is no one- or two-way. This, or the

higher-order ways, are the only ways. A four-way also in-

cludes onions and a five-way also includes onions and

beans.

CHAPTER THREE

SHORT AND SPECIALIZED PIECES

Fillers/Anecdotes

SUBMISSION TIPS

Submission of other short forms generally follows the guidelines for articles, with a few exceptions. Since these are short pieces, it would be pointless to query editors on them. Simply submit these items with a brief cover letter noting what's enclosed, provide a brief paragraph on your background and politely request a response.

These items usually take up a page or less. When they take more, follow the same guidelines for pagination and headers as you would with articles. It's okay to leave less white space above the item to make it fit on one page.

FORMATTING SPECS

- Use a 1″ margin on all sides.
- Don't number the first page.
- If you need a second page, put a slug, or one- to two-word name at the top left corner of the header. Also put a page number at the top right-hand corner of the second page.
- Include rights offered or negotiated and a word count in the top right corner of the first page.
- Include name, address, phone number, fax, and e-mail in the top left corner of the first page.
- When appropriate, put the working title in all caps or boldface and the subtitle underlined or in italic centered, about one-third of the way down the page from the top margin.
- Don't include a byline. Such short items rarely get them. Occasionally, an editor will give the writer credit in a tag line, but you don't need to include your name with the manuscript.
- Drop four lines, indent and begin the item.
- Double-space the entire text of the item.
- Keep type size 10-12 points.

OTHER DOS AND DON'TS

- Don't use a notation of any kind at the end of the item.
- Don't staple the manuscript to the cover letter; insert them loose-leaf.
- Don't use a separate cover page.
- Do put one item per page when making multiple submissions.
- Don't insult the editor's intelligence or intentions by putting a copyright notice on the manuscript. It's copyrighted as soon as you write it.
- Don't use unusual fonts. A simple Times Roman will do fine.
- Don't fax or e-mail your items unless you have permission from the publisher or if the submission guidelines state it is acceptable.

ELECTRONIC SUBMISSIONS

These short items are ideally suited for electronic submissions. Generally, you'll send unformatted text files as attachments or in the body of the e-mail. But don't go clicking away until you've ascertained the electronic submission policies of the publication or syndicate to which you're sending material. Writer's guidelines (see Request for Guidelines Letter on page 22) should spell out the electronic guidelines.

Shorts are common in many types of magazines. Most publications even state in their guidelines that the short is the best way to break in. Perhaps writers haven't given this idea its due. I've broken into my share of major magazines this way. So before you dismiss the short, know that it's a surefire way to show an editor what you can do.

—**Jennifer Nelson, full-time freelancer and contributor to *Writer's Market***

FILLER/ANECDOTE

Jon Newberry
444 W. Eighteenth St.
Cincinnati, OH 45200
(513) 555-3334
newberry@email.com

First North American Rights — Rights offered.
About 225 words — Word count.

Title in all caps, centered, one-third of the way down the page.

CONFESSIONS OF A USED-CAR SALESMAN

No byline.

4 lines

Double-spaced text

1″ margin

On my first day as a used car salesman for a dealership owned by Marge Schott (former owner of the Cincinnati Reds known for dismissing managers and front office staff on, shall we say, whimsical grounds), she fired the guy who had hired me. Another salesman said: ''Don't worry. I've been here for two years, and that's the twentieth sales manager I've worked for.''

Actually, the highlight of my career was my first job at Toyota of Cincinnati, then part of what's now the Performance chain. They rewrote and refined the book on high-pressure sales techniques. First day there, my manager (still the best salesman I've ever seen in action—probably a millionaire by now) was showing me the ropes. He talked some poor girl into putting down a fifty-dollar deposit to hold a car so that we couldn't sell it before she brought her husband back to see it that night. I kept calling them to see when they were gonna come back and at least pick up their deposit, and they said we could keep it. They knew if they set foot back on the lot, they'd own a car when they left. She was terrified.

That summer we finally toppled Jake Sweeney from the top of the list as the number one used-car lot in the city.

Columns and Op-Eds

SUBMISSION TIPS

Columns, be they how-to, business or op-ed pieces, are all styled similarly and generally follow the article format described earlier. The only difference is a brief (usually one-sentence) biographical paragraph appended to the end of the column.

Clearly, you do need to query before landing a regular column assignment with a publication, preferably with three or more ideas. A query isn't necessary for an op-ed submission, though it can certainly help to write ahead for writer's guidelines (especially with magazines) before making a submission.

A brief cover letter introducing either assigned or speculative submissions is in order. Mention the enclosure and provide any other information that may help in editing the piece, including your e-mail address and the best times to reach you at the phone number(s) you provide. Especially with newspapers, editors' hours can vary widely, so give both a daytime and evening phone number. Also provide any information or contact phone numbers that could help in fact checking.

FORMATTING SPECS

- Use a 1″ margin on all sides.
- Use the upper-left corner for your name, address, phone number, e-mail, and other particulars (single-spaced).
- Include rights offered (First North American Rights are generally assumed) and a rough word count (single-spaced) in the upper-right corner.
- Put suggested title or headline in all caps or boldface centered, starting about a third of the way down the page.
- Drop a line and put "by" in lowercase, centered.
- Drop a line and type your name, centered.
- Double-space the rest of the column or op-ed.
- Indent paragraphs, except for your bio at the end of the piece.
- On the second page, use a slug (generally your last name) in the top left corner, and number pages in the top right corner.
- At the end of the column, type a return and then, with no indentation, write your bio. This can be in italic, if you want, but it doesn't need to be. Keep your bio to one sentence, mentioning your name, what you do, where you live, and any other fact that may be of relevance to readers of the column or op-ed. Only in the most compelling circumstances add another sentence.

OTHER DOS AND DON'TS

- Do include daytime and evening phone numbers for submissions to newspapers.
- Do research your column or op-ed as thoroughly as you would anything else you write. Just because it's an opinion doesn't mean you don't need facts. Indeed, the need to verify facts is, if anything, even more pronounced in an opinion piece.
- Do use your real name in an op-ed submission. No worthwhile publication accepts opinion pieces from anonymous contributors.
- Do be brief. About 700 words is generally the top end for opinion pieces. Generally, the shorter the piece, the better its chance of being published, though anything under 250 words is generally letter-to-the-editor material rather than an op-ed piece.
- Don't e-mail or fax your submission unless you have permission from the publication or if the submission guidelines state it is acceptable.

ELECTRONIC SUBMISSIONS

Many newspapers have electronic submission guidelines that can be found on their editorial or op-ed pages. Magazines with regular opinion features will often mail their writer's guidelines to you if you request them (see Request for Guidelines Letter on page 22), and many magazines have their guidelines posted on their Web sites.

> Start sending your work out to local publications, not overlooking the free ones, the neighborhood shopping guides, anything. When you're ready, put together ten sample columns, and send them around to newspapers, asking if they'd like to run your stuff regularly. Pay no attention at first to whether you get paid or how much—that comes later.
>
> —Adair Lara, columnist, *San Fransico Chronicle*

Personal Essays

SUBMISSION TIPS

Personal essays, also known as personal narratives, are found in newspapers and magazines and typically run under two thousand words. They provide a glimpse into a writer's life and can run the gamut from opinionated rants to whimsical observations. As with other short and specialized pieces, a query usually isn't necessary, but you should check a publication's guidelines before you send an unsolicited essay just to make sure.

Include a brief cover letter describing the essay you are sending and provide any other information that indicates why you are qualified to write on the subject you are covering. Be sure to include your e-mail address and a day and evening phone number.

FORMATTING SPECS

- Use a 1″ margin on all sides.
- Put your name, address, phone number, e-mail, and other particulars (single-spaced) in the upper-left corner.
- Put the rights offered (First North American Rights are generally assumed) and a word count (single-spaced) in the upper-right corner.
- Type your suggested title in all caps or boldface, centered, about a third of the way down the page.
- Drop a line and put "by" in lowercase, centered.
- Drop a line and put your name, centered.
- The rest of the essay should be double-spaced.
- Indent paragraphs.
- On the second page, use a slug (usually your last name) in the top left corner; in the top right corner, number the pages.
- At the end of the column, type a return and then, with no indentation, write your one-sentence bio. It should include your name, what you do, and where you live.

OTHER DOS AND DON'TS

- Do use your real name in a personal essay submission.
- Do include daytime and evening phone numbers.
- Don't forget to verify names, places, etc. that you mention in your essay. Just because it's personal doesn't mean it shouldn't be accurate.
- Don't fax or e-mail your essay unless you have permission from the publication or if submission guidelines state it is acceptable.

ELECTRONIC SUBMISSIONS

Check a magazine or newspaper's submission guidelines to see if they accept personal essay submissions via e-mail. If they do, send an unformatted text file of your essay as an attachment or in the body of your e-mail, unless otherwise instructed in the guidelines.

COLUMN/OP-ED/PERSONAL ESSAY

Pete Rightmire
444 Conkles Hollow Lane
Edgewood, KY 44105
Day: (606) 555-3443
Night: (606) 555-4000
pete@email.com

First North American Rights
About 700 words

Include both day and evening phone numbers.

COMMODES COME OUT OF THE CLOSET

by

Pete Rightmire

Title in all caps, centered.

1 line

1 line

4 lines

If you skim through any home-design magazine or visit one of the area's new upscale model home shows, you're likely to notice that builders and buyers continue to place a lot of emphasis on large, luxurious bathrooms. But while whirlpool tubs, showers that double as saunas, and exotic faucets and fixtures have been the stars of these mega-baths for years, the more utilitarian, but arguably, the most important part of any bathroom—the toilet—has pretty much gone unnoticed.

1" margin

Double-spaced

Until recently, that is. It looks as if the toilet has finally come into its own. Last year the National Park Service built a two-stall facility in a Pennsylvania recreational area at a cost of $391,000. That's almost $196,000 a head.

And while no one's as efficient as the federal government at flushing money down the drain, New York City recently took the plunge, building $200,000-plus comfort stations in its city parks. But with four stalls and one urinal each, the total construction cost, per toilet, came to only $45,000, a fraction of what the Park Service spent.

If you're one of those folks who thinks nothing's too good for your pet, you can cough up $215 for the Litter Maid, an electric litter box that cleans itself after every use. This is just for cats, because, as one pet shop owner put it, ''A cat's insulted going to a box that's not scooped.'' Dogs, on the other hand, aren't anywhere near as picky about where they take care of business. Pretty much like most men.

Bio line is flush left, italic (optional) and one sentence.

Pete Rightmire is a freelance writer who lives in Edgewood, KY.

Radio and TV Commentaries

SUBMISSION TIPS

Because many radio and TV commentaries come from people who don't write for a living, and some are submitted in the form of demo tapes rather than manuscripts, the style here is fairly informal. It's best to contact the station directly, find out who deals with commentary submissions and discuss with them what form they prefer.

Generally, the manuscript should indicate how long it will take you to deliver the piece and provide a brief bio and a suggested lead-in for the announcer. Otherwise, commentaries work like other articles and short forms.

FORMATTING SPECS

- Use a 1" margin on all sides.
- Use the top left corner for a title for your piece, your name, address, phone number, e-mail, and other particulars (single-spaced).
- At the top right corner, include a word count and estimated air time.
- Put suggested title in all caps or boldface centered, starting about a third of the way down the page.
- Drop a line and put "by" in lowercase, centered.
- Drop a line and type your name, centered.
- If possible, include a brief, one- or two-sentence lead-in that can be used by an announcer to introduce your piece.
- Double-space the rest of the commentary.
- Indent paragraphs, except for your bio at the end of the piece.
- On the second page use a slug (generally your last name) in the top left corner, and number pages in the top right corner.
- At the end of the column, with no indentation, write your bio. This can be in italic, if you want, but it doesn't need to be. Generally, keep your bio to one sentence, mentioning your name, what you do, where you live, and any other relevant fact.

OTHER DOS AND DON'TS

- Do include daytime and evening phone numbers.
- Do research your commentary as thoroughly as you would anything else you write. Just because it's an opinion doesn't mean you don't need facts. Indeed, the need to verify facts is, if anything, even more pronounced in an opinion piece.
- Do use your real name.

ELECTRONIC SUBMISSIONS

Some stations may accept electronic submissions. Check with the contact person at the station for guidelines.

RADIO AND TV COMMENTARY

Out of the Water Closet   513 words, Time: 2:25   *Word count/*
Pete Rightmire   *estimated air time.*
444 Conkles Hollow Lane
Edgewood, Ky 44105
Day: (606) 555-3443
Include both day   Evening: (606) 555-4000
and evening phone   pete@email.com
numbers.

                                                                                1 line
                    COMMODES COME OUT OF THE CLOSET
                                                                                1 line
                                    by

                              Peter Rightmire

                                                                                4 lines

INTRO: Skim through any home-design magazine or tour any new upscale model homes and you'll discover builders and buyers place a
Lead-in introducing   lot of emphasis on large, luxurious bathrooms. But, as commentator
the piece.   Pete Rightmire noticed, until recently, the spotlight has been
                        focused on all but the most important part of any bathroom.

                                                                                2 lines

            If you visited one of the area's recent home shows, you may have
        noticed that lavish bathrooms are still a hot-selling feature. But
        while whirlpool tubs and exotic faucets and fixtures have been the
        stars of these mega-baths for years, the more utilitarian, but
        arguably, the most important part of any bathroom—the toilet—has
        pretty much gone unnoticed.
            Until recently. It looks as if the toilet has finally come into
1" margin its own. Last year the National Park Service built a two-stall
        facility in Pennsylvania at a cost of $391,000. That's almost
        $196,000 a head. And while no one's as efficient as the federal
        government at flushing money down the drain, New York City recently
        took the plunge, building $200,000-plus comfort stations in its
        city parks. But with four stalls and one urinal each, the total   *Double-spaced*
        per-toilet cost came to only $45,000, a fraction of what the Park
        Service spent.
            And if you can't swing the money for one of these pricey priv-
        ies, do the next best thing and upgrade your current commode. Toto
        offers a seat that features antibacterial glazing, a water spray,
        heat and a fan, for just $800—though you may feel a bit nervous
        settling down onto a seat that's plugged into an electric outlet.
        For the true music lover, manufacturer Jammin Johns offers toilet
        lids shaped like guitars and pianos for $150 to $250.

Bio line is flush
left and one
sentence.   *Pete Rightmire is a freelance writer who lives in Edgewood, KY.*

part 2

FICTION

CHAPTER FOUR

SHORT STORIES

What You Need to Submit

Submitting short stories is quite simple. Unlike with novels (where you typically need to submit a query letter as well as a few sample chapters, an outline and a synopsis), with a short story you only need to send a cover letter and the story (in its entirety). But before you actually submit your story, obtain a copy of the publication's writer's guidelines. To save time, first try to locate the publication's Web site to obtain the guidelines. A search engine such as www.google.com can help locate a publication's Web site. If you can't find the Web site, then proceed to write to the publication.

Request for Guidelines Letter

SUBMISSION TIPS

Send a brief letter stating that you'd like to receive the writer's guidelines. It's also a good idea to ask whether the publication offers the guidelines on its Web site (if there is one).

FORMATTING SPECS

- Address it to the correct editor.
- Use a 1″ margin on all sides.
- Use block or semiblock format.
- Keep it to one paragraph.
- Include your name, address, phone number, e-mail, and fax.
- Enclose an SASE.

OTHER DOS AND DON'TS

- Don't mention anything about your story at this point—all you want are the guidelines.
- Don't mention anything about yourself.
- Don't use "Dear Sir," "Dear Madame," etc. in your salutation.
- Don't address it Mr., Ms., Mrs., or Miss unless you're certain of the person's gender and marital status. If unsure, write, "Dear Pat Smith."
- Do keep the letter brief and to the point.
- Don't fax or e-mail a request for guidelines unless the publication indicates it is acceptable to do so.

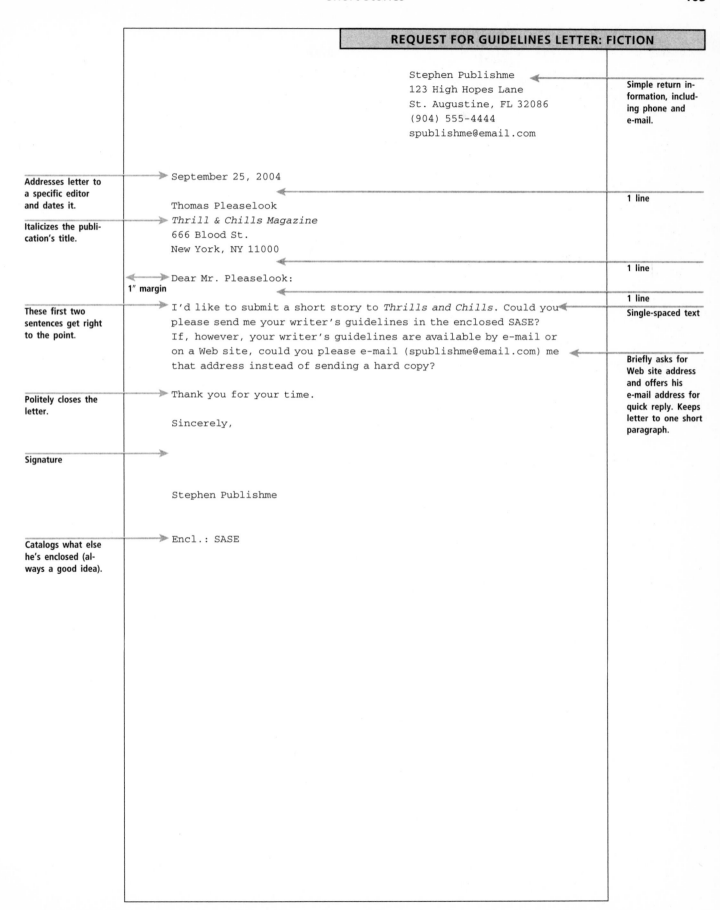

REQUEST FOR GUIDELINES LETTER: FICTION

Stephen Publishme
123 High Hopes Lane
St. Augustine, FL 32086
(904) 555-4444
spublishme@email.com

Simple return information, including phone and e-mail.

September 25, 2004

Addresses letter to a specific editor and dates it.

1 line

Thomas Pleaselook
Thrill & Chills Magazine
666 Blood St.
New York, NY 11000

Italicizes the publication's title.

1 line

Dear Mr. Pleaselook:

1″ margin

1 line

I'd like to submit a short story to *Thrills and Chills*. Could you please send me your writer's guidelines in the enclosed SASE? If, however, your writer's guidelines are available by e-mail or on a Web site, could you please e-mail (spublishme@email.com) me that address instead of sending a hard copy?

Single-spaced text

These first two sentences get right to the point.

Briefly asks for Web site address and offers his e-mail address for quick reply. Keeps letter to one short paragraph.

Thank you for your time.

Politely closes the letter.

Sincerely,

Signature

Stephen Publishme

Encl.: SASE

Catalogs what else he's enclosed (always a good idea).

Cover Letter

SUBMISSION TIPS

Your cover letter is important for two reasons: It lets the editor know who you are and how you write. The best cover letters contain three short paragraphs, in the following order:

- The **introductory** paragraph (state the story's title, then hook the editor with a brief description of your story).
- The **biographical** paragraph (in one or two sentences, explain a bit about yourself that's pertinent to the story, such as previous publishing credits, why you're sending it to this particular publication or how a personal experience influenced your story).
- The **concluding** paragraph (politely close the letter).

While publication will hinge on the story itself, a strong cover letter will ensure your story will at least get a close read. Remember to keep it brief and to the point.

FORMATTING SPECS

- Use a standard font or typeface (avoid bold, script or italics, except for publication titles).
- Put your name, address, phone number, e-mail, and fax in the top right-hand corner or on your letterhead.
- Use a 1″ margin on all sides.
- Address it to a specific editor (call and get the appropriate editor's name, and make sure you know the gender).
- Keep it to one page.
- Use block or semiblock letter format (no indentations or extra spaces between paragraphs).
- Include an SASE or postcard for reply, and state in the letter that you have done so. (The postcard is cheaper and easier for everyone involved. You can have them printed in bulk.)
- Single-space the body of the letter; double-space between paragraphs.
- Give the story's exact word count.
- Thank the editor for considering your story.
- Optional: Mention whether you're soliciting other magazines.
- Optional: Mention how long you'll wait for a response.
- Optional: Mention that your manuscript is disposable and does not need to be returned (this is often just assumed).
- Optional: State that you're able to send your story on disk, CD or via e-mail (this doesn't come up until the editor actually wants to publish your story).

OTHER DOS AND DON'TS

- Do mention if your story has been—or will be—published in another publication.
- Do indicate familiarity with the publication. Make a brief positive comment about the publication, but keep it to a sentence, be sincere and don't go overboard.
- Don't use "Dear Sir," "Dear Madame," etc. in your salutation. Don't use Mr.,

Ms., Mrs., or Miss unless you're certain of the person's gender and marital status. If unsure, write, "Dear Pat Smith."

- Don't state that some other publication has rejected your story.
- Don't ask for advice or criticism—that's not the editor's job at this stage in the game.
- Don't mention anything about yourself not pertinent to the story: you're a first-time writer, you've never been published, or how much time you've spent on the story. Your story must stand on its own.
- Don't bring up payment for the story. It's premature.
- Don't mention copyright information.
- Don't include your social security number.
- Don't staple your cover letter to your story (a paper clip is okay).
- Don't fax or e-mail your cover letter and story unless you have permission from the editor or if submission guidelines state it is acceptable.

Electronic Cover Letter

SUBMISSION TIPS

Before you send a cover letter and story to a publication via e-mail, make sure they accept electronic submissions by contacting the publication directly or checking out their writer's guidelines. Never send a story via e-mail unless you have permission from the editor or if their submission guidelines state it is acceptable.

FORMATTING SPECS

- Include the same information in your cover letter as you would in a paper cover letter—name, address, phone, fax, etc. It's not necessary to include your e-mail address in the body of the e-mail, since the editor can easily click "Reply" to respond.
- Use the subject line to introduce the title of your story.
- Follow the same format you would with a paper cover letter, including the date, salutation, and block paragraph format.

OTHER DOS AND DONT'S

- Don't use all caps or exclamation points in the subject line.
- Don't insert clip art graphics or other images in your cover letter. Keep it simple.

A fiction submission should be accompanied by a cover letter. The cover letter should be addressed to the appropriate editor and include a brief biography with any prior publishing credits, relevant educational background (i.e., workshops, writer's conferences, grants, residencies, other writing experience, degrees, etc.). A SASE is mandatory for a reply.

—**Nan Leslie, fiction editor,** *The Green Hills Literary Lantern*

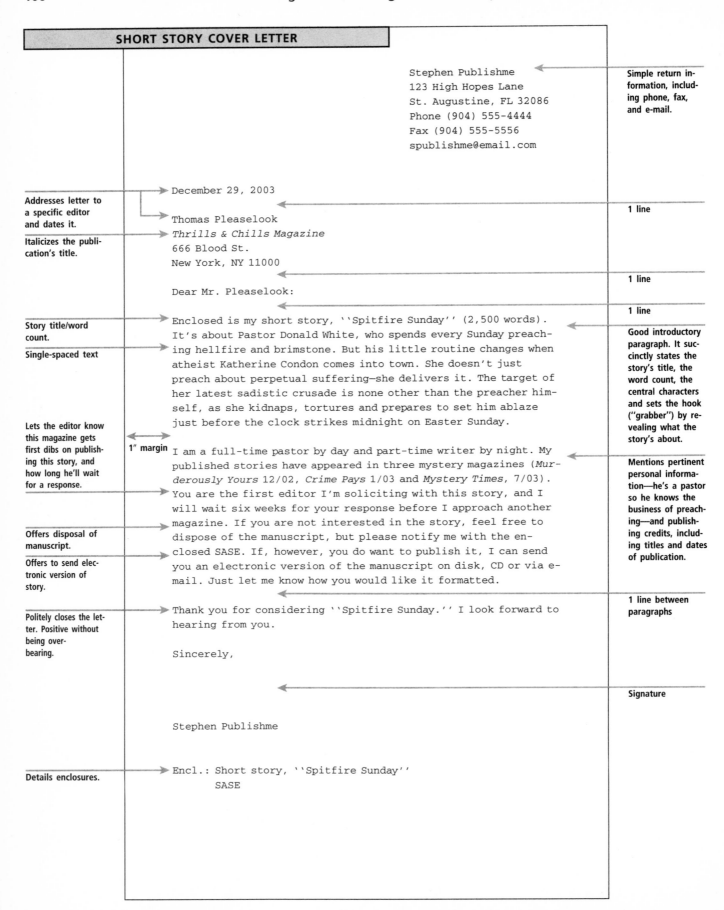

SHORT STORY COVER LETTER

Stephen Publishme
123 High Hopes Lane
St. Augustine, FL 32086
Phone (904) 555-4444
Fax (904) 555-5556
spublishme@email.com

Simple return information, including phone, fax, and e-mail.

December 29, 2003

Addresses letter to a specific editor and dates it.

1 line

Thomas Pleaselook
Thrills & Chills Magazine
666 Blood St.
New York, NY 11000

Italicizes the publication's title.

1 line

Dear Mr. Pleaselook:

1 line

Enclosed is my short story, ''Spitfire Sunday'' (2,500 words). It's about Pastor Donald White, who spends every Sunday preaching hellfire and brimstone. But his little routine changes when atheist Katherine Condon comes into town. She doesn't just preach about perpetual suffering—she delivers it. The target of her latest sadistic crusade is none other than the preacher himself, as she kidnaps, tortures and prepares to set him ablaze just before the clock strikes midnight on Easter Sunday.

Story title/word count.

Single-spaced text

Good introductory paragraph. It succinctly states the story's title, the word count, the central characters and sets the hook (''grabber'') by revealing what the story's about.

1" margin

I am a full-time pastor by day and part-time writer by night. My published stories have appeared in three mystery magazines (*Murderously Yours* 12/02, *Crime Pays* 1/03 and *Mystery Times*, 7/03). You are the first editor I'm soliciting with this story, and I will wait six weeks for your response before I approach another magazine. If you are not interested in the story, feel free to dispose of the manuscript, but please notify me with the enclosed SASE. If, however, you do want to publish it, I can send you an electronic version of the manuscript on disk, CD or via e-mail. Just let me know how you would like it formatted.

Lets the editor know this magazine gets first dibs on publishing this story, and how long he'll wait for a response.

Offers disposal of manuscript.

Offers to send electronic version of story.

Mentions pertinent personal information—he's a pastor so he knows the business of preaching—and publishing credits, including titles and dates of publication.

Thank you for considering ''Spitfire Sunday.'' I look forward to hearing from you.

1 line between paragraphs

Sincerely,

Politely closes the letter. Positive without being overbearing.

Signature

Stephen Publishme

Encl.: Short story, ''Spitfire Sunday''
       SASE

Details enclosures.

COVER LETTER: MISTAKES TO AVOID

Stephen Publishme
123 High Hopes Lane
St. Augustine, FL 32086

No telephone
number or e-mail.

December 29, 2003

Thomas Pleaselook
Thrills & Chills Magazine
666 Blood St.
New York, NY 11000

Salutation is far
too informal.

Dear Tom,

Every sentence in this paragraph begins with "I."

Should begin with
information about
the story, not
himself.
Shouldn't tell the
editor he's never
been published by
a professional
publication.

I have been a man of the pulpit for the last twenty-two years and
I know about faith and evil and sin and redemption. I am also a
published poet and fiction writer. I've had numerous poems published in our local paper and I write weekly stories for the
church bulletin. I get lots of praise from my congregation for
my stories, and other people in the community have made glowing
remarks about my poetry.

Spends too much
time trying to im-
press the editor.

Who cares—what
qualifies them to
give a valued
opinion?

Too colloquial.

Always a bad idea
to tell the editor
how much time
you've spent on the
story—irrelevant.

Should be
"who" not
"that."

Anyhow, I've been working on this one short story for about five
months now that I'd like your magazine to publish. It's about a
minister who gets caught on fire and burned to death by a new
woman in town that doesn't agree with his preaching practices.
I'm sure you'll appreciate this story as it is based on some real
people I have known and therefore it is based in reality but I
made a lot of it up too. It'll scare the heck out of your
readers.

Of course he'd like
the magazine to
publish it—doesn't
need to be stated.

Doesn't tell enough
about the story, but
does reveal the end-
ing! Where's the sto-
ry's hook? Sounds
stupid, obsequious
and manipulative—
fails to let the story
stand on its own.

Never ask for advice
or criticism—that's
not the editor's job
at this stage in the
game.

If for some reason you do not wish to publish this story, I would
appreciate your wise and professional opinion about how to make
it better.

Thank you for your time.

Sincerely,

Stephen Publishme

No mention of the
story in the
enclosures.

Encl.: SASE

Nowhere on this page does the writer mention the word
count, the story's title or the main characters.
This letter is too self-congratulatory, informal, laden with
errors and altogether unappealing.
Even if the enclosed story is spectacular, the editor will
be skeptical when reading it (if he bothers reading it
after wading through this poor cover letter).

Reply Postcards

If you're a bit paranoid about whether your story actually makes it to the publication, you may send a reply postcard along with your story. Having it signed by the editor (or someone on the staff) and sent back to you will alleviate any worries that the package didn't make it to its destination. Two caveats: (1) Not all editors are gracious enough to send your reply postcards back—but most do; (2) Just because you receive a postcard reply from a publication, you cannot assume your story has been read or will be read in the next few days or even weeks. Your reply postcard's only function is to let you know your submission has been received.

Your best bet to ensure an editor will return your reply postcard is to make it neat and simple to use. That means typing your postcard and not asking the editor to do anything other than note your submission has been received. Although it's okay to leave a space for "Comments," keep the space small and never expect it to be filled in—most editors simply don't have the time or a reason to write anything in it. You'll turn off an editor if you ask him to do too much.

Creating a suitable and functional reply postcard is easy. If you create a reply postcard similar to the one below you'll be just fine. Above all, remember to keep things short and sweet—and, of course, always be sure the postcard has a stamp in the top right corner on the side with your address.

REPLY POSTCARD

Stephen Publishme
123 High Hopes Lane
St. Augustine, FL 32086

Your story was received on _____

We need more time to consider your story and will be in touch. ☐

Yes, we are interested in your idea. An editor will be in touch soon. ☐

No, we are not interested in your story at this time. ☐

Comments: _____

_____

_____

_____

Short Story Manuscript

SUBMISSION TIPS

Establish yourself as a professional by following the correct short story format. A separate cover/title page is not necessary; it marks you as an amateur.

FORMATTING SPECS

- Use a 1″ margin on all sides.
- Do not number the first page.
- Include the word count and rights offered in the top right corner of the first page.
- Include your name, address, phone number, fax, and e-mail in the top left corner of the first page.
- Put the story's title, centered in all caps, about one-third of the way down the page from the top margin.
- Skip a line and write "by" in lowercase, then skip another line and put your name in all caps. (If using a pseudonym, put that name in all caps, and then on the next line put your real name in parentheses.)
- Drop four lines, indent and begin your story.
- Double-space the entire text of the story.
- Put a slug or one- to two-word name in the top right corner of every ensuing page (your last name and the page number or the story's title and the page number).
- Optional: Typing "THE END" in all caps when the story is finished. (Some editors like this because it closes the story; other editors prefer the story just end and consider it an insult for you to tell them it's the end. It's your call.)

OTHER DOS AND DON'TS

- Do paper clip pages together in the top left corner (butterfly clamps work well for stories longer than ten pages).
- Do keep an original copy of the story for yourself.
- Don't put your social security number on the manuscript.
- Don't use a separate cover/title page.
- Don't justify the text or align the right margin. Ragged right is fine.
- Don't insult the editor's intelligence or intentions by putting a copyright notice on the manuscript. It's copyrighted as soon as you write it.
- Don't include or submit a disk or CD version of your story unless the editor asks for it.
- Don't use unusual fonts. A simple Times Roman, Arial or Courier is fine.
- Don't e-mail or fax your story to a publication unless you have permission from the editor or if their submission guidelines state it is acceptable.

Electronic Short Story Manuscript

SUBMISSION TIPS

E-mail submissions are only acceptable when you have permission from the publication or if their submission guidelines indicate it is acceptable. Don't forget to include your cover letter in the body of your e-mail.

FORMATTING SPECS

- Before you send the manuscript, find out how the editor prefers to receive files.
- Follow the same formatting specs as above for a paper manuscript submission.
- If the editor doesn't specify a particular file format, save the article as a text file. Most word processing programs can read basic text files.
- If you are sending the manuscript via e-mail, send it as an attachment to your e-mail unless the editor requests otherwise.

OTHER DOS AND DONT'S

- Don't use all caps in your subject line.
- Do ask for specific file format guidelines to make sure the editor can open your files.
- Don't use a separate cover/title page.
- Don't justify text or align the right margin.
- Don't put any copyright information on the manuscript. It's copyrighted when you write it, and the editor is aware of this.
- Don't put two spaces after sentences within the manuscript.
- Don't use hard returns to double- or triple-space the manuscript.

The more standard your format, the less editors are distracted from what is really important: the story itself. Manuscript format is not a place to innovate.

—George Scithers, editor *Weird Tales* magazine

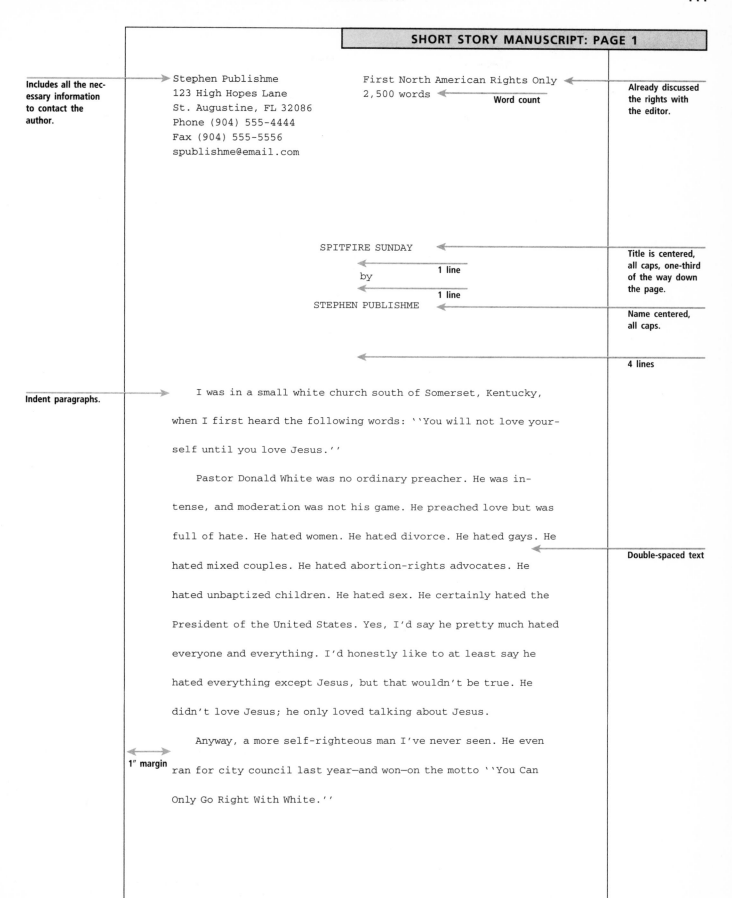

SHORT STORY MANUSCRIPT: PAGE 1

Includes all the necessary information to contact the author.

Stephen Publishme
123 High Hopes Lane
St. Augustine, FL 32086
Phone (904) 555-4444
Fax (904) 555-5556
spublishme@email.com

First North American Rights Only
2,500 words

Word count

Already discussed the rights with the editor.

SPITFIRE SUNDAY

1 line

by

1 line

STEPHEN PUBLISHME

Title is centered, all caps, one-third of the way down the page.

Name centered, all caps.

4 lines

Indent paragraphs.

    I was in a small white church south of Somerset, Kentucky, when I first heard the following words: ''You will not love yourself until you love Jesus.''

    Pastor Donald White was no ordinary preacher. He was intense, and moderation was not his game. He preached love but was full of hate. He hated women. He hated divorce. He hated gays. He hated mixed couples. He hated abortion-rights advocates. He hated unbaptized children. He hated sex. He certainly hated the President of the United States. Yes, I'd say he pretty much hated everyone and everything. I'd honestly like to at least say he hated everything except Jesus, but that wouldn't be true. He didn't love Jesus; he only loved talking about Jesus.

    Anyway, a more self-righteous man I've never seen. He even ran for city council last year—and won—on the motto ''You Can Only Go Right With White.''

Double-spaced text

1" margin

SHORT STORY MANUSCRIPT: LAST PAGE

Upper-left corner is
blank; the
manuscript is often
held together with
a paperclip in the
upper-left corner.

Publishme 15

Slug line is in
upper-right corner
for short stories.

As she poked and prodded him with that scalding hot branding

iron, he danced amidst the flames, cursing and wailing at her.

''You shall not be torn between loving yourself and loving Je-

sus,'' he said. ''For Jesus is life, and if you do not love Jesus

you cannot love your own life. You can hate me and torture me all

you want. I know you're only doing it because you don't love Je-

sus. You don't love yourself!''

Katherine couldn't bear to hear one more word. She took the

branding iron and pressed it to his mouth. He could not speak; he

could barely scream. A look of horror fell over his face as he

collapsed in the ring of fire. Then she pointed the gun at him. I

thought she was finally going to shoot him, to put an end to this

poor man's suffering. But she didn't. She dropped the gun,

watched him burn, and smiled. Once his screaming stopped, Kather-

ine picked up the pistol as if to finish the act, to make sure

he'd be dead.

To my surprise, she put the pistol in her mouth and fired.

Optional, but
perfectly placed if
used.

THE END

CHAPTER FIVE

NOVELS

The Novel Proposal
WHAT YOU NEED TO SUBMIT

There are a few ways to submit your novel proposal to an agent or publisher, depending on the individual agent's or publisher's submission guidelines. Some want only a query letter, others request a query letter and the complete manuscript, others demand a query letter plus three sample chapters and a synopsis, and still others request that you submit a query letter as well as a few sample chapters, an outline, and a synopsis. All want an SASE (self-addressed stamped envelope) with adequate postage, unless they request an electronic submission.

To determine what you need to submit, consult the current edition of *Novel & Short Story Writer's Market* or *Writer's Market*. Both books have submission specifications that come straight from the editors and agents telling you just what to send, how to send it, when to expect a response and other information unique to the agent or editor you will be soliciting.

Expect to send at least a query letter, a synopsis, and three consecutive sample chapters. These are the most important—and most requested—parts of your novel proposal. However, some agents and editors might request an outline, as well as an author biography and an endorsements page. If you don't know whom you'll be soliciting and what they demand, try to have the following prepared before you start sending out submissions:

- A darn good query or cover letter
- A synopsis
- At least three consecutive sample chapters
- A chapter-by-chapter outline
- An author biography
- Endorsements

We will explore each of these six components in detail throughout the ensuing pages (the sample chapters are in The Novel Manuscript section on page 142), including specific submission tips, formatting specs, other dos and don'ts, and samples for each. Know that your novel proposal will probably mix and match several of these six components. Rarely will you need to send them all in the same submission package, since each agent and editor has his or her own preferences. But you probably will need to use each of them at one time or another, so try to prepare everything before you actually start submitting your novel. Finally, include a Novel Proposal Contents Page (see page 127) with your novel proposal, just to keep things organized. This is especially helpful when submitting two or more proposal items, particularly when one is a chapter-by-chapter outline (so it doesn't get confused with the sample chapters). And, of course, always include an SASE if you're sending your submission through the mail.

Query Letter to Agent or Publisher
SUBMISSION TIPS

A query letter is your letter of inquiry. It serves two functions: to tell the agent or editor what you have to offer, and to ask if they're interested in seeing it.

Though you can send the query letter attached to a novel proposal, many agents and editors prefer you send the query letter either by itself or with a synopsis and a few sample pages from your novel (not more than twenty). This is called a blind query or a preproposal query, because you're sending it without having been asked to send it. No matter what you call it, it's your three-minute chance to hook the agent or editor on your novel. If she likes your query, she'll call and ask for either specific parts of your novel proposal (a synopsis and three sample chapters, for example) or the entire manuscript. Then she'll make her decision.

Some agents and editors, however, prefer you accompany your initial query letter with other parts of your novel proposal. If that's the case, include the required materials (a synopsis, sample chapters, outline, etc.) specified by the particular agent or publisher (in the listing in *Novel & Short Story Writer's Market, Writer's Market,* and *Guide to Literary Agents*). When you accompany your query with your novel proposal, the query also becomes your cover letter.

Whether you submit the query by itself or accompanying other material, it is vital. You must make it compelling, interesting, even funny—*anything* to make it outstanding to the agent or editor you're soliciting. But limit it to a page or a page and a half.

Although every winning query works its own magic, all good queries should contain the following:
- A "grabber" or hook sentence that makes the reader want to get his hands on the actual novel.
- One to three paragraphs about your novel.
- A short paragraph about you and your publishing credentials (if you have any).
- A good reason why you're soliciting the person you're soliciting. (Why this agent or publisher instead of another?)
- The length of the novel.
- A sentence or two about the intended audience.
- An indication that an SASE is enclosed if you are sending it through the mail.

Arguably the most important aspect of any query is the grabber, the hook that lures the reader into wanting to see—and, of course, read—your novel. Your grabber should be part of the paragraphs you devote to telling about the novel. Another good idea is to point out why your novel is different from all the others. Then spend a few sentences telling about yourself, in which you list your publishing credentials (if you have any) or toss in a personal anecdote that's pertinent to the novel (explain that you spent two years in the Peace Corps in Somalia if that's where your story takes place). In another paragraph, mention why you're sending your query to this particular agent or editor. Feel free to allude to an author the publisher publishes (or the agent represents) whose work is similar to yours. Doing this is not just name-dropping, but proof you've done your research. Finally, always include an SASE if you're sending your query through the mail.

FORMATTING SPECS

- The basic setup for a query to an agent or publisher is similar to a short story or article query.
- Use a standard font or typeface.
- Use a 1″ margin on all sides.
- Use block or semiblock letter format.
- Use letterhead or put your name, address, phone number, e-mail, and fax in the top right corner.
- Address your query to a specific agent or editor (call to get the appropriate name).
- Try to keep the query to one page, but it's acceptable to go as long as 1½ pages.
- Single-space the body of the letter; double-space between paragraphs.
- Catalog every item you're sending in your enclosures.

OTHER DOS AND DON'TS

- Do state any previous publishing credits.
- Do mention if your novel isn't finished, and state the date your manuscript will be complete.
- Do tell if you're sending simultaneous submissions to other agents and editors.
- Do address your letter to a specific agent or editor.
- Don't e-mail or fax your query unless a publisher or agent requests it or if their guidelines state it is acceptable.
- Don't mention that you're a first-time writer or that you've never been published.
- Don't spend much time trying to sell yourself. Your manuscript will stand on its own.
- Don't state that some other agent or editor has rejected your novel.
- Don't ask for advice or criticism—that's not the agent's or editor's job at this stage in the game.
- Do summarize any relevant experience you have.
- Don't mention anything about yourself not pertinent to the novel.
- Don't bring up payment expectations (advances, royalties, etc.).
- Don't mention copyright information.
- Don't staple your query letter to your manuscript.
- Don't go over two pages.

> I prefer to receive concise, one-page query letters (with SASEs) that tell me a bit about the kind of book it is—i.e., what genre it falls in, other titles that the author might compare it to—and something brief about its plot or distinguishing hook. I also like such letters to include basic information about the author; I especially want to know if the author has ever been published or represented before (if so, when, where and by whom), and any other distinguishing information relevant (even in a quirky way) to his or her profile as an author.
>
> **—Theresa Park, agent, Sanford J. Greenburger Associates**

Electronic Query Letter to an Agent or Publisher

SUBMISSION TIPS

Many publishers and agents now accept queries via e-mail. Before you send a query off to a publisher or agent electronically, however, you must either have permission to send it via e-mail or make sure that their guidelines indicate that it is acceptable.

Communicating with a publisher or agent via e-mail should be just as formal and respectful as if you were sending it through the mail. The basic tone and format of the electronic query shouldn't be much different from a query sent on paper.

FORMATTING SPECS

- Include the same information you would in a paper qery, including your name, address, phone, and fax, etc. The top right-hand corner or top center position is fine for this, though you can also include this information in a signature line at the end. It isn't necessary to include your e-mail address in the body of the e-mail, however, since the editor can reply easily with the click of a button.
- Put a description of your novel or its title in the subject line.
- Follow the same format you would with a paper query, including the date, salutation to a specific editor, and block paragraph format. See the above tips for submitting a paper query; the same rules apply.

OTHER DOS AND DON'TS

- Don't use all caps or exclamation points in the subject line.
- Don't submit an e-mail query unless specifically requested by the publisher or agent or if it is stated clearly in their guidelines that it is acceptable.
- Don't insert clip art graphics or other images into your query letter.
- Do maintain formal communication, just like you would in a paper query.

I look for concise intelligent description of the author's work . . . and a good sense of humor never hurts either.

—Harvey Klinger, agent, Harvey Klinger, Inc. Literary Representation

QUERY TO AGENT: NOVEL

Nicholas Sparks
111 Query Rd.
Bookdeal, SC 44444
(333) 555-1234
sparks@email.com

July 5, 1995

Diane Cleaver
Diane Cleaver, Inc.
% Sanford J. Greenburger Associates, Inc.
55 Fifth Ave.
New York, NY 10003

Dear Ms. Cleaver,

I would like to introduce you to my second literary novel entitled *The Notebook*.

My first novel, *Wokini*, in which I collaborated with William Mills, was published by Orion Books, a division of Random House in 1994. An inspirational work, it was characterized by Al Neuharth, founder and former chairman of *USA Today*, as ''a powerful picture on the meaning of life,'' while Peter Ueberroth called it ''overwhelming and insightful.'' A moderate commercial success, by May 1995, it had sold over 56,000 copies.

This novel, *The Notebook*, is a love story inspired by two special people who recently passed away after sixty years of marriage. They were no one you would know, but there was a grand romance between them, an underlying passion and understanding that had taken a lifetime to develop. In this day and age, the unconditional love they felt for one another makes for a wonderful story, one that is all too rare and much too beautiful to let die without being told.

Like *Romeo and Juliet* or *The Bridges of Madison County*, however, all great love stories need tragedy and separation, as well as love, to fully touch the reader, and their story was no exception. Alzheimers became part of their lives during their final years together and my most vivid memories are those of my grandfather sitting by a bedside and reading to his wife of sixty years, a woman who no longer remembered him. Seeing them this way nearly broke my heart, but never once did he bemoan his plight. ''In my mind,'' he used to tell me, ''she's the young woman I married long ago and nothing will ever change that.'' This story is their story, a story of love, the most faithful love I have ever seen.

The Notebook is a tender novel set in the deep South, a love story written in lyric prose. Like most Southern literary novels, *The Notebook* envelopes all that is special about the region and its people: tradition, loyalty, kindness, love and remembrance. Yet, this novel stands alone in two important ways.

Always address your query to a specific agent.

1″ margin

1 line

1 line

1 line

1 line between paragraphs

Provides important information about previous writing history—lists publication dates, publisher and notable reviews.

Single-spaced text

Summarizes the ''hook'' of the novel—a story about a love that lasts a lifetime, that defies both illness and death.

Very important: Here the author points out what distinguishes this particular book from the thousands of other love stories and novels out there, while still making a strong case for the universality of its appeal. How will this book be fresh and different, yet familiar enough for everyone to relate to?

QUERY TO AGENT: NOVEL PAGE 2

First, it is one of the few passionate love stories written about the elderly, and it reveals a rare but dignified portrait of a couple struggling with the ultimate reality that their lives will be ending soon. Even more importantly, however, *The Notebook* is the first novel that describes the heart-wrenching effects of Alzheimers disease on two people who had loved each other all their lives. The result is a moving eulogy to old age itself—a story of love and grief which pretty much sums up the notable context of most lives.

As a young writer in South Carolina, I am looking for an experienced agent based in New York and your reputation is impeccable. Your varied experiences as an editor at Doubleday, Straight Arrow, Scribner's and Simon & Schuster are impressive, and it would be an honor to work with you on this novel.

> The author has done significant research on the agent and chose her for specific reasons. He is a professional who had spent some time thinking about the kind of agent he thought would be most appropriate for his work.

I have included a short biography for your review. The novel is 52,000 words and fully complete. May I send you a copy of the manuscript? I look forward to hearing from you soon.

Sincerely,

> Including a brief biography is always a good idea— educational background, publications (if any), anything else relevant to your profile as an author.

> Signature

Nicholas Sparks

P.S. Because 22 percent of the people in this country (40+ million) are over 52 years old and 4.5 million people suffer from Alzheimers, this book is unique and marketable to a wide audience. In addition, at 52,000 words, it is short enough not to be cost-prohibitive to most publishing houses.

> An extremely important postscript—here the author tells me who the potential market for this book is, and why it might be particularly attractive to a publisher, from a marketing perspective.

This letter was initially addressed to Diane Cleaver, an agent at Sanford J. Greenburger Associates, without the knowledge that Diane had passed away three months earlier. The letter was passed on to Theresa Park of Sanford J. Greenburger Associates who provided these comments. Before you send a query, make sure that the agent or editor you are addressing is still there. A quick phone call can confirm it.

QUERY LETTER TO AGENT: MISTAKES TO AVOID

839 Wrong Way Drive
Unpublished, OH 40511
July 24, 2004

The author's name, phone number, and e-mail are missing. Be sure to include all pertinent contact information.

Big Time Literary Agency
200 W. Broadway
New York, NY 10125

ALWAYS address your query to a specific agent.

Dear Agent:

I have just completed my first novel and would like to sell it to a publisher. I have never had a book published but I know this novel will be a bestseller. I'm looking for an agent to help me. I would really appreciate it if you could read over the enclosed chapters and give me some advice on whether you think this a good novel and if it needs any extra work to make it a bestseller.

Never mention that you're a first-time writer or that you have never been published—it singles you out as an amateur.

1" margin

Don't ask an agent for advice or criticism—that's not the agent's job nor the purpose of the query letter.

The Subject of Susan is about 60,000 words long and is geared toward an adult audience. It is all about a headstrong woman named Susan and her trials and tribulations throughout the 1950s and beyond as she makes her way in the legal world after graduating from law school as the only woman in her graduating class.

This is vague and tells the agent very little about the book. There is no "hook" to capture the agent's attention.

This is my first novel and while I am not familiar with the legal world, since I'm not a lawyer, I find the subject fascinating and think readers will too. I've written a lot of short stories dealing with women's lives but they were much more romanticized than the story of Susan. Susan is someone you would know in real life. I have spent the last 20 years of my life raising my children and think I have what it takes to become a successful writer.

Don't draw attention to your lack of experience as a writer, and don't mention anything about yourself that is not pertinent to the novel. Keep all your information focused on the book itself.

I own the copyright on this book and would like to discuss possible advances and royalties with you sometime soon.

Don't mention copyright information or payment expectations. This is a query to assess an agent's interest in your novel.

Thank you very much,

Donna Dudley

There is nothing here to indicate how this book will distinguish itself from the thousands of other similar books that have been published. How will this book be different?

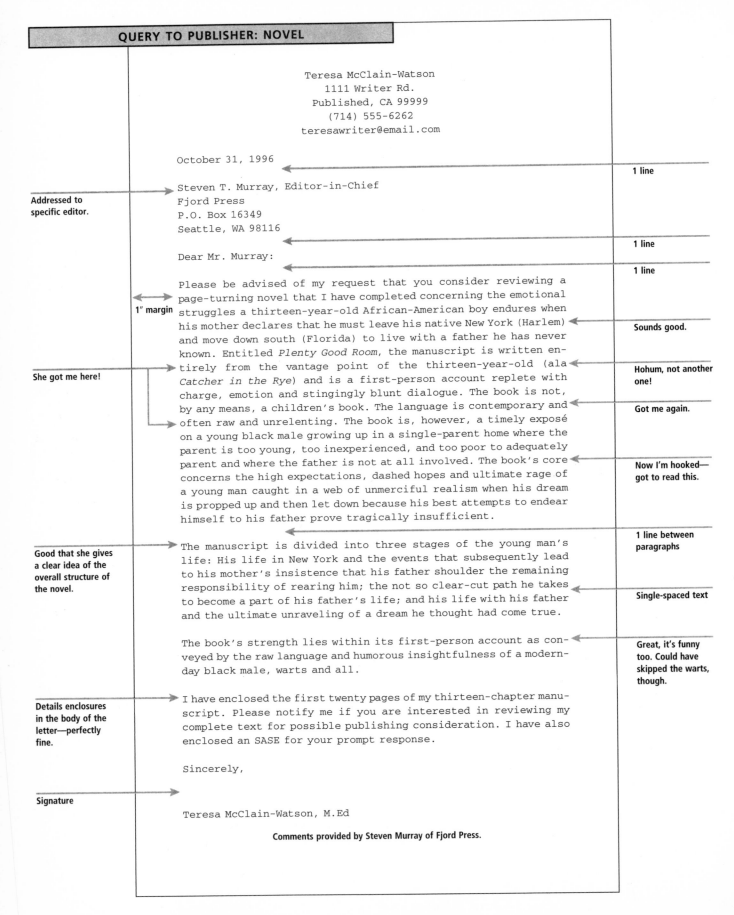

QUERY TO PUBLISHER: NOVEL

Teresa McClain-Watson
1111 Writer Rd.
Published, CA 99999
(714) 555-6262
teresawriter@email.com

October 31, 1996   ◄   1 line

Steven T. Murray, Editor-in-Chief
Fjord Press
P.O. Box 16349
Seattle, WA 98116   ◄   1 line

Addressed to specific editor.

Dear Mr. Murray: ◄   1 line

     ◄   1 line

1″ margin

Please be advised of my request that you consider reviewing a page-turning novel that I have completed concerning the emotional struggles a thirteen-year-old African-American boy endures when his mother declares that he must leave his native New York (Harlem) and move down south (Florida) to live with a father he has never known. Entitled *Plenty Good Room*, the manuscript is written entirely from the vantage point of the thirteen-year-old (ala *Catcher in the Rye*) and is a first-person account replete with charge, emotion and stingingly blunt dialogue. The book is not, by any means, a children's book. The language is contemporary and often raw and unrelenting. The book is, however, a timely exposé on a young black male growing up in a single-parent home where the parent is too young, too inexperienced, and too poor to adequately parent and where the father is not at all involved. The book's core concerns the high expectations, dashed hopes and ultimate rage of a young man caught in a web of unmerciful realism when his dream is propped up and then let down because his best attempts to endear himself to his father prove tragically insufficient.

Sounds good.

Hohum, not another one!

Got me again.

Now I'm hooked— got to read this.

She got me here!

The manuscript is divided into three stages of the young man's life: His life in New York and the events that subsequently lead to his mother's insistence that his father shoulder the remaining responsibility of rearing him; the not so clear-cut path he takes to become a part of his father's life; and his life with his father and the ultimate unraveling of a dream he thought had come true.

1 line between paragraphs

Single-spaced text

Good that she gives a clear idea of the overall structure of the novel.

The book's strength lies within its first-person account as conveyed by the raw language and humorous insightfulness of a modern-day black male, warts and all.

Great, it's funny too. Could have skipped the warts, though.

I have enclosed the first twenty pages of my thirteen-chapter manuscript. Please notify me if you are interested in reviewing my complete text for possible publishing consideration. I have also enclosed an *SASE* for your prompt response.

Details enclosures in the body of the letter—perfectly fine.

Sincerely,

Signature

Teresa McClain-Watson, M.Ed

Comments provided by Steven Murray of Fjord Press.

QUERY TO PUBLISHER: MISTAKES TO AVOID

Contact information is missing.

July 24, 2004

Get Published Books
P.O. Box 554
Success, NY 11584

Find out the name of a specific editor at the publisher who deals with the type of books you write.

Never mention that you're a first-time writer or that you have never been published.

Dear Editor:

As a first-time novelist with no publishing credits, I hope you can help me. I have a great manuscript that I am working on and would like you to take a look at it and let me know what you think.

1" margin

Don't ask for advice or criticism—that's not the purpose of the query letter.

My novel is called *The Subject of Susan* and tells the story of a woman and her trials and tribulations throughout the 1950s and beyond. She is the only woman in her law school class, which leads to some interesting conflicts.

This is vague and tells the publisher very little about the book. There is no "hook" to capture the editor's attention.

I don't know a lot about the legal world, but I've read a lot of John Grisham's books and think lawyers are fascinating—if I didn't get married so young I might have gone to law school my-self. I've been a stay-at-home mom for more than fifteen years and have had a lot of time to work on the book. My husband and my friends think the book is really a page-turner and encouraged me to try and get it published.

Don't draw attention to your lack of experience as a writer, and don't mention anything about yourself that is not pertinent to the novel.

I own the copyright on this book and am looking for an advance in the area of ten thousand to twenty thousand dollars.

Don't mention copyright information or payment expectations. This is a query to assess a publisher's interest in your novel.

Thank you very much,

Donna Dudley

There is nothing here to indicate how this book will distinguish itself from the thousands of other similar books that have been published. How will this book be different?

Cover Letter

SUBMISSION TIPS

A cover letter accompanying a novel proposal is a tightened version of a query letter. Like the query letter, your cover letter lets the editor know who you are *and* what you have to offer. But, because so much information is included in the rest of the proposal, and because you should have already queried the agent or editor, the cover letter can be fairly brief—no more than 1-1½ pages.

With a cover letter, you don't need to spend as much time explaining why what you have to offer is worthwhile; you just need to introduce the material. Why spend a lot of space synopsizing your novel and telling about yourself when you've included a synopsis, three sample chapters and an author bio? Of course, you still want to hook the editor or agent into believing your novel is worth considering, but you don't need to go into as much detail as you would in a blind query letter.

A good rule of thumb is to keep your cover letter to three or four short paragraphs and organize it in the following order:

- The **introductory** paragraph (state the novel's title, then hook the editor with a brief description of your novel).
- The **biographical** paragraph (in one or two sentences explain anything about yourself that's pertinent to the novel, such as previous publishing credits, or why you're sending it to this particular agency or publisher).
- The **concluding** paragraph (politely close the letter).

FORMATTING SPECS

- Use a standard font or typeface (no bold, script, or italic).
- Place your name, address, phone number, e-mail, and fax in the top right corner.
- Use a 1″ margin on all sides.
- Address it to a specific editor (call and get the appropriate editor's name).
- Keep it to 1-1½ pages.
- Use block or semiblock letter format.
- Single-space the body of the letter; double-space between paragraphs.
- Catalog every item you're sending in your enclosures (three chapters, synopsis, SASE).

OTHER DOS AND DON'TS

- Do thank the editor.
- Do give the novel's exact word count.
- Do mention whether you're soliciting other agents or editors.
- Do include an SASE or postcard for reply, and state in the letter that you have done so.
- Don't mention that you're a first-time writer, or that you've never been published, or that someone else has rejected your novel.

At Harlequin/Silhouette, when we request authors to send a query letter, we'd like to see a one-page cover letter with a two-page, single-spaced synopsis of the story along with a self-addressed stamped envelope.

         —Isabel Swift, vice president of editorial, Harlequin Books

- Don't start your pitch all over again in the cover letter. If your query made enough of an impression to spark the editor or agent's interest, alluding to their request to see the proposal is enough. Your novel will stand on its own.
- Don't ask for advice or criticism—that's not the agent's or editor's job at this stage in the game.
- Don't mention anything about yourself that isn't pertinent to the novel.
- Don't bring up payment (advances, royalties, etc.); it's premature.
- Don't mention copyright information. What you've written is already copyrighted, and you don't need to imply that the editor or agent is out to steal your idea.
- Don't include your social security number.
- Don't staple your cover letter to your novel proposal. A butterfly or clamp-style paperclip can hold the proposal elements together, and the cover letter stands alone in front.
- Don't put a page number on the cover letter.

Electronic Cover Letter

SUBMISSION TIPS

If a publisher requests that you submit your book proposal electronically, don't forget to include the cover letter. Just like a paper cover letter, keep it brief, and stick to the format of an introductory paragraph, a biographical paragraph, and a concluding paragraph. You can submit your book proposal along with your cover letter exactly as you would if you were sending it via mail (see pages 125 to 141 for specific formatting guidelines), except, it will be sent as an attachment to your e-mail. Make sure you check with the publisher or agent as to which file format they prefer to receive electronically.

FORMATTING SPECS

- Include the same information you would in a paper query, including your name, address, phone, and fax, etc. The top right-hand corner or top center position is fine for this, though you can also include this information in a signature line at the end. It isn't necessary to include your e-mail address in the body of the e-mail, however, since the editor can reply easily with the click of a button.
- Put a description of your novel or its title in the subject line.
- Follow the same format you would with a paper query, including the date, salutation to a specific editor, and block paragraph format. See the above tips for submitting a paper cover letter; the same rules apply, with the exception of including an SASE.

OTHER DOS AND DON'TS

- Don't use all caps or exclamations in the subject line.
- Don't submit an e-mail cover letter and proposal unless specifically requested by the editor.
- Don't insert clip art graphics or other images into your cover letter.
- Do read the Dos and Don'ts listed above for a paper cover letter submission—the same rules apply, with the exception of including an SASE.

COVER LETTER: NOVEL PROPOSAL

John Law
123 Gairlock Dr.
Allentown, PA 18100
Phone (610) 555-4444
Fax (610) 555-5556
jlaw@email.com

Simple return information, including phone, fax, and e-mail. You don't need to include your e-mail address here if you are sending your cover letter via e-mail.

March 2, 2004

Addresses letter to a specific editor (and dates it).

1 line

Sam Editor
A&B Publishing
187 Seventy-second St., 5th Floor
New York, NY 10000

1 line

Dear Mr. Editor,

In my novel, *Officer on the Run*, the town of Little Hills, Ohio, gets a jolt when Police Chief John Murphy's body is found with a bullet between the eyes and deep fingernail scratches down his back. The primary suspects are women, particularly the Chief's seven mistresses (he calls them his ''Seven Deadly Sins''). But none of their DNA matches the killer's. Is it possible that the murderer could be none other than the man who's next in line for the Chief's job, Lieutenant Robert Lieberman? It's up to detective David Black to solve the case.

Good introductory paragraph—states the novel's title, sets the hook (grabber), reels the editor in (makes him want to read the novel).

Strong grabber sentence.

Single-spaced text

States publishing credits and pertinent professional background.

1 line between paragraphs

1" margin

I am a published mystery writer whose short stories have appeared in *Over Your Dead Body* and *A Dime for Crime*. I am also a prosecuting attorney, and I have brought my writing and professional interests together in *Officer on the Run*. The novel weighs in at 70,000 words. I think it will fit quite well with your successful series by Patty Smith and your current bestseller *The CIA Murders*, by Terry Clark, both of which point to the continued popularity of detective novels.

Tells exact word count.

Mentions the intended audience and why the book will fit in well on this publisher's list.

Thank you for considering *Officer on the Run*. I look forward to hearing from you.

Politely closes the letter.

Sincerely,

Signature

John Law

Encl.: Contents page
        Chapters 1, 2, 3
        Synopsis
        SASE

Catalogs every item being sent in the proposal package (including SASE). You can remove the SASE if you are sending your proposal via e-mail.

Cover Page

SUBMISSION TIPS

The cover page includes the title, an estimated word count, and either your contact information (if you're submitting directly to an editor) or your agent's contact information (if you're submitting through an agent).

FORMATTING SPECS

- Put your contact information in the top left corner if you're submitting to a book editor.
- If you're using an agent, put the agent's contact information in the bottom right corner and don't put your name and address on the cover.
- Put an estimated word count (for the entire book, not for the proposal) in the top right corner.
- Center the title, subtitle, and author's name in the middle of the page.
- Conventionally, the title is in all capital letters and the subtitle is up-and-down. If you want to use boldface for the title and italics for the subtitle, that's fine, too.
- Find out what file format a publisher or agent prefers if they have asked you to send your proposal via e-mail or on disk or CD.

OTHER DOS AND DON'TS

- Don't include both your contact information and the agent's. Use one or the other, depending on the situation.
- Don't use a header or number the cover page.
- Don't fax or e-mail your proposal to a publisher or agent unless they specifically request it.

I like full proposals, not just query letters. I can't make a judgment about a work from a one-page letter. By a full proposal, I mean a brief cover letter, the first three consecutive chapters (or about fifty pages of text), and a three- to five-page synopsis. That's sufficient material for me to make a reasonable decision. I like the synopsis to give me the crux of the story—the highlights—from beginning to end. I certainly hate when someone fails to mention the ending. Tell the entire story. Don't play footsie with your editor.

—Melissa Ann Singer, senior editor, Tor Books

COVER PAGE: NOVEL PROPOSAL

Include author's name and address on proposal to editor. Don't include author's name and address on agented proposal.

John Law
123 Gairlock Dr.
Allentown, PA 18100
Phone (610) 555-4444
Fax (610) 555-5556
jlaw@email.com

70,000 words

Always include the novel's word count.

Center the title in the middle of the page.

OFFICER ON THE RUN

A Novel   1 line

by   1 line

John Law   1 line

Table of Contents

SUBMISSION TIPS

Your novel proposal's contents page should let the editor know precisely what's in your proposal package, including the synopsis, sample chapters, a chapter-by-chapter outline, about the author, and endorsements (if any).

FORMATTING SPECS

- Use a slug line (also called a header) in the top left margin. It should contain your last name, a slash, your novel's title in all capital letters, another slash, and the word Contents. It should look like this: Law/OFFICER ON THE RUN/ Contents.
- Next, drop about six lines and put the heading "Proposal Contents" or "Contents," flush with the left magin in bold (and in a large font, if you wish).
- Then, list all the contents.
- Be sure to catalog every item you're sending in your proposal (synopsis, sample chapters, chapter-by-chapter outline, about the author, endorsements) and the corresponding page numbers as they appear in your proposal.

OTHER DOS AND DON'TS

- Do make your contents page neat and easy on the eyes.
- Do organize your contents page according to sections (see sample) and use double-spacing.
- Don't number the contents page.

Take the time to show editors that you care about your work and are serious about publishing. By following a publication's or book publisher's submission guidelines and practicing standard submission etiquette, you can better ensure your chances to read your work and consider it for publication.

—Novel & Short Story Writer's Market

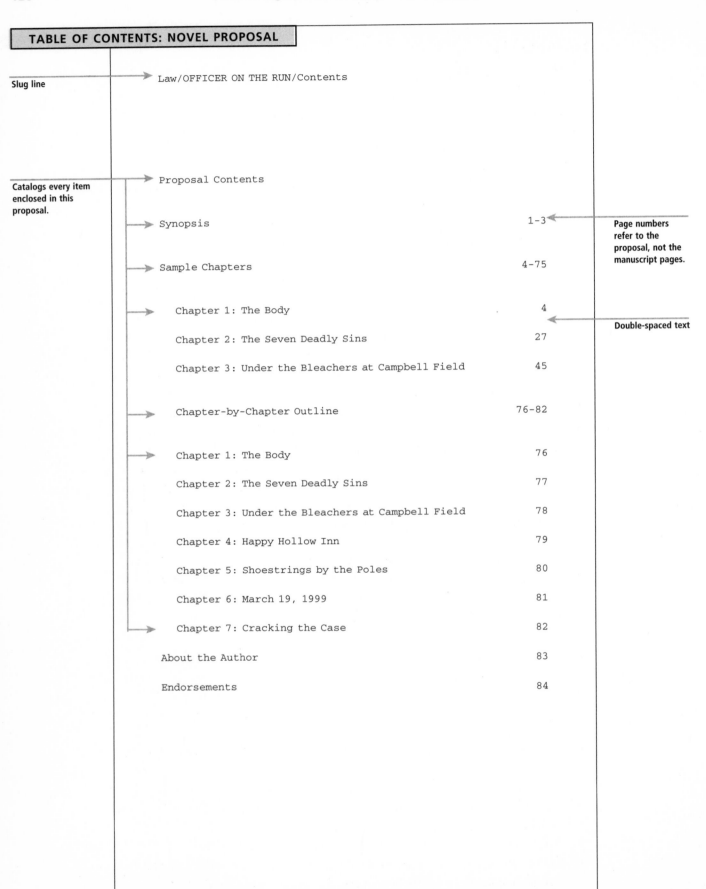

TABLE OF CONTENTS: NOVEL PROPOSAL

Slug line → Law/OFFICER ON THE RUN/Contents

Catalogs every item enclosed in this proposal. →

Page numbers refer to the proposal, not the manuscript pages.

Double-spaced text

Synopsis

SUBMISSION TIPS

The synopsis supplies key information about your novel (plot, theme, characterization, setting), while also showing how all these coalesce to form the big picture (your novel). You want to quickly tell what your novel is about without making the editor or agent read the novel in its entirety.

There are no hard and fast rules about the synopsis. Some editors and agents look at it as a one-page sales pitch, while others expect it to be a comprehensive summary of the entire novel. There's conflicting advice about the typical length of a synopsis. Nearly all editors and agents prefer a synopsis that runs from one to two single-spaced pages, or three to five double-spaced pages. Most editors and agents agree: "The shorter, the better."

On the other hand, some plot-heavy fiction, such as thrillers and mysteries, might need more space and can run from 10 to 25 double-spaced pages, depending on the length of the manuscript and the number of plot shifts. If you opt for a longer synopsis, aim for one synopsis page to every 25 manuscript pages (a 250-page manuscript should get a 10-page synopsis), but try to keep it as short as possible.

Your best bet on knowing how long to make your synopsis is to follow the guidelines in the agency's or publisher's listing (consult *Guide to Literary Agents, Novel & Short Story Writer's Market* or *Writer's Market*). If the listing provides no specific information about the length of the synopsis and you're still unsure, check the publisher's or agent's Web site for guidelines or call and ask. You might have to compose a few versions of your synopsis to meet the demands of various agents and editors.

When writing your synopsis, focus on the essential parts of your story, and try not to include sections of dialogue unless you think they are absolutely necessary (it is okay to inject a few strong quotes from your characters, but keep them brief). Finally, even though the synopsis is but a condensed version of your novel, it must seem complete. Keep events in the same order as they happen in the novel (but don't break them down into individual chapters). Remember that your synopsis should have a beginning, a middle, and an ending (yes, you must tell how the novel ends to round out your synopsis).

That's what's required of a synopsis: You need to be concise, compelling, and complete at the same time.

FORMATTING SPECS

- Use a 1″ margin on all sides.
- Justify the left margin only.
- Type your name, address, phone number, fax, and e-mail on the top left margin of the first page, single-spaced.
- Type the novel's genre, the word length and then the word "Synopsis" on the top right margin of the first page, single-spaced.
- Do not number the first page (but it is considered page one).
- Put the novel's title, centered and in all caps, about one-third of the way down the page (from the top margin).
- Drop four lines below the title and begin the text of the synopsis.
- The text throughout the synopsis should be double-spaced (unless you intend to keep your synopsis to one or two pages, then single-spaced is okay).

- Use all caps the first time you introduce a character.
- After the first page, use a slug line in the top left of every page. The slug line should contain your last name, a slash, your novel's title in all capital letters, another slash and the word "Synopsis."
- Also after the first page, put the page number in the top right corner of every consecutive page, on the same line as the slug line.
- The first line of text on each page after the first page should be three lines (about ¾″) below the slug line and page number.

OTHER DOS AND DON'TS
- Do keep in mind that this is a sales pitch (make it a short, fast, exciting read).
- Do establish a hook at the beginning of the synopsis (introduce your lead character and set up a key conflict).
- Do try to introduce your most important character first.
- Do provide details about your central character (age, gender, marital status, profession, etc.), but don't do this for every character, only the primary ones.
- Do try to include the characters' motivations and emotions.
- Do highlight pivotal plot points and reveal the novel's ending.
- Don't go into detail about what happens; just tell what happens.
- Don't inject long sections of dialogue into your synopsis.
- Do write in third person, even if our novel is in first person.

Electronic Synopsis
SUBMISSION TIPS
Some editors or agents might ask you to submit your synopsis via e-mail or on a disk or CD. The editor or agent can provide you with specific formatting guidelines indicating how they want the synopsis sent and the type of files they prefer. If you are sending it via e-mail, you can attach your file to your e-mail message. Don't forget to include your cover letter in the body of your e-mail and your cover letter and table of contents in the file along with the synopsis.

FORMATTING SPECS
- Find out how the editor or agent prefers to receive files before you send them. If the editor or agent doesn't specify a particular file format, save the synopsis as a text file. Most word processing programs can read basic text files.
- Follow the same formatting specs as above for a paper synopsis submission.
- When sending your synopsis via e-mail, put the name of your novel in the subject line.
- If you are sending the synopsis via e-mail, send it as an attachment to your e-mail unless the editor or agent requests otherwise.

OTHER DOS AND DON'TS
- Don't use all caps in your subject line.
- Don't submit a synopsis electronically unless the editor or agent requests it.
- Don't justify text or align the right margin.

SYNOPSIS, PAGE 1: NOVEL PROPOSAL

Note: Does not number the first page.

Name, address, phone, fax, and e-mail on the top-left margin of first page.

Justifies left margin only.

John Law
123 Gairlock Dr.
Allentown, PA 18100
Phone (610) 555-4444
Fax (610) 555-5556
jlaw@email.com

Mystery
70,000 words
Synopsis

Novel's genre, word length, and the word "Synopsis."

OFFICER ON THE RUN

Title is centered and in all caps.

Four lines between the title and the text of the synopsis.

Uses all caps the first time a character is introduced.

1" margin

Investigative officer DAVID BLACK doesn't know where to be-gin when he gets word Police Chief JOHN MURPHY is found dead on his bed—with a silver bullet between his eyes and half-inch nail marks running down his back. Black has to answer two questions: Who would kill the Chief, and why?

Establishes a good hook, introduces important characters and sets up a key conflict.

It turns out quite a few people aren't too pleased with the Chief. He'd been on the force for twenty-three years and no doubt made some enemies. All the townspeople called him Bulldog because he looked like a pit bull, and certainly acted like one. Countless stories passed through City Hall about how the Chief wouldn't hesitate to roll up his cuffs and beat suspects into sub-mission until they would confess to a crime. That was his method and it worked. He could take control of any person and any situation.

Double-spaced text

Except his wife and his marriage. On that front, the Chief was completely out of control. He'd lost all affection for his wife, MARY, who was once the apple of his eye but now weighs in at 260 lbs. That was fine with the Chief—the less he had to see Mary, the more time for his own pursuits. But he really had only one pursuit: younger women. That fact he didn't hide. He'd often brag to guys on the force about being the only Chief in the his-tory of law enforcement to ''burn through seven dispatchers in just as many years.'' He even called them his ''Seven Deadly Sins.'' Little did he know that one day they'd all be suspects for his murder.

Uses all caps the first time a character is introduced.

SYNOPSIS, PAGE 2: NOVEL PROPOSAL

Law/OFFICER ON THE RUN/Synopsis   2

Slug line with last name, title (in all caps) and the word "Synopsis."

Page number goes on the same line as the slug line.

First line of text is three lines below the slug line and page number.

    Black interviews all seven women and finds no leads until MARLENE PRESTON, the Chief's ''Seventh Deadly Sin,'' reveals how the Chief repeatedly would handcuff her arms and legs to four metal poles under the bleachers at the school football stadium. Marlene says she's never told anyone about any of it. Black then interrogates the six other ''sins,'' to see if they had also been physically mistreated. They all say the Chief never tried anything like that with them.

Paragraphs are short and fast reads, mentioning only the essentials of the story.

    Black drinks himself into a stupor and pours out his problems to a young barmaid, SARAH, who just happens to be the best friend of the Police Lieutenant's daughter, KELLY LIEBERMAN. Sarah tells Black the Chief deserved to die and that he was a jerk, especially to Kelly when she'd baby-sit for the Chief and his wife. According to Sarah, the Chief used to talk dirty to Kelly and then threaten her not to tell her father because LIEUTENANT LIEBERMAN was in line for a promotion.

A new scene/twist begins with start of a new paragraph.

    Black interviews Kelly. She denies the Chief did anything but make a few lewd comments on occasion. When Black approaches Kelly's father, Lieutenant Lieberman says Kelly never mentioned a word about the Chief. Black returns to talk with Kelly and asks why she's never mentioned anything to her father. She says she's afraid he'd get upset at her for bringing it up. Black presses further, asking Kelly if the Chief ever did anything other than verbally harass her. Kelly says no.

    Black decides to walk back under the bleachers to the spot where Marlene says the Chief repeatedly handcuffed her. There, he notices two sneaker shoestrings on the ground by the four poles Marlene pointed out. The strings had been tied in knots and then cut. Black shows the strings to Marlene and asks if the Chief ever tied her to the poles with them. ''Not once,'' she says. ''Handcuffs every time.''

SYNOPSIS: MISTAKES TO AVOID

1

Don't forget to include your phone number, fax, and e-mail address.

Peter Perp
342 Crooked Lane
Philadelphia, PA 19441

The first page should NOT be numbered.

The genre of the novel is not mentioned here, nor is the word length. These elements should be included in the synopsis.

Officer on the Run

The title of the book should be in all caps.

The first time a character is introduced, the name should be in all caps.

The text should be double-spaced.

Investigative officer David Black doesn't know where to begin when he gets word Police Chief John Murphy is found dead on his bed—with a silver bullet between his eyes and half-inch nail marks running down his back. Black has to answer two questions: Who would kill the Chief, and why?

It turns out quite a few people aren't too pleased with the Chief. He's been on the force for twenty-three years and no doubt made some enemies. On the home front, the Chief was completely out of control. He'd lost all affection for his wife, Mary, who was once the apple of his eye.

Black interviews all of the women that the Chief had affairs with, whom he called his ''Seven Deadly Sins,'' and finds no leads until Marlene Preston, the Chief's seventh ''sin.'' She reveals how the Chief repeatedly would handcuff her arms and legs to four metal poles under the bleachers at the school football stadium. Black drinks himself into a stupor and pours out his problems to a young barmaid, who tells him that the Chief deserved to die.

Pivotal plot points are glossed over— they should be highlighted.

Black continues investigating the Chief and uncovers all kinds of sordid details. The killer is revealed at the end, and it is a total shock and surprise to all, especially Black.

The characters' motivations and emotions aren't conveyed at all in this synopsis, leaving the editor or agent to think, why should I care about these characters?

Be sure to reveal your novel's ending.

This synopsis is too short and doesn't give enough information about the characters or the plot to make it compelling.

Outline

SUBMISSION TIPS

An outline is often used interchangeably with a synopsis. For most editors and agents, however, there is a distinction. While a synopsis is a brief, encapsulated version of the novel at large, an outline makes each chapter its own story, usually containing a few paragraphs per chapter. In short, you're breaking down the novel and synopsizing each chapter individually. Try to keep each chapter to about a page, and begin each new chapter on a different page (See Outline Novel Proposal on page 136).

Never submit an outline unless an agent or editor specifically asks for it. Keep in mind that fewer and fewer agents and editors want outlines these days. Most just request a cover letter, a few sample chapters and a short synopsis (or sometimes the entire manuscript). Outlines most often are requested by genre fiction editors, because genre books run for many pages and have numerous plot shifts.

FORMATTING SPECS

- Use a 1″ margin on all sides.
- Justify the left margin only.
- Use a slug line in the top left of every page. The slug line should contain your last name, a slash, your novel's title in all capital letters, another slash and the word "Outline."
- Put the page number in the top right corner of every page.
- Drop four lines below the slug line, center and bold or underline the words "Chapter-by-Chapter Outline."
- Drop four more lines and type the chapter number (Chapter 3).
- Drop two lines and put the chapter's title on the left margin and the number of manuscript pages that chapter runs on the right margin.
- Drop two lines and begin the text of the outline.
- Double-space the text throughout the outline.
- Use all caps the first time you introduce a character.
- Use a separate page for each chapter.

OTHER DOS AND DON'TS

- Do keep in mind that your outline is an extended, more detailed, and structural version of your synopsis.
- Do explain the gist of each chapter.
- Do highlight pivotal plot points.
- Do provide a hook for each chapter.
- Do reveal how the chapter begins and ends.
- Do make sure each succeeding chapter picks up where the previous chapter left off.
- Don't include extended dialogue.

Electronic Outline

SUBMISSION TIPS

Some editors or agents might ask you to submit your outline via e-mail or on a disk or CD. The editor or agent can provide you with specific formatting guidelines indicating how they want the outline sent and the type of files they prefer. If you are sending it via e-mail, you can attach your file to your e-mail message. Don't forget to include your cover letter in the body of your e-mail and your cover page and table of contents in the file along with the outline.

FORMATTING SPECS

- Before you send the outline, find out how the editor or agent prefers to receive files.
- Follow the same formatting specs as above for a paper outline submission.
- When sending your outline via e-mail, put the name of your book in the subject line.
- If the editor or agent doesn't specify a particular file format, save the outline as a text file. Most word processing programs can read basic text files.
- If you are sending the outline via e-mail, send it as an attachment to your e-mail unless the editor or agent requests otherwise.

OTHER DOS AND DON'TS

- Don't use all caps in your subject line.
- Don't submit an outline electronically unless the editor or agent specifically requests it.
- Do ask for specific file format guidelines to make sure the editor or agent can open your files.
- Don't justify tex or align the right margin.

I very much prefer e-mail versus regular mail; it's fast, efficient, saves time, postage, and paper too!

—Harvey Klinger, agent, Harvey Klinger, Inc. Literary Representation

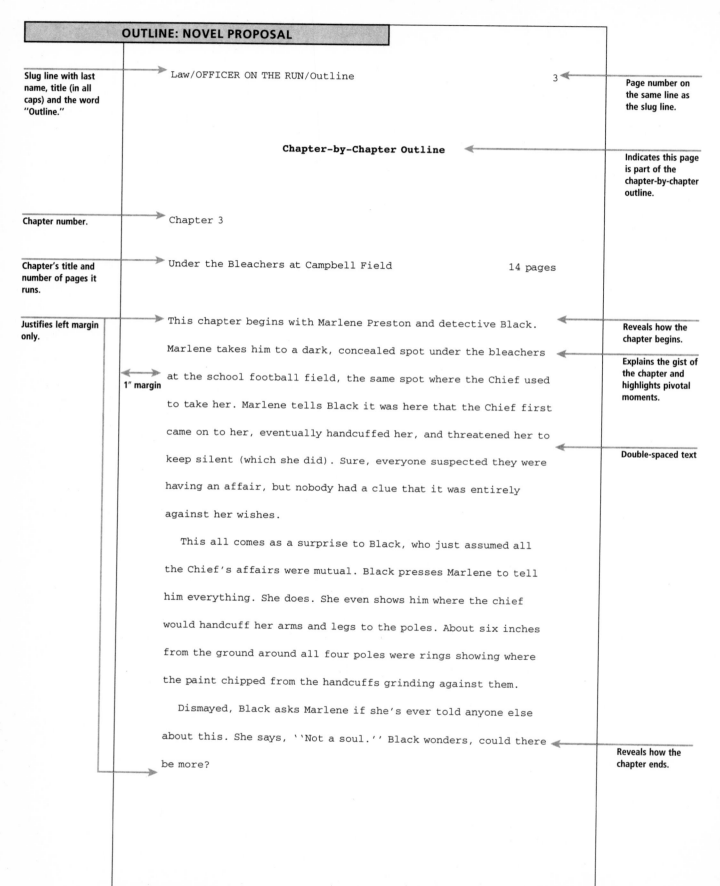

OUTLINE: NOVEL PROPOSAL

Slug line with last name, title (in all caps) and the word "Outline."

Law/OFFICER ON THE RUN/Outline   3

Page number on the same line as the slug line.

Chapter-by-Chapter Outline

Indicates this page is part of the chapter-by-chapter outline.

Chapter number.

Chapter 3

Chapter's title and number of pages it runs.

Under the Bleachers at Campbell Field   14 pages

Justifies left margin only.

This chapter begins with Marlene Preston and detective Black.

Marlene takes him to a dark, concealed spot under the bleachers

1" margin

at the school football field, the same spot where the Chief used

to take her. Marlene tells Black it was here that the Chief first

came on to her, eventually handcuffed her, and threatened her to

keep silent (which she did). Sure, everyone suspected they were

having an affair, but nobody had a clue that it was entirely

against her wishes.

    This all comes as a surprise to Black, who just assumed all

the Chief's affairs were mutual. Black presses Marlene to tell

him everything. She does. She even shows him where the chief

would handcuff her arms and legs to the poles. About six inches

from the ground around all four poles were rings showing where

the paint chipped from the handcuffs grinding against them.

    Dismayed, Black asks Marlene if she's ever told anyone else

about this. She says, ``Not a soul.'' Black wonders, could there

be more?

Reveals how the chapter begins.

Explains the gist of the chapter and highlights pivotal moments.

Double-spaced text

Reveals how the chapter ends.

The slug line should also include the author's last name and the title of the book in all caps.

Outline

The outline should have page numbers in the top right corner of every page.

Chapter-by-Chapter Outline

The chapter's title should be included here.

Chapter 3   23 pages

The text should be double-spaced.

 This chapter begins with Marlene Preston and detective Black. Marlene takes him to the bleachers and tells Black that this is where the Chief first came on to her against her wishes but he threatened her. Black is shocked. Marlene says she never told anyone about her affair with the Chief.

How does the chapter end? What would make a reader want to move on to the next chapter?

This outline is too short to convey what happens in the 23 pages of this chapter. Pivotal moments should be highlighted and the character's motivations and emotions revealed.

Author Biography

SUBMISSION TIPS

Your author bio is about you, but only in the context of what makes you the perfect person to tell this story. Don't include any information that doesn't directly help the pitch. Including educational information is okay if you have an advanced degree. Unless there's something strikingly unusual about your family, don't mention them. It's okay to say where you live and to whom you're married. Mention your profession if it's pertinent to the novel. Definitely include any previous publishing credits. Remember, your bio should always be less than a page and should never include information not directly relevant to your novel's publication.

FORMATTING SPECS

- Have a slug line in the top left corner with your last name, then backslash, then the novel's title in all caps, then backslash again, then "Author Biography."
- Put the page number in the top right corner on the same line as the slug line.
- Double-space the text.
- Write in third person.
- Use present tense.
- Keep it to one page. Standard length is 200–250 words.

OTHER DOS AND DON'TS

- Don't mention your membership in any writer's organizations, unless it can help promote your novel (e.g., if you write a mystery, tell that you belong to the Mystery Writers of America, etc.).
- Do mention any publicity or promotion you've received, such as appearances on national TV or radio programs, or interviews in national magazines.
- Don't mention any "minor" publishing credits unrelated to your novel (e.g., that you had two poems published in your local paper).
- Don't spend too much time complimenting yourself.
- Do stick to the facts (don't exaggerate or lie).
- Don't include an author bio if you're a beginning writer with no publishing credits.
- Do have separate bios if you're collaborating with another author, but make sure both bios fit on the same page.

Somebody who gets to the point is most appreciated. I don't need your life story, and I already heard your jokes. At this point, I just need a simple introduction telling me who you are in very simple terms.

—Jamie S. Rich, editing consultant, Oni Press

AUTHOR BIOGRAPHY INFORMATION

Slug line → Law/OFFICER ON THE RUN/Author Biography   83 ← Page number (on the same line as the slug line).

Tells what this page is. → About The Author

Reveals information that's pertinent to the novel (he's a lawyer, which shows he's probably a good person to write this book). →

John Law has been a prosecuting attorney for Big Lake

County, Pennsylvania, since 1985. He garnered regional media at- ← Double-spaced text

tention during the late 1990s by winning the case that put all- ← Keeps the word count between 40 and 400 words.

star Pittsburgh Steelers quarterback Warren St. Christofer in

prison for sexually harassing his sports agent.

Mentions previously published material. →

Mr. Law's writing credits include stories published in mys-

tery magazines *Over Your Dead Body* and *A Dime for a Crime*, as

1" margin

well as numerous articles in law-enforcement trade journals,

such as *Police Time*, *By the Book*, *Today's Attorney* and *Beneath*

the Badge.

Briefly tells a bit about himself. →

He received his B.A. in Comparative Literature from Kent ← Writes in third person.

State University and his law degree from Case Western Reserve.

Mr. Law lives with his wife and three children in Allentown,

Pennsylvania. This is his first novel.

Endorsements Page

SUBMISSION TIPS

An endorsements page is like a dishwasher—it's not essential, but it helps to have one. Putting the page together is simple because it's nothing more than a list of quotes. The trick, however, is that these quotes must come from noteworthy people, typically prominent industry insiders (well-known authors, agents, editors, experts on the topic) who've read your manuscript and have decided to comment favorably on it. Forget about including what your husband or neighbor or writing group said about your novel. While their words of praise matter to you, they don't matter to an agent or publisher—such opinions won't help sell your novel.

Unless you have contacts, it is difficult to obtain a quote from someone noteworthy. Sure, you can send your manuscript to someone like Philip Roth and hope he'll take the time to read it and comment on it, but the chances of that happening are terribly slim. It's best not to include an endorsements page unless you have at least two good quotes from well-known, well-respected sources. Don't fret if you don't have an endorsements page—very few authors include one with fiction manuscripts. Most endorsements will come once the galleys go out to reviewers.

FORMATTING SPECS

- Have a slug line in the top left corner with your last name, followed by a backslash, followed by the novel's title in all caps, followed by another backslash, then the word "Endorsements."
- The page number should be in the top right corner on the same line as the slug line.
- Single-space the text within each quote.
- Triple-space between quotes.
- Attribute the quotes (double-check for correct spelling of names and titles).
- Keep each endorsement short (fifty words or less).

OTHER DOS AND DON'TS

- Don't worry too much about obtaining endorsements; fiction manuscripts stand on their own.
- Don't expect a response if you send your manuscript to some prominent person you don't know (certainly don't wait more than a few weeks for a response).
- Do get the source's permission to include the endorsement.
- Do send a thank-you note if someone provides a laudatory quote.

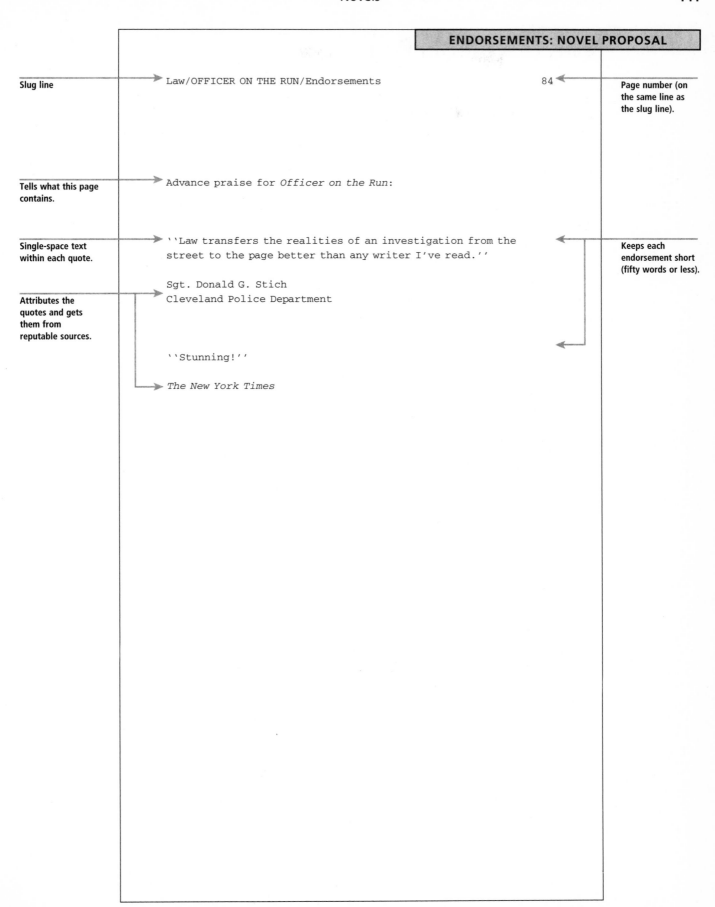

ENDORSEMENTS: NOVEL PROPOSAL

Slug line → Law/OFFICER ON THE RUN/Endorsements   84 ←

Page number (on the same line as the slug line).

Tells what this page contains. → Advance praise for *Officer on the Run*:

Single-space text within each quote. → ``Law transfers the realities of an investigation from the street to the page better than any writer I've read.''

Keeps each endorsement short (fifty words or less).

Sgt. Donald G. Stich
Cleveland Police Department

Attributes the quotes and gets them from reputable sources.

``Stunning!''

The New York Times

The Novel Manuscript

Your novel manuscript is easy to format and submit. What's most important is that you know when and what to submit. Never send an entire manuscript until you've been requested to do so. Unsolicited manuscripts are often ignored and returned (and sometimes even recycled or thrown away) when sent to an agent or publisher who does not accept them. Don't waste your time, energy, paper, and postage; check the particular agent's or publisher's requirements to see if unsolicited manuscripts are accepted.

SUBMISSION TIPS

When a request for your manuscript does come, you'll need to know precisely what to send and how to organize it.

PROPOSAL

If an agent or editor wants to consider representing or publishing your manuscript, here's what to send:
- Cover letter
- Title/Cover page
- Table of Contents
- Chapters
- SASE or postcard reply (not needed with electronic submissions)

OPTIONAL FRONT MATTER:
- Author Biography (see page 138)
- Endorsements Page (see page 140)
- Epigraph (see page 154)

ACCEPTED PROPOSAL

If a publisher agrees to publish your novel, submit:
- Cover letter
- Title/Cover page
- Table of Contents
- Chapters
- SASE or postcard reply (not needed with electronic submissions)

OPTIONAL FRONT MATTER:
- Acknowledgments (see page 151)
- Author Biography (see page 138)
- Dedication Page (see page 154)
- Endorsements Page (see page 140)
- Foreword (see page 156)
- Preface (see page 156)

Manuscript Pages

FORMATTING SPECS

- Use a 1″ margin on all sides.
- Use a title page, set up the same as the title page in your proposal.
- Don't number the title page. Begin numbering with the first page of the text of the book, usually the introduction, prologue or chapter one.
- Use a slug line in the top left corner.
- Start each new chapter on its own page, one-third of the way down the page. The chapter number and chapter title should be in all caps, separated by two hyphens (CHAPTER 1--THE BODY).
- Begin the body of the chapter four to six lines below the chapter title.
- Indent five spaces for each new paragraph.
- Double-space the entire text.
- Underline anything that needs to be italicized.
- Use 10- or 12-point plain font: Times New Roman, Arial or Courier.
- Use 20-lb. bond paper.

OTHER DOS AND DON'TS

- Don't staple anything.
- Don't punch holes in the pages or submit it in a three-ring binder.
- Do submit the manuscript loose-leaf in an envelope. That's why the slug line and page numbers are there.
- Don't number the page or use a slug line on the title/cover page.
- Don't justify or align the right margin.
- Don't put any copyright information on the manuscript. It's copyrighted when you write it, and the editor or agent knows this.
- Do find out what file format the editor or agent prefers if they request that you send the manuscript on a disk or CD.

Electronic Novel Manuscript

SUBMISSION TIPS

If an editor or agent is interested in your proposal, they might ask you to submit your manuscript via e-mail or on a disk or CD. The editor or agent can provide you with specific formatting guidelines indicating how they want the manuscript sent and the type of files they prefer. If you are sending it via e-mail, you can attach your manuscript file to your e-mail message. Don't forget to include your cover letter in the body of your e-mail.

FORMATTING SPECS

- Before you send the manuscript, find out how the editor prefers to receive files.
- If the editor doesn't specify a particular file format, save the article as a text file. Most word processing programs can read basic text files.
- Follow the same formatting specs as above for a paper manuscript submission.

- When sending your manuscript via e-mail, put the name of your book in the subject line.
- If you are sending the manuscript via e-mail, send it as an attachment to your e-mail unless the editor requests otherwise.
- When formatting the manuscript, don't put two spaces after sentences, and don't double- or triple-space by using hard returns.

OTHER DOS AND DON'TS
- Don't use all caps in your subject line.
- Don't submit a manuscript electronically unless the editor specifically requests it.
- Do ask for specific file format guidelines to make sure the editor can open your files.
- Don't justify text or align the right margin.
- Don't put any copyright information on the manuscript. It's copyrighted when you write it, and the editor is aware of this.
- Do call after you've sent a file to make sure the editor has received it.

Cover Letter
SUBMISSION TIPS
A cover letter accompanying a finished novel is brief. All you must do is let the editor know what's enclosed and how to contact you. Be cordial, of course, and feel free to thank the editor for working with you on the project, but don't go into great lengths about the novel or anything else. At this point in the game your editor is focused on one thing: grabbing your novel and reading it in its entirety. So get to the point in your cover letter and let the editor proceed at will.

FORMATTING SPECS
- Use a standard font or typeface (no bold, script or italic).
- Place your name, address, phone, e-mail, and fax in the top right corner.
- Use a 1″ margin on all sides.
- Keep it to one short page—a short paragraph will be fine.
- Use block or semi-block letter format.
- Single-space the body of the letter; double-space between paragraphs.
- Catalog every item you're sending in your enclosures (manuscript, reply postcard, etc.)

OTHER DOS AND DON'TS
- Do address the cover letter to the editor who requested it.
- Do thank the editor.
- Do tell the novel's exact word count.
- Do include a postcard for reply, and state in the letter that you have done so (but you'll probably already have a phone relationship with the editor at this point).
- Don't tell how much time you've spent on the novel.
- Don't bring up payment (advances, royalties, etc.).
- Don't staple your cover letter to your novel.
- Don't put a page number on the cover letter.

COVER LETTER: NOVEL

John Law
123 Gairlock Dr.
Allentown, PA 18100
Phone (610) 555-4444
Fax (610) 555-5556
jlaw@email.com

Nice, simple return address with phone, fax, and e-mail.

September 28, 2004

1 line

Addresses a specific editor.

Sam Editor
A&B Publishing
187 Seventy-second St., 5th Floor
New York, NY 10000

1 line

Dear Mr. Editor:

1 line

1" margin

Enclosed is the manuscript for *Officer on the Run*.

1 line

Brief and to the point.

1 line between paragraphs

Also enclosed is a self-addressed stamped postcard. Would you please indicate that you received this material in good condition and return the postcard to me? Feel free to call or e-mail me as well, if either of these modes of communication is more convenient for you.

Single-spaced text

I look forward to hearing from you.

Politely closes the letter.

Sincerely,

Signature

John Law

Encl.: Manuscript, *Officer on the Run*
SASE

Catalogs every item being sent with the manuscript submission package (you can omit the SASE if you're sending the manuscript via e-mail).

Title Page

SUBMISSION

The title page includes the title, an estimated word count and either your name and contact information (if you're submitting directly to an editor) or your agent's name and contact information (if you're submitting through an agent).

FORMATTING SPECS

- Put the word count in the top right corner of the page, flush with the right margin.
- Center the title of your novel, in bold and in all caps, about halfway down the page.
- Double-space again and type "A Novel" (do not type the quotation marks).
- Double-space again and type your name (if your novel is written with another person, use an ampersand between your names).
- In the lower right-hand corner, put your name, address, and phone/fax/e-mail, single-spaced, in regular text (not all caps). If you have an agent, put the agent's name, address and phone/fax/e-mail here and put your name, address and phone/fax/e-mail in the top left corner.

OTHER DOS AND DON'TS

- Do put your agent's name and contact information in the lower right-hand corner if you have one.
- Don't use a header or number the title page.
- Don't e-mail your manuscripts to a publisher or agent unless they specifically request it.

> Create a simple title page for your manuscript. . . . Sometimes manuscripts are rejected simply because of how they look. Why have a strike against you before you've begun.
> —Evan Marshall, agent and author, *The Marshall Plan for Getting Your Novel Published*

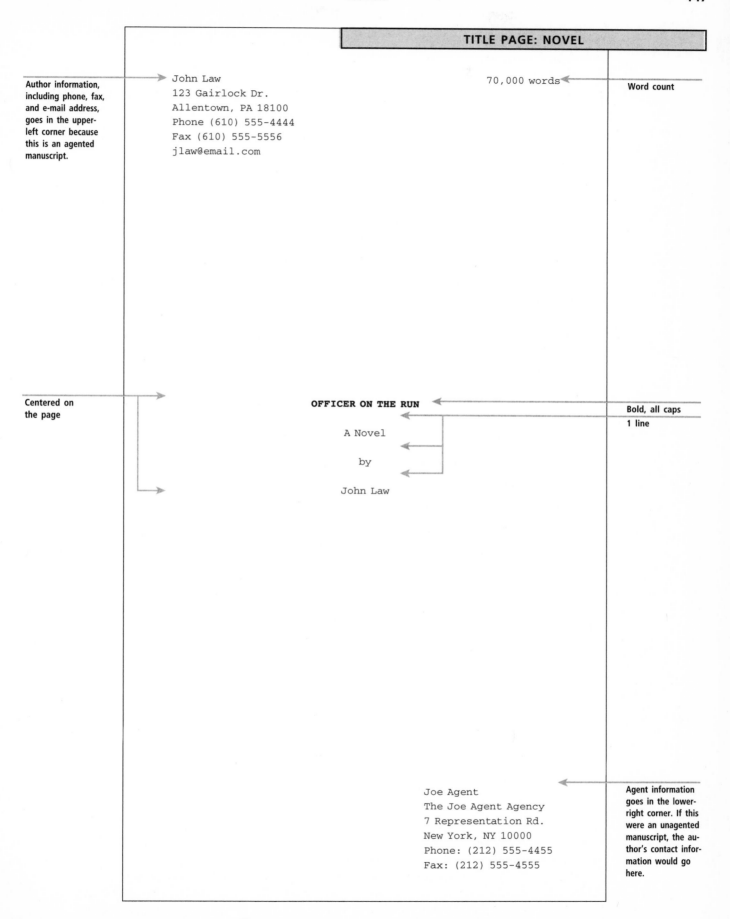

TITLE PAGE: NOVEL

Author information, including phone, fax, and e-mail address, goes in the upper-left corner because this is an agented manuscript.

John Law
123 Gairlock Dr.
Allentown, PA 18100
Phone (610) 555-4444
Fax (610) 555-5556
jlaw@email.com

70,000 words

Word count

Centered on the page

OFFICER ON THE RUN

A Novel

by

John Law

Bold, all caps
1 line

Joe Agent
The Joe Agent Agency
7 Representation Rd.
New York, NY 10000
Phone: (212) 555-4455
Fax: (212) 555-4555

Agent information goes in the lower-right corner. If this were an unagented manuscript, the author's contact information would go here.

MANUSCRIPT, PAGE 1: NOVEL

Law/OFFICER ON THE RUN   1

Slug line with
novel's title in
all caps.

CHAPTER 1--THE BODY

Chapter number and
chapter title in all
caps, separated by
two hyphens, one-
third of the way
down the page.

Marlene Preston walked like a freak but sang like a bird.
With aspirations to become a star, she sang in a band on weekends
but was a nightshift dispatcher during the week. She was the

Justifies left
margin only.

Chief's latest affair, his Seventh Deadly Sin. He would joke
about her with the other officers and refer to her as Lucky No.
7. To her face he only called her Lucky. She never figured out
why. She just wanted him to call her Marlene.

Page number (on
the same line as
the slug line).

Double-spaced text

Marlene grabbed the Chief's attention her second day on the
job, when she arrived at work after a rare midweek gig. Because
the band played until 11:30 and she had to start her shift at midnight, Marlene didn't have time to change into suitable work

1" margin

clothes. To everyone's surprise, she showed up at the station in
skin-hugging black leather tights, six-inch silver pumps and a
white halter top. Her long, dark, untamed hair wrapped around
her shoulders, and her perfume smelled like a rose. Marlene Preston blazed a trail of lust.

Every officer on the force was checking out Marlene. That

Indents five spaces
for each new
paragraph.

was for her one of the perks of the job—being the only woman in
the company of men. She loved the attention, especially from the
Chief. He was, after all, The Man—the guy all the other officers
aspired to be. Marlene was flattered by his flirtations. She
knew she was looking good, and it pleased her that the Chief noticed. And notice he did.

MANUSCRIPT, PAGE 2: NOVEL

Slug line with novel's title in all caps.

Law/OFFICER ON THE RUN 2

Page number (on the same line as the slug line).

At 12:50, a call came in about a robbery. Two guys held up a 24-hour convenience store and shot a clerk in the shoulder. The Chief immediately directed all four officers on duty to hit the streets, two at the crime scene and two to find the getaway car. As soon as the station cleared, the Chief was alone with Marlene. And he let her know he liked that.

Starts each change of dialogue on a new line, with a five-space paragraph indent.

''So, Marlene, this is your first major dispatch, isn't it?''

''Well yeah.''

''You handled that call really well Marlene. Like a pro.''

''Thanks.''

''But then again you look like you could handle just about anything. You're so calm.''

''Thanks.''

''You gotta admit it's kind of exciting, isn't it?''

''Yeah. But it's really sad somebody would go and shoot a poor clerk just for some cash register change.''

''People do crazy things for personal gain, Marlene. Stay on this job and it won't take you long to figure that out.''

''I guess not. I mean it's only my second day and already a robbery. What's next?''

''Oh, who knows. Maybe it could be something really exhilarating . . . like a murder. Like maybe an angry wife murdered her husband because he was having an affair with a colleague. Now that sounds fun.''

The Chief then walked out the door and left Marlene to ponder such a scenario. She was nervous. What did he mean by that? Marlene thought about that for a while but decided she was probably just reading too much into it. Everyone knew the Chief was a happily married man, a father of two lovely children and well respected in the community. Surely she must have misunderstood.

Reply Postcard

If you're a bit paranoid about whether your novel actually makes it to the publisher, you may send a reply postcard along with your novel. Having it signed by the editor (or someone on the staff) and sent back to you will alleviate any worries that the package didn't make it to its destination. Two caveats: (1) Not all editors are gracious enough to send your reply postcards back—but most are. (2) Just because you receive a postcard reply from an editor, you cannot assume your novel has been read or will be read in the next few days or even weeks. Your reply postcard's only function is to let you know your package has been received.

Your best bet to ensure an editor will return your reply postcard is to make it neat and simple to use. That means typing your postcard and not asking the editor to do anything other than note your submission has been received. Although it's okay to leave a small space for "Comments," keep the space very small and never expect it to be filled in—most editors don't have the time or a reason to write anything in it. You'll turn off an editor if you ask him to do too much.

Creating a suitable and functional reply postcard is easy. If you create a reply postcard similar to the one on the following page you'll be just fine. Above all, remember to keep things short and sweet—and, of course, always be sure the postcard has a stamp in the top right corner on the side with your address.

REPLY POSTCARD: NOVEL

John Law
123 Gairlock Dr.
Allentown, PA 18100

John Law, 123 Gairlock Dr., Allentown PA 18100, (610) 555-4444
Date: _____
Your novel *Officer on the Run* was received in my office on

_____.

Other comments:

Signature _____

Company _____

Acknowledgments Page

SUBMISSION TIPS

The acknowledgments page, which is optional, is the place where you spend time thanking everybody who helped you throughout the process of writing the book. Most people thanked in an acknowledgments page are friends who gave you ideas and offered criticisms, family and friends who supported you, an institution that awarded you a grant or sabbatical, and, of course, your agents and editors. Sometimes, what would normally go into an acknowledgments page ends up in a preface, if you have one—unless there are more people an/or institutions than can be acknowledged in the preface.

FORMATTING SPECS

- Put the acknowledgments page on its own page.
- Do not number the page; use a slug line and double-space the text.
- Be sure to drop about a third of the way down the page and use a centered heading that says, "<u>Acknowledgments</u>" underlined.
- At the end of your acknowledgments, you may sign your initials and indicate the place and date.

OTHER DOS AND DON'TS

- Don't forget anyone who helped in preparation of the book when you write acknowledgments, unless they don't want to be mentioned.
- Do keep a running file of names and ways that people helped so you don't have to scramble for this information at the end.

Table of Contents

SUBMISSION TIPS

The table of contents for fiction manuscripts is often pretty spare—merely listing the chapter title and page numbers.

FORMATTING SPECS

- Center the heading "Table of Contents" or "Contents" at least a third of the way down the page.
- Provide an extra-wide margin, at least 1½".
- Don't number pages as part of the manuscript.
- Use a slug in the same place in the header as the rest of the manuscript.
- At the very least, include the chapter titles.
- Include such front-matter elements as prefaces, forewords, and prologues.
- Don't include acknowledgments, dedications, and other short bits of front matter.

OTHER DOS AND DON'TS

- Don't include page numbers with front matter elements.
- Do capitalize all important words in chapter titles.
- Do skip four lines between "Table of Contents" and list of chapters unless it will cause you to go over a page.

ACKNOWLEDGMENTS: NOVEL

No page number

Slug line

Law/OFFICER ON THE RUN/Acknowledgments

Acknowledgments

Heading is centered and underlined, one-third of the way down the page.

Completing and publishing a novel of this magnitude is no easy task, and there are many to thank. Without the following, this book would not be in your hands today.

1" margin

First and foremost, I would like to thank my editor, John Doe, whose insightful comments and criticisms vastly improved this book after I turned it in. Although we occasionally wrestled a bit over which chapters, pages, paragraphs, sentences and words to keep and which to do away with, in the end John was usually right. In my moments of bullheadedness, I'm glad he took me by the horns. I also want to thank my agent, Joe Agent, who believed in this project from the beginning, has guided me through every stage in the process, and has handled all the business aspects of publishing.

Double-spaced text

The Pittsburgh police department deserves a big thanks for allowing me access to the workings of a top-notch investigative team. Numerous car trips, conversations and boxes of jelly donuts have gone into this book.

Finally, and above all, I am indebted to my beloved wife, Jennifer, for giving me the idea to write this book and supporting me throughout. Her enduring love and patience did as much—if not more—to make this book complete than did the sweat of my own brow.

TABLE OF CONTENTS: NOVEL

Slug line → Law/OFFICER ON THE RUN/Contents ← No page number

Table of Contents ← Centered, one-third of the way down the page.

Wide margins (2")

Double-spaced text →

Page numbers correspond to manuscript pages.

Dedication Page
SUBMISSION TIPS
The dedication page, which is optional, is a brief inscription in which you express affection or respect for a person (or persons) who may or may not be directly related to the subject matter of your book. This is the place for you to write things like, "For Jennifer—the light of my life."

FORMATTING SPECS
- Keep your dedication short (only a few lines).
- The dedication gets its own page (do not number) and must have a slug line that should look like this: Law/OFFICER ON THE RUN/Dedication.
- The dedication should be centered about a third of the way down the page.
- Do not put a heading that labels this page a "Dedication."

Epigraph
SUBMISSION TIPS
The epigraph, which is optional, is a short quotation used at the beginning of the novel and/or at the beginning of each chapter. Its content should have relevance to the contents of the book.

FORMATTING SPECS
- Be sure to cite the source of the epigraph.
- When used at the beginning of the novel, type the epigraph on a separate page (do not number).
- Be sure if the epigraph is on its own page to use a slug line that should look like this: Law/OFFICER ON THE RUN/Epigraph.
- The epigraph should be centered about a third of the way down the page.
- Do not put a heading that labels this a page and "Epigraph."
- When used at the beginning of a chapter, type on the same page as the chapter begins (do not number the page).

> Use a plain style. Don't try using weird fonts or graphics. A twelve-point Courier or Geneva font works fine.
>
> —Bob Mayer, *The Novel Writer's Toolkit*

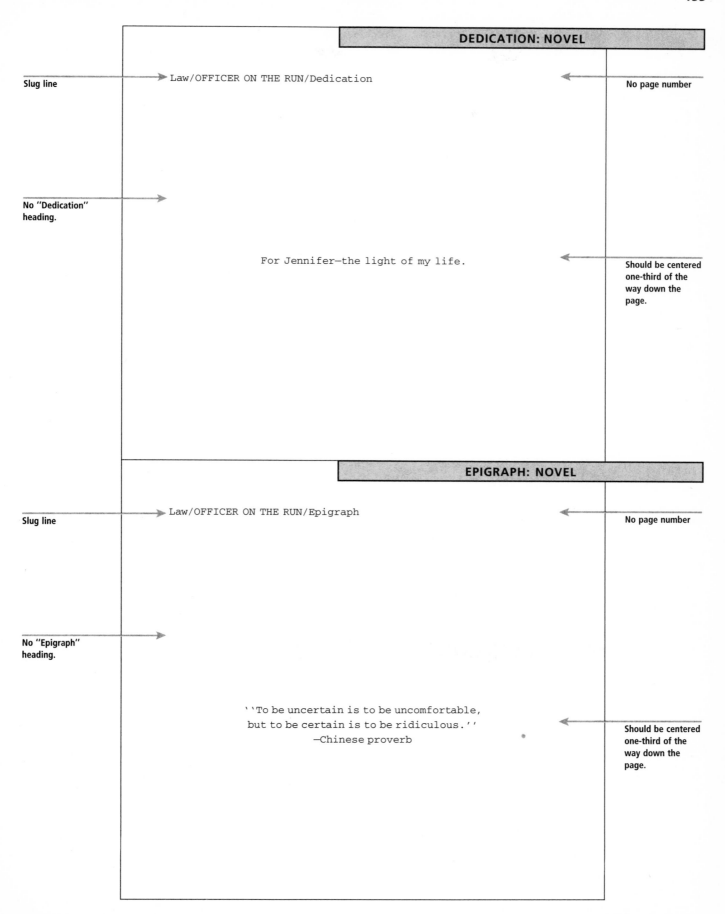

DEDICATION: NOVEL

Slug line → Law/OFFICER ON THE RUN/Dedication ← No page number

No "Dedication" heading. →

For Jennifer—the light of my life. ← Should be centered one-third of the way down the page.

EPIGRAPH: NOVEL

Slug line → Law/OFFICER ON THE RUN/Epigraph ← No page number

No "Epigraph" heading. →

''To be uncertain is to be uncomfortable,
but to be certain is to be ridiculous.''
—Chinese proverb

← Should be centered one-third of the way down the page.

Foreword

SUBMISSION TIPS

The foreword, which is optional, is a brief commentary included in a book's front matter in which someone remarks on the book's contents. The foreword is sometimes written by a well-known author or authority to add credibility and sales appeal to the work. Although the publisher often makes arrangements for the foreword to be written, the author's suggestions about experts in the book's particular subject field are usually welcome.

FORMATTING SPECS

- Like the rest of the front matter, the foreword has a slug but no page numbers.
- Use 1″ margins.
- Be sure to use a heading that explicity states "Foreword" about one-third of the way down the page.
- The name of the foreword's author goes flush right at the end of the text, followed by title and affiliation.
- The foreword's author may want to indicate the city, year, and place the foreword was written.

Preface

SUBMISSION TIPS

The preface, which is optional, is usually written if the author feels the need to explain why he or she wrote the book. It's rarely done with fiction, so talk with your agent or editor about it. The preface can also be used as an acknowledgments page—to thank the people and/or institutions that helped you bring the book to fruition. You, the author, write the preface.

FORMATTING SPECS

- Type the preface on a separate page and double-space the text.
- Do not number the page.
- Use 1″ margins.
- Be sure to use a slug line.
- Use a heading, starting about a third of the way down the page, that reads Preface, centered and underlined.
- Make sure you sign your initials, tell the place you're writing from and include the date.

FOREWORD: NOVEL

Slug line
(Notice Mansell's
name, not Law's.)

No page number

Mansell/OFFICER ON THE RUN/Foreword

1" margin

Foreword

Heading is centered
and underlined, one-
third of the way
down the page.

Double-spaced text

I will never forgive John Law for sending me a copy of *Officer on
the Run*. I was staring down a deadline for my latest manuscript,
Can't Find Solace, and I ended up paying more attention to John's
manuscript. I had a few spare seconds to read the first sentence,
so I did. Then I decided I could take a well-deserved break and
finish the chapter. Before I knew it, I was reading ''The End,''
and the only mystery left was how to explain why my manuscript
wouldn't be on my agent's desk the next morning.

Meg Mansell

San Francisco, California

June 28, 2004

Name, place, and
date go in bottom
flush with the right
margin.

PREFACE: NOVEL

Slug line

No page number

Law/OFFICER ON THE RUN/Preface

Preface

Heading is centered
and underlined, one-
third of the way
down the page.

1" margin

This book would not have been possible without generous assistance
from Detective Carly Benham and her top-notch staff at the Heartland
police department. They helped me brainstorm ideas and made sure I
got every last detail right. Also, many thanks to my co-workers at
the Heartland prosecuting attorney's office for keeping the hot
coffee and unconditional encouragement flowing.

Double-spaced text

John Law

Allentown, Pennsylvania

July 12, 2004

Name, place, and
date go in the bot-
tom flush with the
right margin.

CHAPTER SIX

ROMANCE

Romance Novels

The romance novel is a category of fiction in which the love relationship between a man and a woman pervades the plot. The story concerns the heroine and the hero, who fall in love, encounter a conflict that hinders their relationship, and resolve the conflict. Though marriage is not necessarily the outcome of the story, the ending is always happy.

Romance is the overriding element of this kind of story: The couple's relationship determines the plot and tone of the book. Despite all this emotion, however, both the characters and plot must be well developed and realistic. Contrived situations and flat characters are unacceptable. Throughout a romance novel, the reader senses the sexual and emotional attraction between the heroine and hero. Lovemaking scenes, though sometimes detailed, are generally not too graphic; more emphasis is placed on the sensual element than on physical action.

There are many different categories of romances; Harlequin, for example, has thirteen different series of romances, and their Silhouette line has five different series. They run the gamut from historical to humorous to hot and heavy—their American Romances series focuses on upbeat, lively romances about "the pursuit of love in the backyards, big cities, and wide open spaces of America"; Harlequin Blaze books are steamy, passionate, "red-hot" reads; Harlequin Medical Romances are set in the world of medicine; Harlequin Flipside offers a lighthearted, irreverent look at contemporary romance; and Silhouette's Intimate Moments are set in a world of suspense and adventure.

Today's adult romance novel differs from its counterpart of the past in that it reflects a respect for independent, strong women. "Bodice-rippers" and "rape sagas," though still being published in the historical romance field, are becoming less popular than category romances, as authors and readers increasingly subscribe to the values fostered by the women's movement. The emergence of "Chick Lit," a genre that straddles the line between romance and mainstream fiction, shows an increased interest in stories about contemporary, urban single women that exude a humor, energy, and hipness not seen in the romance novels of the past.

Each publisher of romances has detailed, specific guidelines regarding their specific lines. The publisher will stipulate, for example, whether the heroine may engage in sex outside of marriage, whether marriage will occur at the novel's end, and whether the heroine is in her twenties, thirties, or another age group. In addition, publishers specify lengths for romances, which usually are from 50,000 to 60,000 words; books in some lines, however, such as Harlequin's SuperRomances, are longer and run about 85,000 words.

ROMANCE WRITERS OF AMERICA (RWA)

This organization was established in 1979 and is the largest organization of its kind in the world. Writers need not be published to join RWA, whose more than 8,400 members include individuals in foreign countries and more than 150 local chapters across the United States, Canada, and Australia. RWA strives to increase interest in romantic fiction, to support and encourage writers in their careers, and to provide market information. The Golden Heart Award, presented annually, recognizes an RWA member who is an unpublished writer of romantic fiction. The RITA Award, presented annually, recognizes the best in published romantic fiction. RWA publishes a monthly newspaper, *Romance Writers Report*, and holds an annual conference and regional conferences.

Visit the RWA's Web site at www.rwanational.org, or contact them at 16000 Stuebner Airline Road, Suite 140, Spring, Texas 77379; info@rwanational.org; (832) 717-5200.

Romance Novel Query

SUBMISSIONS TIPS

The most important thing to remember about submitting to romance publishers is to make sure your story or novel fits the exact category of the publisher you are submitting to. For instance, don't send your historical romance set in England in the 1730s to Harlequin's American Romances line, which features stories about finding love in the contemporary United States. Also, know the length of specific lines as well; don't send a 50,000-word novel to Silhouette's Intimate Moments, which are much shorter. The romance market has many more subgenres than other fiction genres, so you have to do your homework to make sure you are submitting to a publisher that works with the type of story you have.

FORMATTING SPECS

To submit and format your short stories and novels in the romance genre, consult the appropriate pages for fiction submissions (page 102 for short stories; page 113 for novel proposals).

OTHER DOS AND DONT'S

- Don't believe the myth that romance novels don't have to be as well written as mainstream novels. Today's romance novels are meticulously crafted, character-driven stories that are continually on the top of the bestseller lists.
- Do obtain a copy of a publisher or agent's guidelines. Romance guidelines are extremely specific as to characters, plotlines, and page length, so make sure your story or novel fits their guidelines before sending.
- Do indicate which series you think your novel will be perfect for if you are submitting to a publisher that has several different series of romances.
- Do indicate in your query letter the names of authors that your work is similar to in order to give the editor or agent a point of reference; if possible, reference an author who is published or represented by the publisher or agent you are sending your query to. This will show that you're knowledeable about the genre and the publisher or agent's authors.
- Don't send a query or proposal via e-mail or fax unless a publisher or agent specifically requests it.

QUERY TO ROMANCE PUBLISHER

Simple return
information,
including phone
number and e-mail
address.

Louise Love
134 Amorous Lane
Perfect, SD 93834
(605) 555-4321
louiselove@email.com

Addresses the
letter to a specific
editor at a
publisher that
deals with the type
of book the writer
is submitting—a
historical romance.

Robin Roman
Leisure Books
276 Fifth Ave.
Suite 1008
New York, NY 10001

Dear Ms. Roman,

Is there a 12-step program for Romance Addicts? A Dear Abby column for those who promise they'll read ''just one'' romance this week and end up on an all-night binge? Please, just say ''No.'' As a confessed RA (Romance Addict), I don't want to be cured!

A "grabber"
sentence to get the
attention of the
editor. It's clear
from this paragraph
that the writer
loves the romance
genre, and her
enthusiasm is
infectious.

Like many RAs, I began churning the stuff out myself one day when the local supply ran short. I sometimes wonder what my friends and family will say, yet that devilish inner voice tells me I've created a ''fix'' too good to keep to myself. I want all RAs to experience the ''high'' of falling in love with Cedric of Murtane, a ruthless warlord capable of stealing any woman's heart. Imagine a ''trip'' to 13th century England. Put yourself in the trembling shoes of Morgan Steele, a feisty heiress destined to marry a man known best as the ''Killer of Kent.'' Yet think of your relief when you discover that the man has been horribly misjudged by others and needs you as much as you need him. The only trouble lies in an evil stepmother and an illicit connection to the throne. Yet there's never a dull moment. THE WARRIOR will give no one a ''bad trip.''

A nice, brief
paragraph gives a
quick outline of
the novel yet gives
a good idea of the
novel.

Details enclosures
in the body of the
letter—they are
exactly what
Leisure Books'
guidelines indicate
they want.

With this novel I hope to join the ''kingpins'' of Romance, authors such as Madeline Baker, Rebecca Brandewyne and Patricia Gaffney. Toward this goal, I've enclosed a sample of THE WARRIOR, hoping the first three chapters will whet your appetite for more, along with a synopsis. There are twenty-two chapters in this completed novel, a total of 125,000 words to satisfy the RA craving completely. Your response to THE WARRIOR would mean a great deal to me.

Mentions other
Leisure Books
authors—this
shows that the
writer has done
her homework and
is familiar with the
books that Leisure
publishes, and
gives the editor a
frame of reference
for her work.

Indicates the
length of the
novel, and that it's
completed.

Sincerely,

Louise Love

Enc.: Chapters 1, 2, 3
Synopsis
SASE

QUERY TO ROMANCE PUBLISHER: MISTAKES TO AVOID

June 24, 2004

Author contact information is missing. Name, address, phone, and e-mail should be on the letter.

Editor

Love Spell

276 Fifth Avenue

New York, NY 10001

Never address a letter to "Editor"—find out the name of a specific editor and address your submission to her.

Dear Romance Editor,

I've written a romance novel that I think you'll like. It's all about a contemporary woman, a doctor, who has been unlucky in love. She meets a wonderful doctor at the hospital she works at and they fall in love and get married, hoping to start a family.

Love Spell publishes time travel, paranormal, and futuristic romance novels. This novel is a contemporary romance—be sure the publisher you are submitting to works with the kind of books you write.

Don't mention that you're a first-time writer or that you've never been published.

This is the first book I've ever written, but I think it will be very popular. My mother, sister, and sister-in-law have all read it and loved it. If you are not interested please let me know by next week so I can send it on to another publisher.

Don't give the editor an unrealistic deadline to get back to you. If she's interested, you'll hear from her.

Thank you for you time.

Never say that family members "loved" your book. This means nothing to an editor, and singles you out as an amateur.

Nancy Nohope

215-555-4242

Watch out for typos!

This tells the editor very little about the book and why it is different from other romances on the market. Who are the characters? What are their motivations? What is the conflict? What is the length of the book?

CHAPTER SEVEN

MYSTERY

Mystery Genre

The mystery is a form of fiction in which one or more elements remain unknown or unexplained until the end of the story. The modern mystery story contains elements of the serious novel: a convincing account of a character's struggle with various physical and psychological obstacles in an effort to achieve his or her goal, good characterization, and sound motivation. Publishers of mysteries, be they short stories in mystery publications such as *Ellery Queen's Mystery Magazine* or complete novels, often look for one or more of these eleven categories:

- **Amateur sleuth.** In an amateur sleuth story, the main character does the detection but isn't a professional private investigator or police detective. Two detectives work together in a bickering team or cohort mystery series. The crime is the main focus, but the relationship—be it marriage or friendship— is also developed.
- **Caper.** A caper is a crime story usually told from the viewpoint of the perpetrator. The tone may be lighthearted and the crime is often theft rather than murder.
- **Cozy.** A murder mystery set in a small English or New England town that features an amateur sleuth is called a cozy or English cozy. The "detective" is usually a genteel old lady or gentleman.
- **Gothic.** A gothic mystery is one with a dark and brooding tone. It contains elements of romantic suspense and is usually set at an old estate.
- **Hardboiled.** A story that features a streetwise and hardened detective is a hardboiled detective story. This character type was popularized in the 1940s and 1950s.
- **Heist.** More serious than a caper, a heist focuses on solving the theft, as well as on the planning and execution of the theft.
- **Malice domestic.** A mystery involving a family member's murder is a malice domestic.
- **Police procedural.** A police procedural is a mystery featuring a police detective or officer who uses standard professional police practices to solve a crime.
- **Romantic suspense.** In a romantic suspense, strong elements of romance appear, usually between the detective and the victim or the detective and the suspect.
- **True crime.** Nonfiction about real murders and serial killings is true crime.
- **Whodunit.** The focus is on discovering the identity of the murderer in a whodunit.

MYSTERY WRITERS OF AMERICA (MWA)

This organization of more than 2,500 members is the leading association for professional mystery writers. The membership includes published writes, novice writers, screenwriters, dramatists, and people in writing-related fields, such as publishers, editors, and agents. There are four categories of membership: *Active* members are published, professional writers of fiction, nonfiction, or drama in the crime/mystery/suspense field. *Associate* members are professionals in allied fields (editors, publishers, news reporters, critics, agents, etc.). *Affiliate* members are writers of crime/mystery/suspense fiction that have not been professionally published. *Corresponding* members are writers qualified for active membership that live outside the United States.

Annual activities of the MWA include a convention, presentation of the Edgar Allen Poe and Raven Awards, and publication of an anthology of members' work. A newsletter, *The Third Degree*, is issued ten times a year. You can visit the MWA Web site at www.myst erywriters.org or contact them at 17 East Forty-seventh Street, Sixth Floor, New York, New York 10017; mwa@mysterywriters.org; (212) 888-8171.

Mystery Query

SUBMISSION TIPS

The most important thing to remember is to make sure the publisher you are submitting to publishes the type of mystery you write. Do your homework! You wouldn't send your hardboiled crime novel to a publisher that is known for only publishing English cozy mysteries. The mystery market has quite a few subgenres, so you really have to do some research to make sure you are submitting to a publisher that works with the type of story you have written.

FORMATTING SPECS

To submit and format your short stories and novels in the mystery genre, consult the appropriate pages for fiction submissions (short stories appear on page 102; novel proposals on page 113).

OTHER DOS AND DON'TS

- Do obtain a copy of a publisher or agent's guidelines before submitting.
- Do indicate in your query letter the names of authors that your work is similar to in order to give the editor or agent a point of reference; if possible, reference an author who is published or represented by the publisher or agent you are sending your query to. This will show that you're knowledgeable about the genre and the authors that the publisher or agent works with.
- Don't send a query or proposal via e-mail or fax unless a publisher or agent specifically requests it.

In a cover letter, I like to see some background on the author, such as publication history and areas of expertise if it bears on the story.

—Linda Landrigan, editor, *Alfred Hitchcock's Mystery Magazine*

QUERY TO MYSTERY PUBLISHER

Simple return information, including phone and e-mail.

George Gumshoe
976 Main St.
Lake Charles, LA 52121
(402) 555-5424
gumshoe@email.com

June 29, 2004

Addresses letter to a specific editor (and dates it).

1" margin

Steven Sleuth
Silver Dagger Mysteries
P.O. Box 1216
Johnson City, TN 37605

Dear Mr. Sleuth:

Good introductory paragraph. States the novel's title, set the hook (grabber), and makes the editor want to read the novel.

In my novel, *Mystery Lake*, the sleepy southern town of Hathaway, Louisiana, is shocked when the dismembered body of its most prominent citizen washes up on the shores of Mystery Lake. Miriam Linnel was well loved by all the citizens of Valley Mills, and a motive for the murder can't be found. However, everyone has notice a mysterious drifter who arrived in town just days before the murder—could he have done it? Or is the secret hidden in Miriam's will? It's up to detective Joshua Dunham to find out.

Strong grabber sentence.

I have had short stories published in several mystery magazines, including *Hardboiled*, *Alfred Hitchcock's Mystery Magazine*, and *Ellery Queen's Mystery Magazine*. I have also been a police detective on the Lake Charles, Louisiana police force for 15 years.

States publishing credits and pertinent professional background.

Tells the exact word count—the author has done his homework, as Silver Dagger's guidelines state that they are looking for books of 60-80,000 words.

The novel is 65,000 words. I think it will fit in well with the other police procedural books you publish, such as *Killer Looks* by Laura Young and *Justice Betrayed* by Daniel Bailey.

Mentions the intended audience and why the book will fit in well on this publisher's list.

Thank you for your time in considering *Mystery Lake*. I look forward to hearing from you.

Sincerely,

George Gumshoe

Catalogs every item being sent in the package—this is exactly what the publisher requests in their guidelines.

Encl.: Outline
    Chapters 1, 2, 3
    Synopsis
    Author bio
    SASE

| **QUERY TO MYSTERY PUBLISHER: MISTAKES TO AVOID** |

Mark Mistakes
Johnson, Utah
401-555-8585

Silver Dagger Mysteries
P.O. Box 1261
Johnson City, TN 37605

To Whom It May Concern:

I have written a romantic suspense novel that I think you'll be
interested in. A young woman in the Pacific Northwest is framed
for a murder she didn't commit. The local police detective is
the only person who believes in her innocence, and as he tries to
solve the crime and clear her of all guilt they find themselves
falling in love with each other.

This is my first novel so it probably needs some help, so if you
could take a look at it and let me know how I can make it better
that would be great. Right now the word count is 30,000 words. I
think that with some professional help this can be a bestselling
mystery novel.

Once you're finished reading the novel, please get back to me
and let me know what you think. I'll be waiting!

Sincerely,
Mark Mistakes

Enclosure: Manuscript

Never address a letter "To Whom It May Concern." Make sure you have a contact name to address your query to.

Silver Dagger only publishes mysteries that take place in the American South, and they emphasize cozies, police procedurals, and hardboiled stories—not romantic suspense.

Tells very little about the story and why anyone should be interested in publishing it. What makes it suspenseful? Who are the characters?

All of the author's contact information should be listed here—name, address, phone, and e-mail. The date should be here, too.

Don't mention that you're a first-time writer.

Silver Dagger looks for books in the range of 60-80,000 words.

Don't ask the editor for advice or help with the novel—that is not the purpose of the query.

Don't send the entire manuscript unless the editor specifically requests it. Do enclose an SASE. The publisher's guidelines will state if they want a synopsis, sample chapters, etc.

CHAPTER EIGHT

SCIENCE FICTION/ FANTASY/HORROR

Science Fiction and Fantasy

Science fiction can be defined as literature involving elements of science and technology as a basis for conflict, or as the setting for a story. The science and technology are generally extrapolations of existing scientific fact, and most (though not all) science fiction stories take place in the future. There are other definitions of science fiction, and much disagreement in academic circles as to just what constitutes science fiction and what constitutes fantasy. This is because in some cases the line between science fiction and fantasy is virtually nonexistent. Despite the controversy, it is generally accepted that, to be science fiction, a story must have elements of science. Fantasy, on the other hand, rarely utilizes science, relying instead of magic, mythological and neo-mythological beings and devices, and outright invention for conflict and setting.

Some of the basic elements of science fiction have been in existence for thousands of years. There have always been fortune-tellers, prophets, clairvoyants, and other extraordinary people who sought to foretell the future. The grand adventure in an exotic setting is a recurring story theme in science fiction and has been a literary theme almost as long as the desire to know the future. Tales of mythological gods and their involvement with humans are echoed by modern-day science fiction of encounters with alien beings. The heroic quest, occurring so often in mythology, is paralleled by stories of pioneering space explorers.

Contemporary science fiction, while maintaining its focus on science and technology, is more concerned with the effects of science and technology on people. Since science is such an important factor in writing science fiction, accuracy with reference to scientific fact is important. Most of the science in science fiction is hypothesized from known facts, so in addition to being firmly based in fact, the extrapolations must be consistent. Science fiction writers make their own rules for future settings, but the field requires consistency. For example, if a future is established in which mass transit is the only form of personal transportation, a character cannot be shown driving a personal vehicle just because it is convenient to the plot.

Whatever the background, science fiction, as other forms of fiction, is dependent upon the "standard" elements of storytelling—plot, characterization, theme, motivation, etc.— for success. Many would-be science fiction writers miss this fact and attempt to dazzle readers with gimmicks and gadgets, to no effect. Beyond inconsistency and an overabundance of gadgetry in place of a good story, there are few taboos in science fiction.

There are several subcategories of science fiction, including dark fantasy, sociological science fiction, space opera, military science fiction, alternate history, and cyberpunk, each having its own peculiarities. Extensive reading in the field can aid in identifying these subcategories and is recommended for anyone wishing to write science fiction.

SCIENCE FICTION AND FANTASY WRITERS OF AMERICA (SFWA)

This organization was founded in 1965 and more than 1,200 members, made up of science fiction/fantasy writers, artists, editors, and allied professionals. The SFWA has four categories of membership: *Associate* is for beginning writers with one professional publication; *Affiliate* is for allied professionals, such as agents, editors, artists, and publishers; and *Institutional*, which is for organizations such as schools and universities. All members receive the quarterly bulletin, the annual membership directory, the *SFWA Handbook* and copies of model paperback and hardcover contracts. Active and associate members also receive the *SFWA Forum*, an in-house journal, six times a year. SFWA presents the Nebula Awards for the best science fiction or fantasy short story, novelette, novella, and novel of the year.

Visit the SFWA's Web site at www.sfwa.org or contact them at SFWA Inc., P.O. Box 877, Chestertown, Maryland 21620; execdir@sfwa.org.

SUBMISSION TIPS

The most important thing to remember about submitting to science and fantasy publishers is to make sure your story or novel fits the exact category of the publisher you are submitting to. The science fiction and fantasy market has different subgenres, so you really have to do some research to make sure you are submitting to a publisher that works with the type of story you have written.

FORMATTING SPECS

To submit and format your short stories and novels in the science fiction and fantasy genre, consult the appropriate pages for fiction submissions (short stories appear on page 102; novel proposals on page 113).

OTHER DOS AND DON'TS

- Do obtain a copy of a publisher or agent's guidelines. Some publishers or fiction magazines only publish certain types of science fiction and fantasy, so make sure your story or novel fits their guidelines before sending.
- Do indicate in your query letter the names of authors that your work is similar to in order to give the editor or agent a point of reference; if possible, reference an author who is published or represented by the publisher or agent you are sending your query to. This will show that you're knowledgeable about the genre and the publisher or agent's authors.
- Don't send a query or proposal via e-mail or fax unless a publisher or agent specifically requests it.

Horror

Howard Phillips (H.P.) Lovecraft, generally acknowledged to be the master of the horror tale in the twentieth century and the most important writer of this genre since Edgar Allan Poe, maintained that "the oldest and strongest emotion of mankind is fear, and the oldest and strongest kind of fear is fear of the unknown. These facts few psychologists will dispute, and their admitted truth must establish for all time the genuineness and dignity of the weirdly horrible tales as a literary form."

Lovecraft distinguishes horror literature from fiction based entirely on physical fear and the merely gruesome. "The true weird tale has something more than secret murder, bloody bones, or a sheeted form clanking chains according to rule. A certain atmosphere of breathless and unexplainable dread of outer, unknown forces must be present; there must be a hint, expressed with a seriousness and portentousness becoming its subject, of that most terrible concept of the human brain—a malign and particular suspension or defeat of the fixed laws of nature which are our only safeguards against the assaults of chaos and the daemons of unplumbed space." It is that atmosphere—the creation of a particular sensation or emotional level—that, according to Lovecraft, is the most important element in the creation of horror literature.

Some horror writing has elements of science fiction and fantasy, and the lines between these genres can get blurred. Dark fantasy is a horror genre that combines the traditional elements of horror with the fantastical elements of fantasy. A good way to research current trends in horror is to study anthologies such as *The Year's Best Horror and Fantasy*, published yearly by St. Martin's Press.

HORROR WRITERS ASSOCIATION (HWA)

This organization was formed in the late 1980s to "encourage public interest in and foster an appreciation of good horror and dark fantasy literature. It has more than 1,000 members in the three categories: *Active* for published writers, *Affiliate* for nonpublished writers with "a demonstrable interest in writing horror," and *Associate* for non-writing professionals with an interest in the field, including illustrators, editors, agents, booksellers, etc.

HWA awards the Bram Stoker Award for Superior Achievement annually. It publishes a bimonthly newsletter and a membership directory. Visit www.horror.org or contact them at HWA, P.O. Box 50577, Palo Alto, California 94303; hwa@horror.org.

You must seize, then hold, your readers' and your editor's interest and attention, then repay the readers' time and the editor's money by having something to say and sharing it with them. The awful truth of the matter is, as Rear Admiral Pinney once put it, "If you don't get the reader's attention in the first paragraph, the rest of your message is lost." This applies even more to fiction than to U.S. Navy correspondence; you MUST capture the reader's attention on the first page (or better, in the first few words).

—George Scithers, editor, *Weird Tales* magazine

SUBMISSION TIPS

Before you submit your query, story, or proposal, be sure that your story fits the type of horror stories or novels that the publisher works with. Do your homework! Don't send your traditional ghost story to a publisher that only publishes dark fantasy.

FORMATTING SPECS

To submit and format your short stories and novels in the horror genre, consult the appropriate pages for fiction submissions (short stories appear on page 102); novel proposals on page 113).

OTHER DOS AND DON'TS

- Do obtain a copy of a publisher or agent's guidelines. Make sure your story or novel fits their guidelines before sending.
- Do indicate in your query letter the names of authors that your work is similar to in order to give the editor or agent a point of reference; if possible, reference an author who is published or represented by the publisher or agent you are sending your query to. This will show that you're knowledgeable about the genre and the publisher or agent's authors.
- Don't send a query or proposal via e-mail or fax unless a publisher or agent specifically requests it.

Mistakes writers make include using undersized type (twelve-point Courier is the best); failing to double-line-space the text; failing to number the pages; and failing to include a stamped return envelope for the editors' comments.''

—George Scithers, editor, *Weird Tales* magazine

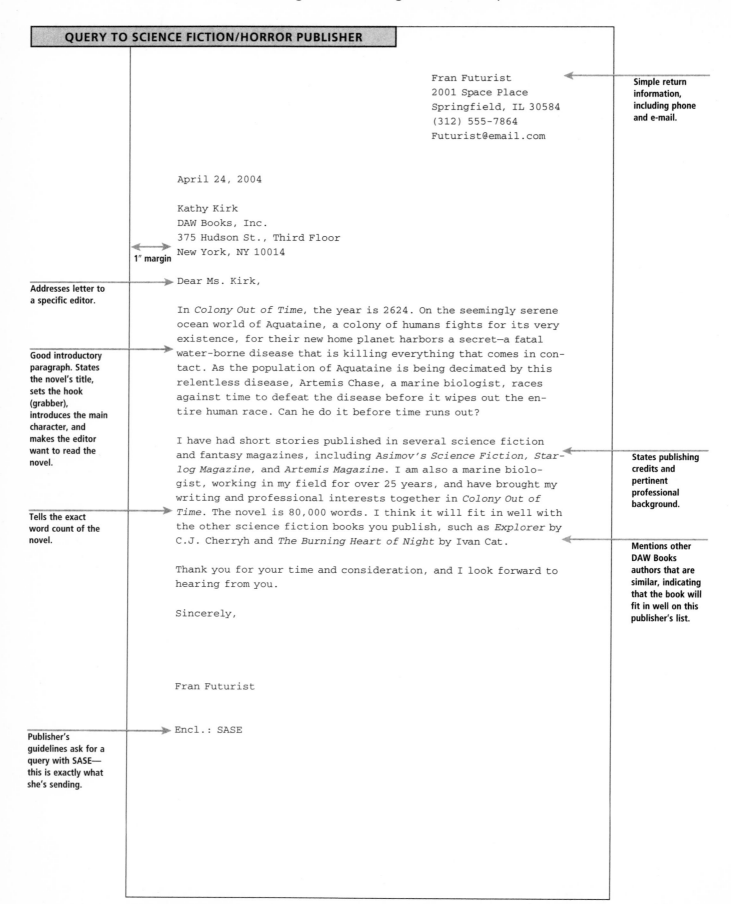

QUERY TO SCIENCE FICTION/HORROR PUBLISHER

Fran Futurist
2001 Space Place
Springfield, IL 30584
(312) 555-7864
Futurist@email.com

Simple return
information,
including phone
and e-mail.

April 24, 2004

Kathy Kirk
DAW Books, Inc.
375 Hudson St., Third Floor
New York, NY 10014

1" margin

Addresses letter to
a specific editor.

Dear Ms. Kirk,

In *Colony Out of Time*, the year is 2624. On the seemingly serene
ocean world of Aquataine, a colony of humans fights for its very
existence, for their new home planet harbors a secret—a fatal
water-borne disease that is killing everything that comes in contact. As the population of Aquataine is being decimated by this
relentless disease, Artemis Chase, a marine biologist, races
against time to defeat the disease before it wipes out the entire human race. Can he do it before time runs out?

Good introductory
paragraph. States
the novel's title,
sets the hook
(grabber),
introduces the main
character, and
makes the editor
want to read the
novel.

I have had short stories published in several science fiction
and fantasy magazines, including *Asimov's Science Fiction, Star-
log Magazine*, and *Artemis Magazine*. I am also a marine biologist, working in my field for over 25 years, and have brought my
writing and professional interests together in *Colony Out of
Time*. The novel is 80,000 words. I think it will fit in well with
the other science fiction books you publish, such as *Explorer* by
C.J. Cherryh and *The Burning Heart of Night* by Ivan Cat.

States publishing
credits and
pertinent
professional
background.

Tells the exact
word count of the
novel.

Mentions other
DAW Books
authors that are
similar, indicating
that the book will
fit in well on this
publisher's list.

Thank you for your time and consideration, and I look forward to
hearing from you.

Sincerely,

Fran Futurist

Encl.: SASE

Publisher's
guidelines ask for a
query with SASE—
this is exactly what
she's sending.

QUERY TO SCIENCE FICTION/HORROR PUBLISHER: MISTAKES TO AVOID

September 23, 2004

DAW Books, Inc.
375 Hudson St., Third Floor
New York, NY 10014

Dear Editor,

I have written a horror story that I swear will scare the hell out of you. Deep in the dark woods of New Bedford, Iowa, an evil lurks. Two teenagers happen upon it one night and wind up dead. One by one young people in this small town are being found dead. Wait until you find out what's doing all the killing!

I've never written anything before but I know this is just as good as anything Stephen King has ever written.

Let me know when you want to publish the book and we can talk compensation. I own the copyright to this book.

Thanks,

Bob Badquery
North Platte, NE
Bob@email.com

1" margin

Enclosure: Manuscript

Encl.: SASE

Always address a query to a specific editor.

DAW Books publishes science fiction and fantasy—this query is for a horror novel. Be sure to read publisher's guidelines to make sure they publish the type of novel you've written.

Don't mention that you're a first-time writer, and don't boast that your work is just as good as a bestselling, well-known author—your query and novel should speak for itself.

All of the author's contact information should be listed here—name, address, phone, and e-mail.

Don't tell an editor what he or she will feel when reading your book.

This is not the time to talk compensation.

Don't mention copyright—you're stating the obvious.

Don't send the entire manuscript unless the editor specifically requests it. Do enclose an SASE. The publisher's guidelines will state if they want a synopsis, sample chapters, etc.

This tells very little about the story and why anyone should be interested in publishing it. Who are the characters? How is it different from other books in this genre?

CHAPTER NINE

COMICS AND GRAPHIC NOVELS

Although many use the terms interchangeably, there are a few key differences between a comic book and a graphic novel. Graphic novels are book-sized volumes of material not previously published in traditional "comic book" periodical form. A distinction can also be made regarding plot accessibility. Comics periodicals are generally part of a lengthy, ongoing series, so someone new to a title might have to read six or eight back issues just to understand the story. Graphic novels, on the other hand, are usually self-contained, novel-length books that stand alone (with a few exceptions, such as Neil Gaiman's *Sandman* series). Even though they're called graphic "novels," graphic novels do not have to be works of fiction. "Graphic novel" is a format, not a genre, that encompasses works of nonfiction as well.

Comics and Graphic Novel Manuscript
SUBMISSION TIPS

Before you submit to any comics or graphic novel publisher, read their submission guidelines carefully (you can usually obtain a copy by sending a SASE to the publisher with your request or check out the publisher's Web site). You should also become familiar with techniques and terminology used in comics, and graphic novels. You might want to consult *Comics and Sequential Art* and *Graphic Storytelling*, both by Wil Eisner (Poorhouse Press).

Depending on the publisher, you may have to send in just a story idea without illustrations or a complete, illustrated comic, or graphic novel. Each publisher's guidelines are different, so read them carefully and submit only what they want to see.

If you are asked to submit a story idea, keep it brief—this story idea is called a springboard, which is a one-page, double-spaced typed story concept/synopsis. When writing your springboard, think of it as the sales copy on a novel's back jacket—if it's well written and interesting, the person reading it will want to look inside. Make sure your springboard story has a beginning, a middle, and an ending, so your story idea seems complete. Don't forget to introduce your main characters, develop conflicts, and have some resolution. The first sentence of your springboard should have a hook to grab the editor's attention and make her want to keep reading. What works best is condensing the gist of your story in one fast, catchy, interesting sentence.

FORMATTING SPECS

If a publisher requests art, follow their guidelines meticulously. NEVER send original art—send copies, slides, or photographs (whatever is requested) and make sure they are clean, sharp, and easy to read.

Full-length comic stories for most magazines tend to run from twenty-two to twenty-five typed pages, depending, of course, on the publication and the required format. Graphic novels are novel-length; the publisher's guidelines will indicate the length of manuscript they usually publish.

When submitting a comic or graphic novel "script," the most accepted format is called the Screenplay Method, because it is very similar to formatting a movie or television script—but a little easier. All you have to do is describe each panel (see sample). Be sure to use Courier 12-point font.

TAB AND MARGIN SETTINGS

(These are approximations—just try to make your pages look neat with consistent tab markings, as in the sample on page 175).
- Left margin: 17 spaces
- NARRATIVE and SCENE headings: 22 spaces
- Speaking character's NAME: 27 spaces
- Dialogue: 38 spaces
- Right margin: 72 spaces

ALL CAPS
- PANEL
- NARRATIVE
- SCENE
- Speaking character's NAME
- Loud sounds (GONG!)

UNDERLINE
- PANEL
- NARRATIVE
- SCENE

SINGLE SPACE
- Within dialogue
- Within scene descriptions
- Within narrative

DOUBLE SPACE
- Between the narrative and scene descriptions
- Between the scene descriptions and dialogue
- Between the speeches of the different characters

TRIPLE SPACE
- Between panels

OTHER DOS AND DONT'S

- Do include your name, address, phone number, and e-mail on each page of your submission and on each piece of art.
- Don't send original artwork!
- Do include an SASE for reply with enough return postage.
- Do type your material and use only one side of the paper.
- Do make your submission professional (neat, typed, spell-checked, brief).
- Do include a short cover letter that briefly states your background in comics or graphic novels, or any related information.
- Don't send portfolios or other expensive packages.
- Don't call a publisher to check on your submission.
- Don't send a résumé along with your submission.
- Don't staple pages together.

ELECTRONIC COMICS AND GRAPHIC NOVEL SUBMISSIONS

It is rare for a publisher to request comics or graphic novels via e-mail, but it might happen. If it does, make sure you get detailed guidelines as to how the script and art should be submitted and follow them meticulously. Find out how they want the art submitted (via e-mail, on a CD) and make sure the art is saved in the proper file format and resolution that the publisher requests.

The best thing to do is to find out what each publisher prefers. Here at SLG Publishing for example, we don't look at art or writing on its own—we only consider projects that have both an artist and a writer attached to it. Other publishers might not take unsolicited submissions or they might have specific procedures for making proposals. As with any other writing market, you should know the submission guidelines before you send something in or approach a publisher.

—Jennifer de Guzman, editor-in-chief, SLG Publishing

COMICS/GRAPHIC NOVEL SCRIPT

Page 3

PANEL 1

    1 line

NARRATIVE: The following morning . . .

    1 line

Single space
with dialogue.

ROBIN: ''My oh my what a great day this is going
to be! I can't wait to wake up Batman to
let him know Lex Luther is back in Gotham
City.''

    1 line

Left margin begins
at space 17.

SCENE: The morning sun is shining through the
window. Robin is sitting up in his bed
talking to himself. Batman is in the bed
right beside his, sound asleep.

    2 lines

PANEL 2

Speaking character's
name is in all caps.

BATMAN: ''What did you just say, Boy Wonder?''

ROBIN: ''I thought you were asleep.''

BATMAN: ''I was until you started talking to yourself. Now what were you mumbling?''

SCENE: Batman wakes up with an angry expression
on his face. He sits up in his bed and
looks over at Robin.

Underline panel, nar-
rative, and scene
headings (and put in
all caps).

PANEL 3

NARRATIVE: Five minutes later . . .

BATMAN: ''Will you get me some cereal and two as-
pirin? I'm hungry and I've got a really
bad headache.''

SCENE: Batman sitting at the kitchen table with
his head in his hands, elbows on the table. Robin is in the background opening
the refrigerator door and he turns toward Batman to see what he wants.

CHILDREN'S WRITING

CHAPTER TEN

PICTURE BOOKS

The Format

Written for children to read or have read to them, a picture book usually contains 150-1,000 words and 32 pages generally with 28 pages of text and illustrations, the other pages being front and back matter (copyright page, title page, etc.). The text of a picture book is well organized and carefully constructed, since its audience has little experience with literature. Because picture books are often read aloud and children have an instinctual fondness for rhythm, poetic techniques (e.g., alliteration, consonance, assonance, and onomatopoeia) can enhance a picture book's story. Other techniques that appeal to children are the repeated anecdote, used in *The Three Little Pigs*, and the refrain, used in *The Gingerbread Man*. Vocabulary in this category of writing is simple, and sentence construction is likewise uncomplicated; it often uses the active voice and mimics speech patterns.

A common misconception among many new writers of picture books is that they must find illustrators for their work before they submit. This is absolutely not the case; in fact most editors frown upon a writer and illustrator teaming up on a submission. Once a publisher accepts your material, the publisher will select an appropriate illustrator for your project. So even if your sister-in-law or co-worker is an illustrator, it's best not to send their illustration samples with your manuscript. Most likely a publisher will not be interested in the whole package, and including those illustrations will only hurt your chances of getting published. Also, if you enclose unprofessional art samples with your manuscript, you're destined for rejection.

Remember that the biggest taboo in picture book publishing is submitting finished artwork with the proposal. This is the unmistakable mark of an amateur—worse, an amateur who has not researched the field. The size, color, and method of printing the art can only be determined after a book is budgeted and designed. Your best bet is to write a great story, forget about the illustrations, make your query or cover letter professional and submit your manuscript.

> A query should be thorough and descriptive enough to give us a sense of the project. A sample passage, especially for a picture book, is ideal because it gives us a sense of the writer's style and tone. A query should state why the project is unique, who the audience is, and any other details that will help us understand the concept—all in a one-page letter!
>
> —**Kristen McCurry**, associate editor, **North Word Books for Young Readers**

Query Letter and Manuscript

SUBMISSION TIPS

The primary difference between submitting a picture book and an adult book is that you generally send the entire manuscript of your picture book, not just a proposal or a few sample chapters. Some publishers do accept and want query letters, though. Check each publisher's specific guidelines before you send anything. Also, even though the text for a picture book is short, publisher's do not want you to submit more than one manuscript at a time.

The cover letter accompanying your manuscript should be brief and professional, yet friendly. It should interest the reader but not overdo it on cuteness or cleverness. Mention the title of the work you are sending, a few sentences about the material, and a brief summary of previous writing experience. If you don't have any previous experience, you shouldn't mention it. Simply thank the editor for her consideration.

FORMATTING SPECS

To submit and format your picture book manuscript, consult page 142 for adult fiction submissions.

OTHER DOS AND DON'TS

- Do obtain a copy of the publisher's guidelines and follow them carefully.
- Don't include a sentence that says, "I read my work to my kids/grandkids/second grade class and they loved it." This definitely does not sway an editor's opinon, and seems amateurish.
- Don't include unnecessary personal information in your query letter.
- Do research the publisher you are querying to make sure you are sending the type of book they publish (fiction, nonfiction, certain age groups, etc.).
- Don't recommend an illustrator for your manuscript—the publisher will decide which illustrator they want to use if they are interested in your book.
- Do indicate in your query or cover letter any previous writing experience or credits you may have, as well as memberships in children's writing organizations such as the Society of Children's Book Writers and Illustrators (SCBWI).
- Don't send a query or manuscript via e-mail or fax unless a publisher or agent specifically requests it.
- Always include an SASE when sending a query or manuscript through the mail.
- Don't indicate page breaks and don't type each page on a new sheet of paper.

ELECTRONIC SUBMISSIONS

Before you send a query or manuscript to a publication via e-mail, make sure they accept electronic submissions by contacting the publication directly or checking out their writer's guidelines. Never send a query or manuscript via e-mail unless you have permission from the editor or if their submission guidelines state it is acceptable. For detailed information on submitting manuscripts electronically, see page 143.

CHILDREN'S PICTURE BOOK QUERY LETTER

Includes complete contact information— name, address, phone, and e-mail.

Verna Victor
93 Success St.
Fulton, MD 54412
(301) 555-3737
verna@email.com

June 23, 2004

Goldie Locks
Just for Kids Books
34 Broadway
New York, NY 10019

1″ margin

Addresses a specific editor.

Dear Ms. Locks,

One of the scariest moments in a small child's life is the first day he has to leave home to attend kindergarten. Helping kids become excited instead of apprehensive about their first day at school is what my picture book, *Ira's Big Day*, is all about.

Good, concise outline of the reasons behind the author writing a book on this topic.

Ira's Big Day follows six-year-old Ira Nelson as he prepares for his first day at kindergarten. His mother, father, and older sister all help Ira plan for the big day—his Mom lays out his new clothes, his Dad gives him a brand-new knapsack filled with school supplies, and his older sister, Paige, tells him all about her first day in kindergarten. Ira asks the hard questions that most kids ask, and his loving and supportive family answers them honestly, thus helping Ira—and the reader—put their minds at ease.

It gives a quick overview of the storyline and introduces the main characters.

Outlines related professional experience and publishing credits.

I have been a kindergarten teacher for 23 years, and have seen firsthand the fears that children bring with them on their first day of school. I have had articles and stories published in *U.S. Kids, Jack and Jill, Highlights, Parenting,* and *Teaching K-8* magazines, most of them dealing with first-day-of-school jitters and other anxieties that kids face in new environments.

Indicates length of the manuscript (which falls within the typical length of a children's picture book) and that it is completed and ready for submission.

Ira's Big Day is 1,000 words and complete. May I send you a copy of the manuscript? I have enclosed an SASE for your reply. Thank you for your consideration, and I look forward to hearing from you.

Politely asks for permission to send the manuscript, indicates that an SASE is enclosed, and thanks the editor for her time.

Sincerely,

Verna Victor

Encloses an SASE for reply.

Encl.: SASE

COVER LETTER: CHILDREN'S PICTURE BOOK

Complete return information—name, address, phone, and e-mail.

Verna Victor
93 Success St.
Fulton, MD 54412
(301) 555-3737
verna@email.com

June 23, 2004

1" margin

Goldie Locks
Just for Kids Books
34 Broadway
New York, NY 10019

Addresses a specific editor.

Dear Ms. Locks,

Introductory paragraph includes the book's title, the word count, the central characters, and tells what the story is about.

Enclosed is my 1,000-word picture book, *Ira's big Day*, which follows six-year-old Ira Nelson as he prepares for his first day at kindergarten. His mother, father, and older sister all help Ira plan for the big day—his Mom lays out his new clothes, his Dad gives him a brand-new knapsack filled with school supplies, and his older sister, Paige, tells him all about her first day in kindergarten. Ira asks the hard questions that most kids ask, and his loving and supportive family answers them honestly, thus helping Ira—and the reader—put their minds at ease.

Mentions pertinent personal information—her background shows why she's qualified to write a book about this subject, and she's included her past publishing credits.

I have been a kindergarten teacher for 23 years, and have seen firsthand the fears that children bring with them on their first day of school. I have had articles and stories published in *U.S. Kids, Jack and Jill, Highlights, Parenting*, and *Teaching K-8* magazines, most of them dealing with first-day-of-school jutters and other anxieties that kids face in new environments.

Thank you for considering *Ira's Big Day*, and I look forward to hearing from you.

Politely closes the letter on a positive note.

Sincerely,

Verna Victor

Enclosure: Manuscript, *Ira's Big Day*
            SASE

Details everything that is included in the submission package. You can omit the SASE if you are sending your manuscript via e-mail.

MANUSCRIPT FOR PICTURE BOOK

Slug line with novel's title in all caps. → Victor/IRA'S BIG DAY

1 ← **Page number (on the same line as the slug line).**

Justifies left margin only. →

When Ira Nelson woke up on Sunday morning, he knew this day was different. What was it? Was it his mother's birthday? No, her birthday was the day after the Fourth of July. Was it his dad's birthday? No, his birthday was just last month. His big sister Paige's birthday? No, her birthday was easy to remember—it was

1″ margin ↔ on New Year's Day. So what was so different about this day? As Ira sat up in bed trying to figure it out, he heard his mother calling him from downstairs.

''Ira, time for breakfast!,'' she said in a sing-song voice. ''We've got your favorite, eggs and bacon and bagels!'' ← **Double-spaced text**

Doesn't indicate page breaks. → ''Come on Ira, we're hungry,'' yelled his big sister Paige.

''Woof,'' said Ira's dog Sparky.

Ira jumped out of bed and headed downstairs to the kitchen. His mother would know what was so different about this day.

''Here's our sleepyhead,'' said Ira's dad. ''Just in time for breakfast.'' Ira took his seat at the end of the table, and Sparky sat down at his feet.

''Mom,'' Ira said as he took a gulp of orange juice, ''What is today?''

''Sunday,'' his mother said.

''I know,'' said Ira as he took a bit of his bagel. ''But what's different about today?''

''Different?'', said his mom. ''Oh, Ira, today's the day before you start kindergarten!''

Ira felt funny. That's what was so different.

''I don't want to go to kindergarten,'' Ira said. ''I want to stay here with you and Sparky.''

CHAPTER ELEVEN

MID-GRADE, YOUNG ADULT BOOKS

The Categories

Books written for children (excluding picture books) are divided into two groups according to the readers' ages: books written for children younger than twelve (mid-grade) and those written for children older than twelve (young adult, or YA). Nonfiction books for mid-grade and young adults should reflect the age of the intended reader; obviously a book on science geared toward fifth graders would be much more simplistic than one written for high school students. Make sure you know the educational level of the book's intended audience and write specifically for them.

The main character in a children's novel should be no younger than the age group of the book's intended audience; however, the character can be a year or two older than the novel's oldest reader.

YA novels revolve around characters aged fourteen to seventeen who are involved in more complex plots and show more depth than those characters in mid-grade novels. Also, YA novels employ a more sophisticated writing style, vocabulary, subject matter and general treatment.

In writing a YA novel, you should remember that this work will be read predominately by young teenagers, since older teenagers are likely to read fiction written for an adult audience. Therefore, the plot and situations of the characters should be identifiable to the child of junior high school age. Reading children's novels and talking to public or school librarians are important steps toward understanding your audience.

Query Letter and Manuscript
SUBMISSION TIPS

Be sure to check each publisher's specific guidelines before you send anything, and make sure that the children's publisher you are submitting to is interested in a mid-grade or YA book—some children's publisher's only work with picture books.

The query or cover letter accompanying your manuscript should be brief and professional, yet friendly. It should interest the reader but not overdo it on cuteness or cleverness. Mention the title of the work you are sending, a sentence or two about the material, and a brief summary of previous writing experience. If you don't have any previous experience, you shouldn't mention it and simply thank the editor for her consideration.

FORMATTING SPECS

To submit and format your mid-grade and YA novels, consult chapter five for fiction submissions. For nonfiction titles, see chapter two.

OTHER DOS AND DON'TS

- Do obtain a copy of the publisher's guidelines and follow them carefully.
- Don't include a sentence that says, "I read my work to my kids/grandkids/second grade class and they loved it." This definitely does not sway an editor's opinon, and seems amateurish.
- Do indicate how your book is different from similar books on the market.
- Do indicate the word count of the book in your query or cover letter.
- Do indicate the age group that your book is intended to reach.
- Do cite works from the publisher that you are sending your query to, if possible, to indicate where your work falls in the publisher's line. This shows your familiarity with the publisher's work and that you've done your homework and know the market.
- Do indicate in your query letter any previous writing experience or credits you may have, as well as memberships in children's writing organizations such as the Society of Children's Book Writers and Illustrators (SCBWI).
- Do indicate where you see your nonfiction book being used and marketed, if relevant (in the classroom, at home, sold through bookstores, museum stores and catalogs, etc.)
- Don't send a query or manuscript via e-mail or fax unless a publisher or agent specifically requests it.
- Always include an SASE unless you are sending it via e-mail.

ELECTRONIC SUBMISSIONS

Before you send a query or manuscript to a publisher via e-mail, make sure they accept electronic submissions by contacting the publication directly or checking out their writer's guidelines. Never send a query or manuscript via e-mail unless you have permission from the editor or if their submission guidelines state it is acceptable. For detailed information on submitting manuscripts electronically, see chapter five for fiction submissions and chapter two for nonfiction submissions.

The biggest mistake writers make when sending queries is not including an SASE because we won't respond without one. Another common mistake is submitting inappropriate material.
—Kristen McCurry, associate editor, Northwood Books for Young Readers

MID-GRADE AND YOUNG ADULT BOOK QUERY LETTER

Cindy Blobaum
9034 Foxhunter Lane
New Book, IA 50311
704-555-8547
Gloria@email.com

September 23, 2004

Pamela Potter
Williamson Publishing Company
Church Hill Road
P.O. Box 185
Charlotte, VT 05445

Dear Ms. Potter,

Do you know how to make a mountain out of a molehill? Kids do. Try to find fun, easy-to-understand geology activities that go beyond making baking soda an vinegar volcanoes. Imagine constructing your own periodic table while cooking *Ingneous Edibles*. Or understanding how fossils form by creating *Sponge Stones*. And it gets really personal when you discover that *You're a Mine Field!*

For 10 years I have researched, developed, and field-tested many hands-on geology activities. Students and teachers have been overwhelmingly enthusiastic about the programs and have requested additional information. I am responding by writing a book—***Geology Rocks!*** This manual of interconnected activities addressing conceptual geology:

- features innovative activities that create the ''AHA!'' experience
- uses inexpensive, everyday materials like candy and building blocks
- provides appropriate background knowledge without burying it in mountains of text
- offers levels of information from beginning to more advanced
- furnishes multiple, flexible ways to learn the same concept
- involves users in simulated geologic processes from cave formation to plate shifting.

Geology rocks! emphasizes learning-by-doing fun, similar to your successful *Kids' Nature Book* and *Kids' Science Book*. This single-subject book, aimed at children ages 7-12, would fit well with your *Kaleidoscope Kids* series. It would be appropriate for kids to use at home, for teachers planning lessons, and for professionals designing enrichment programs. It could easily be marketed through bookstores, scientific supply companies, museum and educational stores, and catalogs, and used in workshops, continuing education, and pre-service methods classes.

The enclosed section, *Make Mine Metamorphic*, highlights the type of activities and information included throughout the book. I have also enclosed an outline and SASE. I look forward to hearing from you.

Sincerely,

Cindy Blobaum

Enc: Section One
      Outline
      SASE

Margin notes:

Includes complete contact information—name, address, phone, and e-mail.

Addresses a specific editor.

This paragraph shows that the author knows the publisher's mission and did her homework. The author is offering something different from what's already on the market.

1″ margin

A quick outline on the content and goals of the book.

Briefly outlines the author's experience in the subject.

Mentions the age group the book is intended for.

References books in the publisher's line where this book would fit in—this shows that the author knows the market.

Outlines where the author sees her book being used and marketed.

Indicates what is enclosed.

MID-GRADE AND YOUNG ADULT BOOK QUERY: MISTAKES TO AVOID

February 2, 2004

Editor
Random House Inc.
Juvenile Books
201 E. 50th St.
New York, NY 10022

Dear Sir,

Being professionally involved in the funeral industry through contract work and having kids of my own has brought an interesting twist to my children's writing.

These experiences have allowed me to approach the subject of death without being threatening to young readers. I have developed a series of stories involving the interaction of different dogs with morticians and undertakers in a vast array of situations, including embalming, funeral planning, grief, and mourning, etc.

If you are interested in a manuscript copy of one of these stories, please contact me.

Thank you for your time.

Sincerely,

Carol Quitnow

The author didn't include her contact information.

A query letter should always be addressed to a specific editor.

This is vague. What is "contract work" in the funeral industry? What children's writing? Has the author been published before?

What is this series? How long is each book in the series? Needs a lot more detail.

If the author had checked the publisher's guidelines, she would know that they request a copy of the complete manuscript with a query.

What age is she specifically targeting?

These are completely inappropriate subjects for children's books, which indicates that the author knows nothing about the market.

At the very least, an SASE should have been included.

CHAPTER TWELVE

CHILDREN'S MAGAZINES

What to Submit

Writing articles for children's magazines is similar to writing articles for any other magazine—you have to know what audience a magazine serves and write for that audience. There are hundreds of children's magazines for sale on newsstands and distributed in schools that are aimed at children of all ages and interests. You should read as many back issues as you can of a magazine that you're thinking of submitting to so you can identify the magazine's "voice." Make sure you know what a publication's focus is before you submit anything. Don't send a short story or poem to a magazine that only publishes news stories for kids. In this and any other magazine market, you have to study what's out there so you don't waste your time submitting inappropriate articles and stories. Whether you are sending a story, article, or poem, your submission should be age-appropriate and follow the publication's guidelines meticulously.

Query Letter and Manuscript

SUBMISSION TIPS

Be sure to check each publisher's specific guidelines before you send anything. The query or cover letter accompanying your manuscript should be brief and professional, yet friendly. It should interest the reader but not overdo it on cuteness or cleverness. Mention the title of the work you are sending, a sentence or two about the material, and a brief summary of previous writing experience. If you don't have any previous experience, you shouldn't mention it and simply thank the editor for her consideration.

FORMATTING SPECS

To submit and format your submission of an article to a children's magazine, consult chapter one on article submissions.

OTHER DOS AND DON'TS

- Do obtain a copy of the publisher's guidelines and follow them carefully.
- Don't include a sentence that says, "I read my work to my kids/grandkids/second grade class and they loved it." This definitely does not sway an editor's opinion, and seems amateurish.

- Do indicate your familiarity with the publication. It's okay to make a positive comment, if it's sincere and appropriate.
- Do indicate in your query letter any previous writing experience or credits you may have, as well as memberships in children's writing organizations such as the Society of Children's Book Writers and Illustrators (SCBWI).
- Do indicate if you are sending simultaneous submissions to other publications.
- Don't send a query or manuscript via e-mail or fax unless a publisher or agent specifically requests it.
- Don't discuss payment terms—this will be discussed if your manuscript is accepted.
- Always include an SASE.

ELECTRONIC SUBMISSIONS

Before you send a query or manuscript to a publication via e-mail, make sure they accept electronic submissions by contacting the publication directly or checking out their writer's guidelines. Never send a query or manuscript via e-mail unless you have permission from the editor or if their submission guidelines state it is acceptable. For detailed information on submitting manuscripts electronically, see chapter one.

Voice is so important in a query! It's a good place to show me that you are savvy when it comes to teen/kid-friendly copy. Your letter should convince me that you can do this—which doesn't mean attaching a page of publishing credits. A few well-crafted sentences can establish your credibility. A lucid, clever query letter can overcome lack of publishing credits.

—Mary Lou Carney, editor-in-chief, *Guideposts for Teens*

CHILDREN'S MAGAZINE QUERY LETTER

Floyd Gotit
123 Published Road
Sunny, FL 31101
(305)555-8541
floyd@email.com

Includes complete contact information—name, address, phone, and e-mail.

April 2, 2004

Jeff Juvenile
U.S. Kids

1" margin P.O. Box 567
Indianapolis, IN 46205

Addresses a specific editor.

Dear Mr. Juvenile,

Opening paragraph is straightforward and to the point. The author doesn't waste time telling the editor how much kids will enjoy reading his article—the editor will be the judge of that.

Enclosed please find a 500-word nonfiction manuscript title ''The First Horse,'' which is about the first horse to go into battle in the Civil War. I would appreciate it if you'd consider it for publication.

Fits right in the the article requirements for *U.S. Kids*.

I'm a professional archaeologist and freelance writer whose mose recent publications include articles in the September 2002 and 2003 issues of *America's Civil War*, the June 2003 issue of *True West*, and the Autumn 2003 issue of *Persimmon Hill*, a publication of the National Cowboy Hall of Fame. I also have pieces appearing in forthcoming issues of *Military History* and *TIME for Kids*.

Briefly outlines the author's experience in the subject and previous publications. The fact that he's been published in both history and children's magazines indicates the accuracy of his work.

The ending is polite and business-like.

I have enclosed an SASE for your reply. Thank you for your consideration. I look forward to hearing from you on this matter.

Sincerely,

Floyd Gotit

Lists what is enclosed.

Enclosure: Manuscript
                SASE

CHILDREN'S MAGAZINE QUERY: MISTAKES TO AVOID

Complete contact information should be included—name, address, phone, and e-mail. Don't forget to include the date, too.

Tina Missedit
123 Never Road
Stop Now, OH 33521

Editor
U.S. Kids
P.O. Box 567
Indianapolis, IN 46205

A query letter should always be addressed to a specific editor.

To Whom It May Concern,

Young children love to use their imaginations. They will block out the world and use their imaginations. The simplest toy or object begins to talk and come alive. The mind of a child is a fantasy adventure. When told to keep busy or take a bath, their world comes alive with fantasy.

This is a dull, pointless opening—the space is better used to describe the manuscript that is being submitted, not obvious statements about children and imagination.

Watch out for typos! Spell check wouldn't have caught this one.

Please find enclosed my manuscript taken fro a picture book, titled *The Adventures of Sir Jerry in the Bath*. When Jerry takes a bath and brings some toys with him, the waters and toys come alive. He becomes a fighter, protector and then the hero. He lets his imagination run wild. It uses playful, humorous language and will appeal to a child's sense of fantasy.

U.S. Kids is a magazine, so why is she pitching a picture book story? The author obviously doesn't know the market.

There is no reason to list the names of other publications you are submitting to. The phrase "This is a simultaneous submission" is enough.

I have submitted simultaneous submissions to *Highlights for Children*, *Humpty Dumpty's Magazine*, *Pockets*, and *Owl Magazine*. I have never been published before but my grandchildren just love my stories.

Sincerely,

Tina Missedit

Don't tell the editor that you've never been published, and don't tell him that your kids/grandkids/neighbors love your work! It screams "amateur."

An SASE should be included for a reply.

part 4

SCRIPTS

Automatic Formatting Software Programs for Scriptwriters and Playwrights

Fortunately for scriptwriters, there are several highly competitive stand-alone and add-on software programs to help format scripts. All will save you time, all will make your writing easier and most work on both Macs and PCs. They don't take up much disk space on your hard drive, either. You should also be able to download a demo of the product from the retailer's Web site (don't buy unless you try). Find out more about these programs by checking the individual Web sites. Below, we break up these programs into their stand-alone and add-on camps, define the differences between these two types of script-aides, and offer information about each program.

STAND-ALONE PROGRAMS

A stand-alone script processor does it all, all by itself—formatting, paginating, indexing, spell-checking, and other chores. You do not need a word processing program to run a stand-alone program. Essentially, it works without a word processor and requires just a few keystroke commands from you and minimal hardware space from your computer. Most programs cost from $75 to $300, and all offer screenplay, sitcom, and stage play formats. While there are individual differences among them, they all make writing scripts and organizing ideas unbelievably easy.

Final Draft (Final Draft Inc., 26707 W. Agoura Rd., Suite 205, Calabasas, CA 91302, [800] 231-4055, www.finaldraft.com) Final Draft offers formatting capabilities for screenplays, sitcoms, or stage plays. The enter and tab keys can handle most of the commands in Final Draft. You can easily change your script from one format to another (just in case you write a sitcom but change your mind and want to turn it into a screenplay). Final Draft imports and exports scripts in both ASCII and RTF file formats, and will export to Movie Magic Scheduling. One problem with Final Draft is that when cutting and pasting text from another program in Windows, Final Draft changes everything into all caps. However, this doesn't happen when importing an RTF file. Final Draft offers an outline view and an index card view, as well as a great spell-checker and thesaurus. For an additional twenty-five dollars or so, you can get an add-on program for television scripts that provides character names and formatting specs for many currently airing shows. A manual is included.

Movie Magic Screenwriter (Write Brothers, Inc., 138 N. Brand Blvd., Suite 201, Glendale, CA 91203 [818] 843-6557, www.screenplay.com)

Movie Magic Screenwriter is perhaps the king of software formatting programs (Write Brothers, Inc. was first to develop scriptwriting software, back in 1983). It offers formatting for screenplays, sitcoms, stage plays, and multimedia scripts. You can do almost all your work with the tab and enter keys. You get a spell-checker, a thesaurus and a Character Name Bank containing thousands of names (in case you need some). Perhaps the most impressive part of Screenwriter is its electronic index card system that lets you build your script scene by scene. The program also controls your script length. All production features (revisions, breakdown sheets, tagging for export to Movie Magic Scheduling) are in one menu. Screenwriter also includes templates with preset margins, sets, character lists and script styles for the most television shows on the air. And it by far has the best manual of all scriptwriting programs (good technical support, too). Foreign-language dictionaries are also available for Screenwriter (Danish, Dutch, French, German, Italian, Norwegian, Spanish, Swedish or UK English).

ScriptWare (Cinovation, Inc., 1750 Thirtieth St., Suite 360, Boulder, CO 80301-1005, [800] 788-7090, www.scriptware.com)

ScriptWare stands out because it is the only software program with two-column A/V formatting features. It also has formatting capabilities for screenplays, television shows, sitcoms, and stage plays. ScriptWare created *Scriptype*, the interface now copied by most other programs—it keeps track of and fixes all margin changes, spacing changes, capitalization and punctuation. All you need to do is control the tab and enter keys. ScriptWare takes care of page breaks and scene and page numbering. You can create scene cards that let you rearrange your scenes in index card mode. ScriptWare has a clear and uncluttered menu and a functional navigation bar with speed buttons. You can export and import a range of files, too. The program's thesaurus and spell-checker are excellent. You also get the best available telephone support with ScriptWare.

ADD-ON SCRIPT PROCESSORS

Add-on programs complement your existing word processing software (usually MS Word). Essentially, they are a bundle of macros that help your word processor process scripts. Add-ons are less expensive than the stand-alone programs listed above ($80 to $175). If you regularly use your word processor and don't have much money to spend on formatting programs, an add-on is a good choice. That said, you should know that add-ons become outdated much sooner than stand-alone programs (if you upgrade your word processing software, you'll likely need to upgrade your add-on, too).

ScriptWerx (Parnassus Software, 1923 Lyans Dr., La Canada, CA 91001, [818] 952-2665, www.scriptwerx.com)

You must have Microsoft Word version 97 or above to use ScriptWerx, which has thirteen add-on templates, including feature film, live sitcom, taped sitcom, and corporate video. Each template has its own set of tool bar buttons and commands that appear under a single ScriptWerx tab on Word's menu. Most formatting can be done with the enter, shift, alt, and tab keys. The program can build lists of characters and locations. ScriptWerx will take care of scene numbering and basic revision. The manual is user-friendly. There's no online help for ScriptWerx within Word.

Script Wizard (Stefani Warren & Associates, 1517 Hillside Dr., The Woodlands, Glendale, CA 91208, [818] 414-8690, www.warrenassoc.com)

If you like working in Word 97/2000/XP or later and you have Windows 98 second edition or higher, you will probably appreciate Script Wizard. The program offers twelve formatting templates for screenplays, sitcoms, A/V scripts, radio scripts, soaps, interactive projects, and variety award shows, and it also has most of the features found in a stand-alone program. Most work in Script Wizard can be done using control, shift, and alt key combinations. Script Wizard is one of the few programs to format a series of shots (montages). It has scene numbering and revision features for shooting scripts. You can create script notes and use Word's outline view to move scenes. Phone support is free to all registered users.

ScriptWright (Indelible Ink, 261 Fifth Ave., Mezzanine, New York, NY 10016, [212] 255-1956, www.indelibleink.com)

ScriptWright is compatible with Word and is designed to format only screenplays, but it does an excellent job. Once you install ScriptWright's own menus and help files, Word won't seem the same to you. Most of the formatting can be done with the enter, tab, and alt keys, but the program offers a unique Smart Enter feature that lets you easily create short macros that'll save you keystrokes. ScriptWright comes equipped with a format check and outliner to make sure your script is in order. It will also automatically adjust your margins to keep your script at the right length. ScriptWright creates a scene breakdown and character report. You also can choose menu options to determine if you want to work only in script mode (without Word features) or if you want to work within Word with script features.

SideBySide (Simon Skill Systems, Box 2048, Rancho Santa Fe, CA 92067, [888] 234-6789, www.simon1.com)

SideBySide makes multicolumn scriptwriting in Word easy. It offers ten different multicolumn formats, including audio/visual, documentary, commercials, speech, storyboard, industrial, and multimedia projects. SideBySide numbers pages, provides a word count, and makes on-screen editing easy. You'll also find that SideBySide creates a narration script for you automatically. This is an ideal add-on for writers working with A/V formats.

CHAPTER THIRTEEN

THE SCREENPLAY

Parts of a Script

Although a screenplay can be difficult to sell, formatting one is pretty simple. Most motion picture scripts run from 90 to 120 pages (comedy scripts usually run about 90 to 105 pages, dramatic scripts 105 to 120 pages). Figure on one minute of screen time for each manuscript page, in a Courier 12-point type (hence a 120-page script will run two hours). Scripts should include dialogue and action descriptions but few to no camera directions, no soundtrack suggestions, and no casting suggestions. Do not number your scenes, and always leave 1"-1½" at the top and bottom of each page.

(Note: Screenplay writers today use one of the many software programs available to format their screenplay. For more information about these programs, see pages 191-193).

Your screenplay can be broken down into six basic parts. Here they are in the order they are likely to appear in your script:

- Transitions
- Slug Line (Scene Heading)
- Action
- Character Cue
- Dialogue
- Parenthetical Comment

Now let's take a closer look at each of these.

TRANSITIONS

Transitions simply indicate that a shot or scene is either beginning, ending, or shifting to another shot or scene. These include such directions as FADE IN:, FADE TO:, CUT TO:, and DISSOLVE TO:. Transitions appear in all caps and are flush with the right margin, except FADE IN:, which is flush with the left margin. Every screenplay begins with FADE IN: at the top left margin.

SLUG LINE (SCENE HEADING)

The slug line sets the scene and specifies the shot. It begins on the left margin (17 spaces from the left edge of the page) and is written in all caps, with a double-spaced line before and after it. Most slug lines begin with either EXT. (exterior shot) or INT. (interior shot). After you determine whether the shot is outside or inside, identify the specifics of the shot, such as a particular building or house, and then if necessary, precisely where the shot takes place. With the slug line, organize the details by going from the more general to the more specific. End each slug line by indicating whether it's day or night. For example:

```
INT. WOODROW WILSON ELEMENTARY SCHOOL—PRINCIPAL'S
OFFICE—DAY.
```

ACTION

The action descriptions are sentences or very short paragraphs that describe what happens during the scene. They should always be written in present tense. The text within the action descriptions begins on the left margin (17 spaces from the left edge of the page) and is single-spaced, with regular capitalization. Do not justify the right margin. There should be one double-spaced line before and after the action text. If you have lots of description, break up the text to leave some white space—try not to allow a block of text to run more than five or six lines without a double-spaced break for the eyes (the more white space in a script, the better).

CHARACTER CUE

The speaking character's name should be typed in all caps, and should appear 43 spaces from the left edge of the page. A double-spaced line should appear before the character's name, but there should be no double-space between the name and the dialogue, or between the name and the parenthetical comment (see below).

DIALOGUE

Dialogue should be in regular text (not all caps) and begin on the line below the speaking character's name. The left margin for dialogue is at space 28, and the right margin is at space 60 (do not justify the right margin). Try to avoid large blocks of dialogue that run seven or more lines. If your character needs to say more than can be fit in seven lines, add a blank line space between the text so it's more visually pleasing (e.g., a fourteen-line section of dialogue should be broken into two blocks of seven lines each).

PARENTHETICAL COMMENT

Parenthetical comments, also known as parentheticals, help the speaker of the dialogue know what emotion you intend for the delivery. Parenthetical comments are typically short (often a word or two), typed in regular text (not all caps), appear one line below the character's name (and thus one line above dialogue) and are set in parentheses. A parenthetical should look like this:

```
          ANN
     (panicking)
What's wrong with Mrs. Browning?
```

Some screenwriters prefer not to use parentheticals and instead detail the emotion in a descriptive action line instead. So the previous parenthetical would look like this:

```
ANN paces back and forth in a panic.


          ANN
What's wrong with Mrs. Browning?
```

Parentheticals are becoming less common so it may be best to use the descriptive line. It's up to you which format to use—just make sure you're consistent throughout the script.

In addition to the aforementioned regular elements of your screenplay, you will probably find yourself in situations where you need some special formatting and cues. Here are some of the more common script tricks you can inject in your screenplay.

NARRATIVE VOICE-OVER

Many films have a first-person narrator who relates parts of the story to the viewer. If your script calls for voice narration, indicate it as such by typing "(V.O.)" next to the name of the character who's narrating. A scene with a voice narration should look like this:

```
INT. ROGER'S CHILDHOOD HOME—LIVING ROOM—DAY


Many young kids are running around the room yelling and
screaming at each other. The mother has no control over the
situation.


          ROGER (V.O.)
Mine wasn't what you'd call a typical childhood. With
ten brothers and sisters running around, I never got
the sense that I was unique. I was always just one of
the boys. My poor mom spent all her time trying to keep
us from killing each other, so making each of us feel
loved and special just wasn't possible. But she did
the best she could.
```

CARRYING DIALOGUE FROM ONE PAGE TO THE NEXT

Do your best not to make a character (actor) flip a page in the middle of dialogue. If, however, you can't avoid carrying a character's dialogue on to the next page, use the indicator "(MORE)" on the bottom of the first page and "(cont'd)" next to the speaker's name at the top of the next page:

```
          ROGER
I'm sorry, Marcia. I've tried and tried to please you
but you never appreciate a damn thing I do.
               (MORE)
```

_____NEW PAGE_____

```
        ROGER (cont'd)
I just can't go on being your slave. You never clean
up after yourself. You never do the laundry. Hell,
you've never given me even a penny for the rent.
```

HAVING A CHARACTER SPEAK OFF-CAMERA

In movies, characters often speak off-camera, and you'll probably write at least one scene in which this happens. When you have a character speaking off-camera, use "(O.C.)" next to the character's name. Let's say Roger is on camera in the bedroom while talking to Marcia, who's off-camera in the bathroom.

```
        ROGER
Marcia, did you just say something? I thought I heard
you say something.
```

```
        MARCIA (O.C.)
I asked if you would bring me a towel. I'm soaking wet
for God's sake. Are you deaf?
```

```
        ROGER
What did you say?
```

EMPLOYING CONTINUING SHOTS

Although as a screenwriter you should refrain from giving camera directions (that's the director's job), you might want to tell part of your story with a series of camera shots without dialogue or narration. These kinds of "moving pictures" usually tell their own little story. They are often accompanied by a musical score and are used to quickly advance the plot. Try doing it like this:

```
SERIES OF SHOTS: ROGER AND MARCIA EXPLORE NEW YORK


(A) On a ferry to the Statue of Liberty.
(B) Eating hot dogs from a vendor on Times Square.
(C) Walking arm in arm through Central Park.
(D) Kissing outside the Guggenheim.
(E) Driving across the George Washington Bridge.


BACK TO SCENE
```

Another way to use continuing shots is with a montage. A montage is pretty much the same as a series of shots except it's used for a briefer sequence of shots and doesn't really have to tell its own story. A montage is formatted a little differently, with a double hyphen instead of letters in parentheses:

```
MONTAGE--ROGER AND MARCIA AT DISNEY WORLD


--They get their pictures taken with Mickey and Minnie.


--They ride Magic Mountain.


--Roger offers Marcia some cotton candy. She makes a mus-
tache out of it and Roger eats it. They laugh.


END MONTAGE
```

With both a series of shots and montages, be sure to end with either "BACK TO SCENE" or "END MONTAGE."

OTHER DOS AND DON'TS

- Do spell out numbers (one through ninety-nine), but use numbers for 100 and over.
- Do spell out personal titles (Father Niehaus, Pastor Karl) except for Mr., Mrs., and Ms.
- Do spell out time indicators: eleven-thirty, not 11:30.
- Do spell out "okay," not OK or o.k.
- Do number your pages and put a period after the number (the page number goes at the top of the page, flush right, about four lines down).
- Do keep dialogue short.
- Don't use special effects directions, such as FX (visual).
- Don't use sound effects directions, such as SFX (sound).
- Don't use camera directions and camera angles.
- Don't number the first page.
- Don't number your scenes.
- Do leave 1"-1½" at the top and bottom of each page.

What follows are formatting specifications for your screenplay as well as a sample screenplay title page and a sample first page of a screenplay.

TAB AND MARGIN SETTINGS

- Left margin: 17 spaces
- Dialogue left margin: 28 spaces
- Parenthetical comments: 35 spaces
- Character cue: 43 spaces
- Dialogue right margin: 60 spaces
- Transitions: 66 spaces
- Page number followed by a period (in top right-hand corner, four lines from top of page): 72 spaces
- Right margin: 75 spaces

ALL CAPS
- Type of shot (INT. and EXT.)
- Setting or scene location (ITALIAN RIVIERA)
- Time of day (DAY or NIGHT)
- The first time you introduce a character (JOHN walks in)
- The speaking character's name (PHIL), followed by dialogue
- Camera directions (PAN, CLOSE-UP, etc.)
- Important sound cues (Ted hears a GUNSHOT in the hallway.)
- Scene transitions (CUT TO:, DISSOLVE TO:, etc.)
- (MORE)

SINGLE SPACE
- within dialogue
- within action/scene descriptions (also called narrative)
- within camera directions, sound cues
- within stage directions
- between the character's name and dialogue

DOUBLE SPACE
- between the scene location and action/scene descriptions
- between the action/scene descriptions and the speaking character's name
- between the speeches of the different characters
- between the paragraphs of lengthy dialogue or action descriptions
- between dialogue and a new speaking character's name
- between dialogue and stage or camera directions

TRIPLE SPACE
- before each new scene

Title Page

SUBMITTING TIPS
Your title page will include the script's title, the author(s), whether or not the script is based on a novel, and your contact information (if you have representation, it will include your agent's contact information instead).

FORMATTING TIPS
- The screenplay title should be in all caps, centered, about one-third of the way down the page.
- Double-space twice, and type either "Written by," "Screenplay by," or just "by" (do not type the quotation marks).
- Double-space again and type your name (if your script is written with another person, use an ampersand between your names).
- If your script is based on a novel, drop six lines and type "Based on *Novel's Title*," drop two more lines and type "by" and "Author's Name" (see the following sample).

- In the lower right-hand corner, put your name, address, phone number, and e-mail, single-spaced, in regular text (not all caps).
- If you have an agent, put "Representation:," skip a line and put the agent's name, address, phone number, and e-mail instead of yours.
- In front of the title page, make sure you include a cover page that includes only the title and author's name.
- Preferred cover page paper is a white, cream, rust or pale blue cover of card stock, 40 to 60 lb.
- The pages should be bound in brass brads, short enough so they don't cut through an envelope when mailed.
- Use a backing page with the same stock as the cover page.

OTHER DOS AND DON'TS

- Don't type the draft number and the date in the bottom left corner for a spec script. Including the draft number is irrelevant and including the date of a script can show that it has been circulating for a long time.
- Don't put any pictures or artwork on you cover page.
- Don't use spiral or other machine-type bindings.
- Do register your script with the Writer's Guild of America (WGA), but you don't need to put the WGA registration number on the cover page.

Research the companies to which you want to submit. Don't submit a romantic comedy to Michael Bay. Don't submit a suspense thriller to Jay Roach. Tailor your submissions to your script. Also, find a personal connection. In a world where everyone is six derees from everyone else, find out whom you know that knows someone that knows someone who's related to someone at the company.

    —**Chad Gervich, manager, talent and development, The Littlefield Company/Paramount Television**

TITLE PAGE: MOTION PICTURE

Script's title is in all caps, one-third of the way down the page.

100K

All this text is centered.

3 lines

Written by

Bill Ward & Jim Precinct

1 line

6 lines

Tells us the script is based on a novel, and credits the author.

Based on the novel *Outrageous Days*

by R.M. Lightfoot

Representation:

Angela Ash
Big Time Agency
111 West Sun St.
Hunter, CA 90001
(323) 555-2222

Shows the writer has representation (includes agent's name, address, and phone number). This always goes in the bottom-right corner.

SCREENPLAY SCRIPT

1" margin on top and bottom.

Transition is in all caps.

FADE IN: 1.

Page number followed by a period (space 72 or flush with right margin—space 75).

INT. CAR—NIGHT

First time a character is introduced, the name is in all caps.

JOHN is drinking a cup of coffee.

                    JOHN
          Looks like it's going to be a long night.

                    CATHY
          How long do you think it'll take us to get there?

                    JOHN
Dialogue left margin is at space 28 (right margin is 60).
          We're looking at maybe three or four hours, consid-
          ering the weather. But that's a blizzard out there.
          We'll be lucky to make it through Lawson Pass.

Dialogue is single-spaced (do keep blocks of dialogue short).

A deer crosses the road right in front of them.

                    CATHY
          Watch out!

                    JOHN
          Oh my God!

Left margin is at space 17.

John slams the brakes and misses the deer, but the car does a
180-degree turn, causing John to spill coffee on his lap.

Picks up with the same character who was speaking before the action break.

                    JOHN (Cont'd)
          Damn that's hot!

                    CATHY
          Are you okay?

Character cue is in all caps (space 43).

                    JOHN
          Yes, I'm fine. Jesus, that was a close call.
          Are you all right?

                    CATHY
            (crying)
          Just a little scared, that's all. Maybe we ought
          to stop at the next motel and stay the night.
          This is just looking too dangerous. Your mom
          will understand.

Parenthetical comments are lowercase (space 35).

                    JOHN
          Yeah, that's a good idea.

Slug line is in all caps.

EXT. MOTEL PARKING LOT—NIGHT   2.

Snow is falling heavily and we see the car pull into a very crowded lot. John gets out, goes inside, and immediately returns to
the car.

Action description is single-spaced and flush with left margin.

                    CATHY
          Boy that was fast. Are they booked?

                    JOHN
          Of course they're booked.

                    CATHY
          I wonder if we should go back home?

                    JOHN
          We're not going back home now. I'll just keep driv-
          ing until we get there. I'll drive all night if I
          have to.

Car speeds out of parking lot.

                                              FADE OUT

Transition is at space 66 (or flush with right margin).

Submitting Your Screenplay to an Agent or Production Company

After you finish your screenplay, you'll want to submit it to an agent or a production company. Ideally, you'll find an agent to represent you, someone who knows the ins and outs of Hollywood. Having a good agent who believes in your work and is willing to go to great lengths to get it sold is invaluable. Almost every screenwriter in Hollywood has an agent, and so should you.

THE VALUE OF AN AGENT

So, what is a good agent? Aside from being someone who believes in your work, a good agent knows who is working where, who has deals with whom and who wants what. A good agent will direct your script to the most suitable producer and will negotiate payments on your behalf. Many beginning writers try to become a client at a major agency, but that's not always such a good idea. Newcomers often don't get much attention at major agencies. Your best bet is to find an agent who will appreciate your writing and do his or her best to champion it—no matter how large or small the agency. Just be sure the agent is a signatory of the WGA—signatory agents have signed and agreed to abide by industry rules and standards. All reputable agencies belong to the WGA; those who do not should be avoided.

FINDING THE RIGHT AGENT FOR YOU

A good way to acquire an agent who will appreciate your writing is to find one who already represents material similar to yours. Seek out movies already made that are similar to yours. See or rent them, and pay close attention to the credits. Write down the names of the writers or the story editors.

Once you get these names, call the Writer's Guild, West (800) 548-4532, request to speak to the agency department, then ask which agency represents those writers or story editors. The agency department will grant your request if you have three names or less (no more). After you get the agency's name, consult the WGA's list of signatory agents to make sure that agent is a signatory. The WGA offers the list free on its Web site (www.wga.org), or you can write or call: 7000 W. Third St., Los Angeles, CA 90048-4329, (800) 548-4532.

Also check the following directories if you wish to do research on agents:

Annual Agency Guide, published by Fade In Books, lists over 1,500 literary agents, managers and entertainment lawyers. The directory indicates if the agency represents motion picture and/or television writers, and if there is a fee involved.

Guide to Literary Agents, published by Writer's Digest Books, contains the most detailed listings of six hundred literary and script agents. The guide divides its listings according to nonfee-charging and fee-charging agents. It also includes a variety of insider information (profiles, interviews, articles) on marketing your work and getting your script in the right agent's hands (4700 East Galbraith Road, Cincinnati, OH 45236, [800] 289-0963).

Hollywood Representation Directory, published by the Hollywood Creative Directory, offers probably the most complete list of agents and managers. It boasts 7,000 names and can be purchased as a book or an online directory. (℅ IFILM Publishing, 1024 N. Orange Dr., Hollywood, CA 90038, [800] 815-0503, www.hcdonline.com).

SELLING THE SCRIPT YOURSELF

You may wish to shop your script to a studio or production company without first finding an agent. This will likely be difficult but it is still an option, and many first-time writers go this route. Fortunately, a few resources do exist for finding information about producers, studio executives, and other industry insiders. In fact, some of the following publications provide extensive lists of studios and production companies that might take an interest in your script:

Hollywood Creative Directory (IFILM Publishing, 1024 N. Orange Dr., Hollywood, CA 90038, [800] 815-0503, www.hcdonline.com) is a great place to locate the person you're looking for. This is the film and television industry bible, with the most complete, up-to-date information about who's who in film and TV development and production. It lists production companies, studios, and networks; their addresses, phone, and fax numbers and e-mail addresses; and provides cross-referencing.

Hollywood Reporter Blu-Book (5055 Wilshire Blvd., Los Angeles, CA 90036, www.hollywoodreporter.com) also provides information about numerous production companies and their needs.

Spec Screenplay Sales Directory, Deluxe Edition (edited by Howard Meibach, available through www.writersstore.com and www.amazon.com) lets you in on what screenplays have been selling, who's buying them, and how much your potential script could be worth. It lists more than six years of sold screenplays, including log line, genre, writer, producer, agent, buyer, attorney, and sales. This is also cross-referenced.

Writer's Market published annually by Writer's Digest books, contains the most detailed listings of over 200 script agents. It also includes a variety of insider information (profiles, interviews, articles, query samples) on marketing your work and getting your script in the right agent's hands (4700 E. Galbraith Rd., Cincinnati, OH 45236, [800] 289-0963, www.writersmarket.com).

If you want to stay tuned to the day-to-day operations in Hollywood, check out *Daily Variety* (www.variety.com) and *The Hollywood Reporter* (www.hollywoodreporter.com), both of which will keep you up on industry news. *Boxoffice* (www.boxoff.com) is a monthly trade magazine geared more toward movie distributors than scriptwriters, but it still offers a lot of information about what kinds of films studios are producing.

After you figure out which studio or production company you're interested in, call and ask for the story department then ask for the name of the story editor. That's it. Don't ask to speak with the story editor—just get his or her name, then get ready to write your letter of inquiry.

> Always do the homework required to first detail what the person you're submitting to requires. Most agents and managers, in fact, don't take new or cold submissions so before you send anything, check. Sometimes the reasons are bound in legal requirements.
>
> —Mark Sevi, screenwriter

The Query Letter

Once you know who to contact (agent, producer, or story editor), send that person a query letter. *Do not submit an outline, a treatment, or a script to anyone in the industry unless you've been asked to do so*—they'll return it because they can't look at anything without a signed release form. In your query letter, say that you've written a script and would like the person you're soliciting to consider it. Don't send a query letter unless you have the script written. If they like your idea, they may want to see the script in as soon as two weeks. Keep your query letter to a few short paragraphs (less than a page). J. Michael Straczynski, in *The Complete Book of Scriptwriting*, suggests mentioning the following:

- That you know the films they produce (or the agency represents, if you're soliciting an agent).
- That you've written an original screenplay that fits in quite well with what they've been producing (or with an agency, representing) over the past few years.
- That you own the rights to the story.
- That you would like to submit your screenplay on a spec basis. (Do not go into detail about the contents of your spec script—you'll ruin your chances of selling it.)
- That when you send your script you will enclose a standard release form or use the production company's or agency's preferred release form.
- That you have writing credits or a professional background that qualifies you to write this screenplay. (If you've spent ten years as an attorney and your screenplay is a legal thriller, mention your background.)

Basically, that's all you need to include in your query. Again, never send an unsolicited script, treatment or synopsis to an agent, producer or story editor—it will be returned, the package unopened. Producers and agents will not look at unsolicited scripts because they are afraid of getting sued for plagiarism. That's why you need to send the release form. Of course, mention your script idea in your query letter, but do so only in general terms.

Follow these formatting specifications when composing your query letter:

FORMATTING SPECS

- Use a standard font or typeface (no bold, script or italic).
- Place your name, address, phone number, e-mail, and fax in the top right corner.
- Use a 1″ margin on all sides.
- Address it to a specific agent, producer, or story editor.
- Keep it to one page.
- Use block or semiblock letter format.
- Single-space the body of the letter; double-space between paragraphs.
- Catalog every item you're sending in your enclosures.

OTHER DOS AND DON'TS

- Do make the letter pointed and persuasive.
- Do include an SASE or postcard for reply, and state in the letter that you have done so.
- Do offer to sign a release form.

- Do offer to send the script.
- Don't use "Dear Sir," "Dear Madame," etc. in your salutation.
- Don't use Mr., Ms., Mrs., or Miss unless you're certain of the person's gender and marital status.
- Don't mention that you're a first-time writer or that you've never sold any piece of writing.
- Don't spend much time trying to sell yourself.
- Don't tell how much time you've spent on the script.
- Don't ask for advice or criticism.
- Don't mention anything about yourself not pertinent to the script.
- Don't bring up payment.
- Don't include your social security number.

Electronic Query Letter

SUBMISSION TIPS

Many agents, producers, and story editors now accept queries via e-mail. Before you send a query via e-mail, however, you must have permission to send it. The basic tone and format of the electronic query shouldn't be much different from a query sent on paper.

FORMATTING SPECS

- Include the same information you would in a paper query, including your name, address, phone, and fax, etc. The top right-hand corner or top center position is fine for this, though you can also include this information in a signature line at the end. It isn't necessary to include your e-mail address in the body of the e-mail, however, since the editor can reply easily with the click of a button.
- Put a description of your screenplay or its title in the subject line.
- Follow the same format you would with a paper query, including the date, salutation to a specific editor and block paragraph format. See the above tips for submitting a paper query; the same rules apply.

OTHER DOS AND DON'TS

- Don't use all caps or exclamation points in the subject line.
- Don't submit an e-mail query unless specifically requested by an agent, producer, or story editor.
- Don't insert clip art graphics or other images into your query letter.
- Do read the Dos and Don'ts above for a paper query—the same rules apply!

If you're going to submit to a company that welcomes submissions, I suggest finding a personal angle. Do some research. Do you have a friend who knows someone at the company? Are you from the hometown (or state) of one of the executives? Did the company produce one of your favorite movies or TV shows? Anything you can do to establish a relationship works to your benefit. Find a personal connection, even a small one, and you increase your script's odds of staying alive.

—**Chad Gervich, manager, talent and development,** *The Littlefield Company/Paramount Television*

QUERY TO PRODUCTION COMPANY: FEATURE FILM

Bill Ward
100 Fourth St.
Newport, KY 41000
Phone (606) 555-4447
Fax (606) 333-6556
ward@email.com

> Nice, simple letter-head with address, phone, fax, and e-mail. You don't need to include your e-mail address if you're sending your query electronically.

April 1, 2004

> 1 line

Cynthia Picture
Story Editor
S&T Productions

> 1" margin

1111 Movie Rd.
Hollywood, CA 90120

> 1 line

Dear Cynthia Picture,

> Addresses letter to a specific story editor.

> 1 line

I've written a screenplay, ''100K,'' that I think fits in quite well with pictures recently produced by S&T Productions (namely, *An Uncivil Action*, which shows the popularity of legal thrillers is growing). The script is 118 pages, and I do own the rights to the story.

> Single-spaced text

> Shows he's familiar with other scripts the production company represents, and he mentions the audience, the script's length and that he owns the rights to the story all in a short space.

In ''100K,'' Cathy McTierney dies after the car she and her husband, John, are traveling in wrecks during a blizzard. The catch is that Cathy's mother and father are claiming vehicular homicide. They think John killed Cathy for the $100,000 dollars she recently inherited from her dying grandfather. A ferocious courtroom battle ensues.

> Briefly tells the gist of his script's story, but only in general terms.

> 1 line between paragraphs

I am a published writer whose articles have appeared in *Legal Times* and other trade journals. I am also a prosecuting attorney. I have brought my writing and professional interests together in ''100K.''

> Mentions writing credits and pertinent professional background.

I would like to submit my spec script for ''100K'' to S&T Productions. I will, of course, send a standard release form with my script submission. If S&T Productions has its own release form, please send it in the enclosed SASE.

> Offers to send the script and sign a release form, and states he's included an SASE.

I look forward to hearing from you soon.

> Politely closes the letter.

Sincerely,

> Signature

Bill Ward

Encl.: SASE

> Notes enclosures (you can skip the SASE if you're sending your query via e-mail).

OUTLINE, PAGE 1: FEATURE FILM

298 Stark Road
Bomb, AR 52423

Dear Story Editor,

After working on it for nearly ten years, I've just completed my very first screenplay. It's a story of my father's life growing up in the Great Depression on a farm in Iowa. I don't have a name for it yet.

The screenplay follows my father's life from his birth in a barn to raising eleven children on the same farm in Iowa. It is a story of epic proportions with lots of drama.

This is my first attempt at any kind of writing, but my father's life was so interesting that everyone in my family has always said it would make a great movie. Can I send you the script and you can tell me what you think about it?

I can see Haley Joel Osment playing my father as a boy and Russell Crowe playing my father as a man. Jessica Lange would be perfect as my long-suffering mother.

Thank you very much for your time and I look forward to hearing from you soon.

Sincerely,

Dan Dismal

This looks like a form letter, as it's not addressed to any particular production company or to a specific person.

Tells very little about the screenplay. What is the title of your screenplay? What makes this story compelling?

Never mention casting suggestions in your query.

Don't forget to include an SASE (unless you're sending the query via e-mail).

Complete contact information should be included here—name, address, phone, fax, and e-mail.

Never mention how much time it's taken you to write your screenplay, and don't mention that you're a first-time writer.

Don't ask for criticism or advice—the purpose of this query is to gauge interest in your screenplay.

Submitting Your Script

If your query letter does what you want it to, you'll receive a request for your script. Before you do anything else, register your script with the WGA (you don't need to be a WGA member to do so). To register, contact the WGA and ask them to send you an application (7000 W. Third St., Los Angeles, CA 90048-4329, [800] 548-4532).

Then you need to get your script ready for submission. Print your script on standard three-hole, 20-lb. paper. Use heavy (40- to 60-lb. bond), colored stock paper (use either cream, gray, rust, or pale blue paper) for your cover/title page and your back cover. Bind your script with two brass paper fasteners (sometimes called brads), one in the top hole and one in the bottom. Enclose a simple letter that says the requested script and release form are enclosed. Also include an SASE. Do not forget to sign and include the release form, and on the outside of the package's envelope be sure to write "REQUESTED RELEASE FORM ENCLOSED." Then send your script and wait four to six weeks for a reply.

Outlines and Treatments

Outlines and treatments are stepping stones on the way to selling your full-length script. Both are summaries of your script, and both share the same format. The outline is a short precursor followed by a longer, more detailed (and more important) treatment. Although your script is composed almost entirely of dialogue, your outline or treatment covers the overarching story behind (and without) the dialogue and scene descriptions.

OUTLINES

An outline briefly synopsizes your script. You likely will not have to show anyone your outline, but you could be asked for one—if so, focus only on the major points of your story, keep the outline informal and write it in paragraph form. With an outline, less is more, especially when you use it as a pitch to sell your idea. You don't want to bore anyone, and the rule of thumb in Hollywood is that "high-concept" story ideas can be described quickly (ideally, one sentence!) and are the most saleable. The outline is an informal but crucial starting point from which you can successfully pitch your story idea, which leads to writing a compelling treatment, which ultimately leads to selling a script.

Most outlines run anywhere from a few pages for a half-hour sitcom to as many as seven or more pages for a feature film. Rarely should your outline go over 5,000 words.

TREATMENTS

Unlike outlines, which tend to be a bit informal and more skeletal, treatments are carefully constructed, extremely well-written summaries of your script (in fact, treatments are similar to a novel synopsis). You get to expand on the outline and go into more detail about your characters, settings, and plot twists. You can even weave some samples of dialogue into the narrative. Try to keep the number of dialogue lines minimal, however, and be sure to inject them only at points where they can tell something significant about the character uttering them.

Treatments can run anywhere from four to twenty or more pages, depending on the type of script at hand. If you're writing a treatment for a half-hour sitcom, it will probably run from four to six pages, whereas a treatment for an hour episodic drama might run six to nine pages, and one for a motion picture feature or television movie might be ten to fifteen pages. No specific stipulations apply to the length of your treatment, but remember that shorter is usually better (especially with spec treatments—try to keep them under ten pages). The two imperatives are that you double-space the text and write in present tense.

Ideally, your treatment should clearly delineate the major scenes in your script, with a new paragraph devoted to each scene or plot shift. Writers typically break up their treatments according to the conventions of the type of script they're writing. You can break up your treatment by using subheads to denote when a new act begins. Doing so shows you've thought out the structure and timing of the script.

- Most sitcoms are divided into two acts; a few are broken down into three acts. Some series use a teaser at the show's beginning and/or a tag at the show's conclusion.
- One-hour dramas typically have four acts; some shows also use a teaser at the show's beginning and/or a tag at the ending.
- Television movies contain seven acts. The act breaks coincide with the seven commercial breaks that typically occur during a two-hour time slot for movies on television.
- Motion picture feature films consist of three acts.

WHY YOU'LL NEED AN OUTLINE AND TREATMENT

Whether you're writing for television or the silver screen, to get your foot in the door you will need a sample spec script that showcases your talent as a writer. (That's why you must send a complete script after you've queried—a mere outline or treatment won't do at this stage in the game because you still need to prove yourself as a writer.) If that spec script impresses the right person (hopefully, the producer), you might be invited to pitch ideas for other scripts. This, by the way, is where knowing how to write an outline comes in handy—you use an outline to ensure you cover all the major points in your pitch. If your pitch is successful, you might get an assignment to write a treatment, and if that goes well, you will be asked to write the script.

To make sure you understand the process, let's walk through a dream-come-true hypothetical scenario. You've written a spec motion picture script called "The Summer of Love," and you've been fortunate enough to get a producer at (since we're dreaming) DreamWorks to read your script. He loves it but he refuses to buy it. Why? Because DreamWorks just bought a similar script called "1967." However, he was so impressed with your writing that he wants you to come up with a few other movie ideas that he might consider optioning. You agree, come up with three ideas, write pitch outlines for each and make an appointment to pitch your story ideas to him. Your first two ideas don't go over so well, but your third one does. He tells you he'll talk to other producers and get back to you. A few weeks go by, and lo and behold, you get a call from the producer telling you that everybody at DreamWorks loves your idea, and DreamWorks would like to offer you a development deal, or a step deal. Are you interested? Of course.

You then sign a contract for the development or step deal, which means that you get a step-by-step commitment—and payment—from the producer as the deal goes through development. It works like this: The producer can stop the development of your script at any step in the process, but he must pay you for what you've already written. And because he's paid you for what you've done, he owns and can do what he wants with it.

So what are the steps in a development deal? The first step is a treatment, next comes the first draft of a script, then a second draft, and finally the perfected script. Once the producer asks you to write the initial treatment for your story idea, he must pay you the negotiated fee for that step (step one) of the process. If, unfortunately, you turn in your treatment and DreamWorks doesn't like it, they have the option to drop you from the project and pass it on to other writers (you still, of course, get paid for the treatment). If they do like it, however, you're asked to write (and get paid for) a complete draft of the script. Even if your final draft goes over well and you get paid lots of money for it, keep in mind that DreamWorks has the right to pass your script on to other writers to make improvements to it—sorry, that's just the way the business works. You'll still get the credit for the screenplay, of course, but your story could get changed quite a bit. Just be prepared.

FORMATTING SPECS

- Use a 1″ margin on all sides.
- Justify the left margin only.
- Type your name, address, phone number, and e-mail on the top left margin of the first page, single-spaced.
- Put the script's title, centered and in all caps, about one-fourth of the way down the page (from the top margin).
- Drop one line below the title and type "A Treatment by" or "An Outline by" (centered).
- Drop one line and type your name (centered).
- Drop four lines and begin the text of the treatment.
- Do not number the first page (but it is considered page one).
- After the first page, use a slug line (also called a header) at the top left of every page. The slug line should contain your last name, a backslash, your script's title in all capital letters, another backslash and either the word "Treatment" or "Outline."
- After the first page, put the page number in the top right corner of every consecutive page, on the same line as the slug line.
- The text throughout the treatment should be double-spaced.
- Use all caps the first time you introduce a character.
- The first line of text on each page after the first page should begin three lines (about ¾″) below the slug line and page number.

OTHER DOS AND DON'TS

- Do use present tense.
- Do write in first person.
- Do keep in mind that you're writing a sales pitch (make it a short, fast, exciting read).
- Do establish a hook at the beginning of the treatment (introduce your lead character and set up a key conflict).
- Do try to introduce your most important character first.

- Do provide details about your central character (age, gender, marital status, profession, etc.), but don't do this for every character—only the primary ones.
- Do try to include characters' motivations and emotions.
- Do highlight pivotal plot points.
- Do reveal the story's ending.
- Don't go into too much detail about what happens; just tell what happens (plot twists, etc.).
- Don't insert long sections of dialogue into your treatment.

Electronic Script Submissions

It is rare for an agent, producer or story editor to request your script via e-mail, but it might happen. If it does, make sure you get detailed guidelines as to how the script should be submitted and follow them meticulously.

Less is more. Although many people like to submit scripts with articles, long bios, letters of recommendation, or reviews of previous work and performances, these materials do more harm than good to your script's presentation. No producer or executive has time to wade through piles of supplementary material. Sure, they want to find the next hot script, but if your script can't stand on its own merits, it has no business being submitted.

—Chad Gervich, manager, talent and development, The Littlefield Company/Paramount Television

OUTLINE, PAGE 1: FEATURE FILM

Simple contact information.

> James Jones
> 111 Treatment Lane
> Sunnyside, CA 90124
> Phone (213) 555-4874
> Fax (213) 555-5985
> jones@email.com

Does not number the first page (but it is considered page one).

Script's title is in all caps and centered, one-fourth of the way down the page.

SUMMER OF LOVE

1 line

An Outline by

1 line

James Jones

4 lines

Uses all caps the first time a character is introduced, and introduces the most important characters first.

STEVE JENKEE, UCLA's leading student activist on race relations, finds his mother, DR. JENKEE (UCLA's Director for Programs in Peace & Justice and avid ally of blacks), has been murdered by an African American, and then in a rage Steve kills the

1" margin   murderer.

There are two major ironies to this script's central story:

1. That Dr. Jenkee, UCLA's Director for Programs in Peace & Justice who's been a champion of blacks and fighting against

Justifies left margin only.

racism since the early 1950s, would be killed by a black student. Moreover, she must withstand violence (not peace) and injustice (not justice).

Double-spaced text

2. That Steve Jenkee, who's been a leading activist against racism, would actually commit the most atrocious act: murdering a person of the race he has been trying to advance and protect.

Notice how an outline is more informal than a treatment (shown on page 215).

TREATMENT, PAGE 1: FEATURE FILM

Simple contact information.

James Jones
111 Treatment Lane
Sunnyside, CA 90124
Phone (213) 555-4874
Fax (213) 555-5985
jones@email.com

Does not number the first page (but it is considered page one).

Script's title is in all caps, centered, one-fourth of the way down the page.

SUMMER OF LOVE

1 line

A Treatment by

1 line

James Jones

4 lines

Uses all caps the first time a character is introduced, and introduces the most important characters first.

It's 1967 and STEVE JENKEE, UCLA's leading student activist on race relations, doesn't know what to do when a crazed African-American student breaks into his mother's (DR. JENKEE) office and slits her throat, eventually killing her.

This first paragraph establishes a hook by setting up a mystery and a conflict.

Steve can't figure it out and he's angry. Not only was his mother loving and caring toward him, she was also UCLA's Director for Programs in Peace & Justice. She's been fighting for desegregation and against racism since the early 1950s. The murder just doesn't make sense. A white student murdering her would make sense (she was deemed the white man's enemy and the black man's Aunt Tom, even though she was white herself), but why would an African-American student kill her? After all, thinks Steve, ''every African-American student and faculty member on campus loves mom.'' All, that is, but one. And now Steve is out to kill him.

1" margin

Double-spaced text

Justifies the left margin only.

Uses present tense.

Incorporates a quote from the script.

Notice how a treatments tells the story instead of just telling what the story is about, which is what an outline does.

CHAPTER FOURTEEN

TV SCRIPTS

Submitting Television Scripts

To get your television script (sitcom, episodic drama, soap opera, television movie) through the Hollywood maze, you need to put your script in the right hands. There are a few ways to go about this. The ideal way is to acquire an agent to represent you, but a few writers sneak through the cracks by contacting the production company first.

Before soliciting anyone, however, you should know a couple peculiarities about submitting scripts for television.

First, you might want to have more than one spec script ready to showcase. Some writers actually have a portfolio of scripts for each *type* of show they want to work on (if they want to write sitcoms, for instance, they'll have one script each for shows like *Everybody Loves Raymond, That '70s Show,* and *Will and Grace*).

Second, in choosing the shows you write spec scripts for, know that you probably will not be able to submit a script for the exact show you want to work on. It sounds crazy, but that's the way television works. So if you want to write for *The Practice*, for example, you'll need to send a *Law & Order* script and vice versa. You must do this because it reduces the chances of plagiarism lawsuits (plus the show's writers and producers might not be objective enough to fairly evaluate your writing). By submitting a similar type of script, you avert these problems while still demonstrating your writing skills in that medium.

Whether you plan to solicit a production company or an agent, you must first target the show you plan to write for, watch it, and pay close attention to the opening and closing credits.

CONTACTING THE PRODUCTION COMPANY

To contact the production company directly, look at the show's credits for the name of the production company and the producer or story editor. (Tape the show if you have to, so you get the correct names and spellings.) Then find the phone number and address of the production company and send the producer or story editor a query letter (see the following sources for information on contacting production companies).

The best way to find the production company's address is to call directory assistance or consult one of the following publications:

Hollywood Creative Directory (℅ IFILM Publishing, 1024 N. Orange Dr., Hollywood, CA 90038, www.hcdonline.com, [800] 815-0503) is great place to locate the person you're looking for. This is the film and television industry bible, with the most complete, up-to-date information about who's who in film and TV development and production. It lists production companies, studios, and networks; addresses, phone and fax numbers, e-mail addresses, and provides cross-referencing.

Spec Screenplay Sales Directory, edited by Howard Meibach (available through writersstore.com and amazon.com), catalogs sales and deals of spec screenplays. This can be quite helpful because it tells what material production companies and studios are buying. The sales information is divided into three sections: screenplay sales, book sales, and pitch/treatment sales. The directory is cross-referenced.

Hollywood Reporter Blu-Book (5055 Wilshire Blvd., Los Angeles, CA 90036, www.hollywoodreporter.com) also provides information about numerous production companies and their needs.

CONTACTING AGENTS

If you don't want to go directly to the production company, contact an agent who represents the show's writers. To do this, pay close attention to the show's credits to find the names of the writers or story editors. Once you get these names, call the Writer's Guild, West (800) 548-4532, request to speak to the agency department, then ask which agency represents those writers or story editors. The agency department will grant your request if you have three names or less, so don't call with a long list of names.

After you get the agency's name, consult the WGA's list of signatory agents to make sure that agent is a signatory (the WGA offers the list free on its Web site: http://www.wga.org), or write or call for the list: 7000 W. Third St., Los Angeles, CA 90048-4329, (800) 548-4532. Signatory agents have signed a membership contract agreeing to abide by industry rules and standards. All reputable agents belong to the WGA; those who do not should be avoided.

Also check the following directories if you wish to find out more about agents:

Annual Agency Guide, published by Fade In Books, lists over 1,500 literary agents, managers, and entertainment lawyers. The directory indicates if the agency represents motion picture and/or television writers, and if there is a fee involved.

Guide to Literary Agents, published annually by Writer's Digest Books (4700 E. Galbraith Rd., Cincinnati, OH 45236, [800] 289-0963, www.writersmarket.com), contains detailed listings of over six hundred literary and script agents. It also includes a variety of insider information (profiles, interviews, articles) on marketing your work and getting your script in the right agent's hands.

Hollywood Representation Directory, published by the Hollywood Creative Directory (% IFILM Publishing, 1024 N. Orange Dr., Hollywood, CA 90038, [800] 815-0503, www.hcdonline.com), offers probably the most complete list of agents and managers—it boasts 7,000 individual names and can be purchased as a book or an online directory.

OTHER TELEVISION RESOURCES

Other excellent publications for breaking into television include: *Written By: The Journal of the Writers Guild of America, West* (7000 W. Third St., Los Angeles, CA 90048-4329, [800] 548-4532, writtenby@wga.org) provides a TV Market List with information about every television show in production, including the person responsible for freelance writers and the phone number of the production company. Non-WGA members may subscribe. Also, *The Hollywood Scriptwriter* (www.hollywoodscriptwriter.com) offers interviews with successful writers as well as agents and market information. If you want to stay tuned to the day-to-day operations in Hollywood, check out *Daily Variety* (www.variety.com) and *The Hollywood Reporter* (www.hollywoodreporter.com), both of which publish charts with television production information and will keep you up on industry news.

The Query Letter

After you've done your research and know how to contact the right agency, producer or story editor, send a query letter. That's all you should send at this point; do not submit your spec script. In your query letter, say you'd like to write for the show and ask if the production company or agency is interested in new writers. J. Michael Straczynski, in *The Complete Book of Scriptwriting* (Writer's Digest Books), suggests mentioning the following:

- That you're enthusiastic about the show and have studied it.
- That you've written a spec script and would like to submit it. (Do not go into detail about the contents of your spec script—you'll definitely ruin your chances of writing for the show.)
- That when you send your spec script you will enclose a standard release form or will use the production company's or agency's release form.
- That you have writing credits or a profession that qualifies you to write for this show. (If you've spent ten years working in an emergency room, mentioning that could really help if you want to write for a show like *ER*.)

That's basically all you need to include in your query. Again, never send a spec script to an agent, producer or story editor unless you are requested to do so. Do not mention any specifics about your story idea in your query letter or it will be returned immediately. Producers and agents refuse to look at unsolicited spec scripts and story ideas because they are afraid of getting sued for plagiarism. Just keep your query letter to a few short paragraphs and ask for permission to send your spec script. Follow these guidelines:

FORMATTING SPECS
- Use a standard font or typeface (no bold, script, or italic).
- Place your name, address, phone number, e-mail, and fax in the top right corner.
- Use a 1″ margin on all sides.
- Address it to a specific agent, producer, or story editor.
- Keep it to one page.
- Use block or semiblock letter format.
- Single-space the body of the letter; double-space between paragraphs.
- Catalog every item you're sending in your enclosures.

OTHER DOS AND DON'TS
- Do include an SASE or postcard for reply, and state in the letter that you have done so.
- Do offer to sign a release form.
- Do offer to send the spec script.
- Don't use "Dear Sir," "Dear Madame," etc. in your salutation.

- Don't use Mr., Ms., Mrs., or Miss unless you're certain of the person's gender and marital status.
- Don't mention that you're a first-time writer or that you've never sold any piece of writing.
- Don't spend much time trying to sell yourself.
- Don't tell how much time you've spent writing the script.
- Don't ask for advice or criticism.
- Don't mention anything about yourself not pertinent to the script.
- Don't bring up payment.
- Don't mention copyright information.

Electronic Query Letter

SUBMISSION TIPS

Many agents, producers, and story editors now accept queries via e-mail. Before you send a query via e-mail, however, you must have permission to send it. The basic tone and format of the electronic query shouldn't be much different from a query sent on paper.

FORMATTING SPECS

- Include the same information you would in a paper query, including your name, addresss, phone, and fax, etc. The top right-hand corner or top center position is fine for this, though you can also include this information in a signature line at the end. It isn't necessary to include your e-mail address in the body of the e-mail, however, since the editor can reply easily with the click of a buton.
- Put a discription of your TV script or its title in the subject line.
- Follow the same format you would with a paper query, including the date, salutation to a specific editor and block paragraph format. See the above tips for submitting a paper query; the same rules apply.

OTHER DOS AND DON'TS

- Don't use all caps or exclamation points in the subject line.
- Don't submit an e-mail query unless specifically requested by an agent, producer, or story editor.
- Don't insert clip art graphics or other images into your query letter.
- Do read the Dos and Don'ts above for a paper query—the same rules apply!

In your cover letter, don't spend a paragraph letting us known you as a person. Why? *We don't care.* We want to find a brilliant script, not an interesting dinner companion. We only want information relevant to our perception of the script (like telling us you worked as a contractor, which validates the world of your story).
    —Chad Gervich, manager, talent and development, The Littlefield Company/Paramount Television

QUERY: TELEVISION SCRIPT

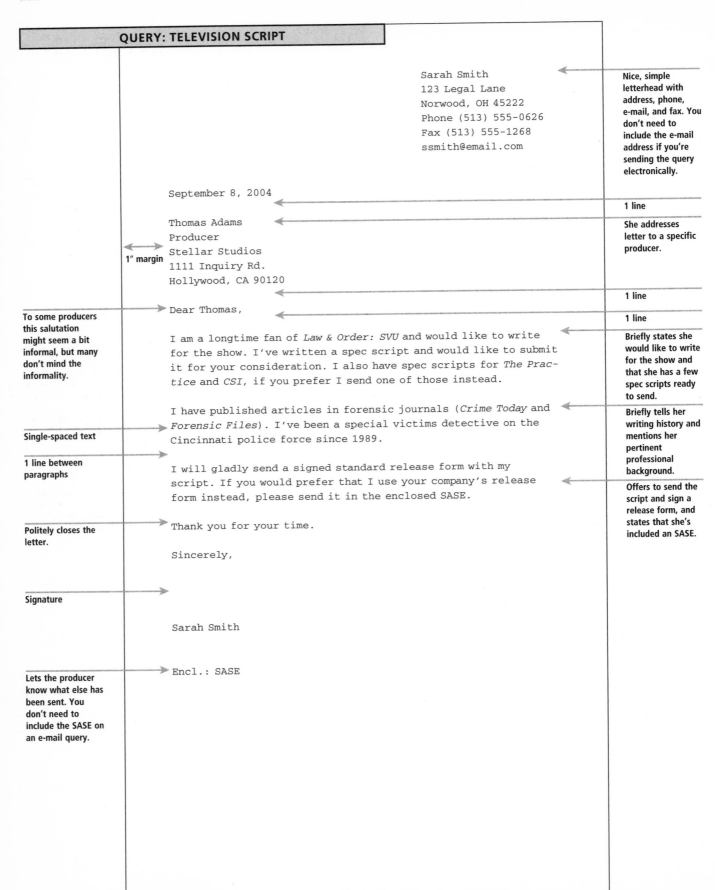

Sarah Smith
123 Legal Lane
Norwood, OH 45222
Phone (513) 555-0626
Fax (513) 555-1268
ssmith@email.com

Nice, simple letterhead with address, phone, e-mail, and fax. You don't need to include the e-mail address if you're sending the query electronically.

September 8, 2004

1 line

Thomas Adams
Producer
Stellar Studios
1111 Inquiry Rd.
Hollywood, CA 90120

1" margin

She addresses letter to a specific producer.

1 line

Dear Thomas,

1 line

To some producers this salutation might seem a bit informal, but many don't mind the informality.

I am a longtime fan of *Law & Order: SVU* and would like to write for the show. I've written a spec script and would like to submit it for your consideration. I also have spec scripts for *The Practice* and *CSI*, if you prefer I send one of those instead.

Briefly states she would like to write for the show and that she has a few spec scripts ready to send.

I have published articles in forensic journals (*Crime Today* and *Forensic Files*). I've been a special victims detective on the Cincinnati police force since 1989.

Briefly tells her writing history and mentions her pertinent professional background.

Single-spaced text

1 line between paragraphs

I will gladly send a signed standard release form with my script. If you would prefer that I use your company's release form instead, please send it in the enclosed SASE.

Offers to send the script and sign a release form, and states that she's included an SASE.

Politely closes the letter.

Thank you for your time.

Sincerely,

Signature

Sarah Smith

Lets the producer know what else has been sent. You don't need to include the SASE on an e-mail query.

Encl.: SASE

TELEVISION SCRIPT QUERY: MISTAKES TO AVOID

Don't forget to
date your letter.

All of your contact
information should
be included—name,
address, phone, and
e-mail address.

Be sure to address
your query to a
specific editor that
works on the
television show you
are submitting your
script for, and
include their address
information.

Briefly state that
you would like to
write for a show
and indicate that
you have spec
scripts ready to
send; your family
situation doesn't
indicate to a story
editor that you're
qualified to write
for it.

Don't mention that
you're a first time
writer, and don't
beg a story editor
to read your script.
And don't ask for
advice or criticism!

Don't forget the
SASE, unless you're
sending your query
via e-mail.

This paragraph
should be used to
outline your writing
history and
pertinent
professional
background. Explain
why you are
qualified to write
for this show.

Also, don't say that
your friends and
family think your
script is great—that
means nothing to a
story editor, and
singles you out as
an amateur.

You should always
mention that you're
willing to sign a
standard release
form.

Fiona Failure
215-555-9696

To Whom It May Conern:

I just love the television show *Gilmore Girls*, and I have a great
idea for a story line for an upcoming episode. Can I send it to
you? I think you'll really like it, I have a similar relationship
with my daughter like Lorelai has with Rory, so I really understand what it's like to have a daughter that's like your best
friend. I also have a husband, which Lorelai doesn't have, but
he always tells me that we're ''just like Lorelai and Rory on *Gilmore Girls*,'' so I thought I'd write an episode.

The episode I've written is from a real-life adventure that my
daughter and I took on a road tip to visit our ailing aunt in the
country. Our car trip was filled with witty banter, just like
the characters on *Gilmore Girls*, so I based the episode on that.
Everyone in my family has read it and thinks it's just wonderful, if not better than the actual episodes that we see every
week on *Gilmore Girls*.

I have taken local writing workshops and while I have never been
published, I think this is my big break into the land of television writing. Please give me a chance. I will send you the entire
script. Since it's my first screenplay, any advice you can give
on how to make it even better would be great!

I'm looking forward to working with you on this fabulous script.
Thanks!

Respectfully yours,

Fiona

Sitcoms

Unlike movie features and one-hour dramas that are shot on film, half-hour sitcoms are shot entirely on videotape and have a unique script format tailored for them. (Actually, each sitcom has its individual formatting quirks, so try to obtain a copy of the show's "bible" and a sample script.) What sets a sitcom script apart from other scripts is that almost everything is in all caps and double-spaced. There are good reasons for these differences, most notably that sitcom scripts often get revised up until the taping sessions (there are usually two sessions in front of live audiences, held on the same day), and sitcoms have directions for three cameras written alongside the script. A script written in a single-spaced format wouldn't allow enough room for the handwritten changes and camera directions. Basically, a sitcom script has a lot of much-needed white space.

STRUCTURE

Most sitcoms have only two acts, with three scenes per act (some shows use a teaser or a tag, which we'll discuss later). Because of all the double-spacing, plan on about thirty seconds per script page. Consider that the viewing time of the average sitcom is about twenty-two to twenty-four minutes, so your script should be forty to fifty pages (with each act running about twenty to twenty-five pages; six to eight pages per scene). Acts are in all caps. At the end of the act, type "<u>END OF ACT ONE</u>" (or two), centered and underlined two or three spaces below the last line of the act.

TEASERS AND TAGS

Many sitcoms today begin with a teaser or end with a tag; some use both. A teaser is a short scene that airs at the beginning of the show, and a tag is a short scene that appears after the final act has been resolved. The tag almost always follows a commercial break and has the show's credits rolling alongside it. Both teasers and tags should run about two pages. Sometimes teasers and tags have little or nothing to do with that episode's story.

FIRST-PAGE PARTICULARS

The series title should be ten lines from the top of the page and centered. Two lines under the series title should be the episode title, with the act number centered eight lines below that (the act number should be completely spelled out). The series title and act number should be in all caps and underlined, whereas the episode title should be in regular text (not all caps), underlined and enclosed in quotation marks. Drop both the series title and the episode title from the first page of act two, but remember to include the act number (spelled out)—it should be fifteen lines from the top of the page and centered.

PAGE NUMBERS

Page numbers should appear in the top right corner of the page, flush with the right margin (about 75 spaces from the left edge of the page), about four lines from the top of the page, and followed by a period (e.g., 17.).

ACT AND SCENE NUMBER NOTATIONS

In the top right corner two lines below the page number should appear an act and scene number notation (although many sitcoms use letters for their scenes—A, B, C—instead of numbering them; check the formatting rules for each show). This notation should be in all caps on the first page of the act:

    First page in act: ACT 2, SCENE 2

After the first page of the act, the heading should be underlined on the rest of the pages, and only the act should be capitalized:

    All other pages in the act: ACT 2, scene 2

CAST MEMBER LISTS

Also in the top right corner of the page is the cast member list. It appears only on the first page of each new scene, in parentheses, two lines under the act and scene notation. The cast member list includes just the names of the actors in that scene, with the names in regular text (not all caps) separated by commas:

    15.

    ACT 2, scene 2

    (Tom, Jerry, Stan)

Some scripts, however, have the character list one line under the slug line (scene heading) on the left margin (see Slug Lines below). Again, check the show's specifications.

TRANSITIONS

Transitions indicate that a shot or scene is either beginning, ending, or shifting to another shot or scene. These include such directions as FADE IN:, FADE OUT, DISSOLVE TO: and CUT TO:. Transitions appear in all caps and are justified with the right margin (about 75 spaces from the left edge of the page), except FADE IN:, which is flush with the left margin (15 spaces from the left edge of the page). FADE OUT is used only at the end of an act and CUT TO: at the end of a scene (to indicate a new scene should begin). Some shows underline transitions.

SLUG LINES

The slug line, also called a scene heading, specifies the scene. It begins on the left margin (15 spaces from the left edge of the page) and is written in all caps and underlined, with a double-spaced line before and after it. Your first slug line should appear two lines below FADE IN:. In sitcoms, the slug line will usually be INT. (interior shot), but occasionally you'll need to use EXT. (exterior shot). With the slug line, organize the details by going from the more general to the more specific. End each slug line by indicating whether the action takes place during the day or at night. For almost every sitcom, the slug line typically contains three parts: INT. or EXT., the scene location and DAY or NIGHT. Your slug line will look like this:

<u>INT. FRASIER'S LIVING ROOM—NIGHT</u>

Some shows have the character list for that particular scene in parentheses one line below the slug line:

<u>INT. FRASIER'S LIVING ROOM—NIGHT</u>
(Frasier, Niles, Daphne)

ACTION DIRECTIONS

The action directions are sentences that describe specifics about what happens, when, where, how, and anything else that's important to the scene. The text within the action sentences begins on the left margin (15 spaces from the left edge of the page), is single-spaced, in all caps and should always be written in present tense (in some scripts, the action is in parentheses). Do not justify the right margin (which is at 75 spaces). Many shows underline entrances and exits (either the entire sentence or just the verb):

<u>JONATHAN ENTERS THE DINING ROOM.</u>

Or:

JONATHAN <u>ENTERS</u> THE DINING ROOM.

There should be one double-spaced line before and after the action description. If you have lots of description, break up the text to leave some white space—try not to allow a block of text to run more than four or five lines without a double-spaced break for the eyes (the more white space in a sitcom script, the better).

CHARACTER NAMES

The speaking character's name (also called the character cue) should be in all caps and should appear 35 spaces from the left edge of the page. A double-spaced line should appear before and after the character's name. Note: The first time you introduce a character into the script, put that character's name in all caps and/or underline it.

JACK
I think I just saw <u>SUSAN</u> walk up the steps. Maybe she's coming up here.

PARENTHETICAL COMMENTS

Parenthetical comments, also known as parentheticals, help the speaker of the dialogue know what emotion or expression you intend with the delivery. A parenthetical is typically short (often a word or two), typed in all caps and appears either on the same line as the first line of dialogue or on a line by itself (in which case it appears flush with the left margin):

VERONICA
(EMBARRASSED) He really said I was cute?

Or:

```
                    VERONICA
                (EMBARRASSED)
            He really said I was cute?
```

DIALOGUE

Dialogue is double-spaced, typed in regular text (not all caps), and begins two lines below the speaking character's name (and parenthetical). The left margin for dialogue is at space 25 and the right margin is at space 60 (do not justify the right margin).

CONTINUATIONS

If you must continue dialogue from one page to the next, use what are called continuations, which are just the words (MORE) and (CONT'D). Use them like this: Put (MORE) under the last line of dialogue on the first page and (CONT'D) to the right of the character's name on the following page:

```
            PAUL
      Ira, if you don't knock before you come in here
                  (MORE)
```

_____NEW PAGE_____

```
            PAUL (CONT'D)
      I'm going to sic Murray on you.
```

USING A NARRATIVE VOICE-OVER

You will rarely need to use a narrative voice-over with sitcoms, but if you do, make sure you indicate it as such by typing "(V.O.)" to the right of the character's name:

```
            DHARMA (V.O.)
      Wait a minute, now how did that happen?
```

HAVING A CHARACTER SPEAK OFF-CAMERA

When you have a character speaking off-camera, type "(O.C.)" to the right of the character's name. Let's say Joey is on camera in the hallway talking to Chandler who's off-camera inside the apartment.

```
            JOEY
      Come on, Chandler. You gotta let me in.
            CHANDLER (O.C.)
      Joey, that's you, right?
```

OTHER DOS AND DON'TS

- Do keep dialogue short (break it up every four or five lines).
- Do spell out one- and two-digit numbers (one, ten, fifty), but use numbers for 100 and over.

- Do spell out personal titles except for Mr., Mrs., and Ms.
- Do spell out time indicators: eleven-thirty, not 11:30.
- Do spell out "okay," not OK or o.k.
- Don't use any font other than Courier 12-point.
- Don't justify right margins.
- Don't date your script.
- Don't include a cast of characters or set list page.
- Don't use camera directions and camera angles.
- Don't use special effects directions, such as FX (visual).
- Don't use sound effects directions, such as SFX (sound).

What follows are formatting specifications for your sitcom script, a sample first page of a mock script for *Frasier*, and a sample sitcom script title page.

TAB AND MARGIN SETTINGS
- Left 15 spaces; right 55 spaces for camera and stage directions
- Left 15 spaces; right 70 spaces for action/scene descriptions
- Left 15 spaces; right 70 spaces for slug line
- Left 25; right 60 spaces for dialogue
- 35 spaces for character name
- 15 spaces for FADE IN
- 60 spaces for transitions

ALL CAPS
- Act and scene headings
- Act breaks
- All action/scene/stage directions
- Speech delivery (e.g., SLURRY)
- Transitions (FADE IN:, FADE OUT)
- Tags
- Teasers
- Slug lines (EXT. or INT., DAY or NIGHT)
- All descriptions
- Character names (except when part of dialogue or character list)
- Continuations (MORE or CONT'D)
- Act and show endings (END OF SHOW)

UNDERLINE
- Act headings
- Scene headings
- Locale designations
- Important sounds
- Slug lines
- When a character is first introduced

SINGLE SPACE
- within action directions
- within scene descriptions

DOUBLE SPACE
- between scene heading and first lines of directions or scene descriptions
- between character's name and dialogue
- within dialogue lines
- between dialogue lines and directions or scene descriptions
- before and after transitions

Electronic Sitcom Script Submissions

It is rare for an agent or story editor to request a sitcom script via e-mail, but it might happen. If it does, make sure you get detailed guidelines as to how the script should be submitted and follow them meticulously.

> The key is to get your script to a company that *needs* your material. Plenty of companies "accept" cold submissions, but you want the company looking specifically for *your script*. An enormously successful production company like Imagine has its own stable of writers and a full slate of projects; the last thing they have time for is reading strangers' material. Target smaller companies that specialize in your genre of material. Hone your crusade to a handful of companies where your script will fulfill a need and you have a shot at forming some personal relationships.
>
> **—Chad Gervich, manager, talent and development, The Littlefield Company/Paramount Television**

SITCOM SCRIPT

Each scene begins on a new page.

1.

ACT I, SC. A

(Frasier, Niles)

Page number followed by a period (space 72 or flush with right margin—space 75).

Act and scene number notation is essential with sitcoms.

Lists the characters in this scene.

Series title in all caps and centered.

<u>FRASIER</u>

Episode's title, centered and in quotes.

``Niles Go Home''

Act number and scene numbers are centered, in all caps and underlined.

<u>ACT ONE</u>

<u>SCENE A</u>

Left margin is at space 15.

Transition is in all caps.

FADE IN:

<u>INT. LIVING ROOM—THE NEXT MORNING</u>

Slug line is in all caps and underlined.

The first time a character is introduced, the name is underlined.

<u>NILES</u> IS DRINKING COFFEE AND READING THE NEWSPAPER. <u>FRASIER</u>, LOOKING TERRIBLY HUNGOVER, COMES IN THE FRONT DOOR, DROPS HIS COAT ON THE FLOOR, IGNORES NILES, AND FALLS ON THE COUCH.

Action line is in all caps and single-spaced.

Character cue is in all caps (space 35).

NILES

My aren't we perky this morning! And where has

Dialogue left margin is at space 25 (right margin is 60).

Dialogue is double-spaced

Frasier been all night?

FRASIER

Parentheticals are uppercase (can fall within dialogue or on a separate line).

(HOLDING HIS HEAD) Oh shut up, Niles.

(MORE)

Indicates the character has more lines on the following page.

1" margin on top and bottom.

SITCOM SCRIPT, PAGE 2

2.

Second page numbered

Picks up with same character who was speaking before the page break.

FRASIER (CONT'D)

You're no ray of sunshine.

NILES

I'm no hungover drunk either.

FRASIER

Well at least I have a home.

NILES

Oh you cruel man. You know my marriage is on the rocks.

You know that MARIS wouldn't let me back in the house if

I sawed my left leg off for her. She's such a cold woman.

Dialogue is double-spaced (keep blocks of dialogue short).

FRASIER

Yeah, but she's your woman. Now go back home.

NILES

Are you saying you don't want me here? Are you saying

you won't help your brother out in a time of need?

FRASIER

That's exactly what I'm saying.

NILES

Dad!

HE GETS UP AND RUNS INTO THE KITCHEN, POUTING.

FADE OUT

Transition goes at space 66 (or flush with right margin).

END OF ACT ONE

Title Page

SUBMISSION TIPS

The title page includes the series' title, the episode's title, the author(s), and the author's contact information (this can be substituted with your agent's name and contact information if you have representation).

FORMATTING SPECS

- The sitcom series should be in all caps, centered, about one-third of the way down the page.
- Drop one line and put the episode title in quotes.
- Drop four lines and type either "Written by" or just "by" (don't type the quotation marks).
- Drop one line and type your name.
- In the lower right hard corner, put your name, address, phone number, and e-mail, single-spaces, in regular text (not all caps). If you have an agent, type "Representation:," double-space then put the agent's name, address, phone number, and e-mail instead of yours.
- In front of the title page, be sure to include a cover page that includes only the title and author's name.
- Preferred cover page paper is a white, gray, cream, rust, or pale blue cover of card stock, between 40 and 60 lbs.
- The pages should be bound in brass brads, short enough so they don't cut through an envelope when mailed.
- Although your script should have three holes punched in it, only the first and third holes should have brads in them.

OTHER DOS AND DON'TS

- Don't put any pictures or artwork on your cover page.
- Don't use spiral or other machine-type bindings.
- Do include a back cover in the same card stock as the cover page.

Too many writers think that anybody can write for television and film . . . Sure, much of it is so bad that it seems like anybody could do it, but you must be an amazing writer with a great sample to break in.

—Richard Krevolin, author of Screenwriting From The Soul and How to Adapt Anything into a Screenplay

(www.profk.com)

TITLE PAGE: SITCOM

Series' title is in all caps, one-third of the way down the page.

4 lines

1 line

FRASIER

``Niles Go Home''

1 line

Epsiode's title in quotes.

Written by

Don Prues & Jack Neff

Byline

Prues & Neff
111 W. Seventy-third St.
New York, NY 11001
(212) 555-2222
pruesandneff@email.com

Writer's name, address and phone always go in bottom right corner, unless you are represented by an agent then include their contact info.

The One-Hour Episodic Drama

STRUCTURE

Your hour-long script will be roughly fifty pages. Most one-hour dramas run forty-eight minutes, and as with the motion picture format, you can average about one minute of viewing time per manuscript page. Nearly all hour-long dramas contain four acts that occur at roughly twelve- to fifteen-minute intervals (so your script should change acts every twelve to fifteen pages). The act breaks will correspond with the network's commercials, which occur about every thirteen minutes. Because networks want viewers to hang around through the commercial breaks, your story needs to have a cliffhanger or an emotional moment at the end of each act. Whether or not such a moment needs to be included in the last act depends on the individual show—does it typically end with a neat resolution or with something to carry over to next week?

TRANSITIONS

Transitions simply indicate that a shot or scene is beginning, ending or shifting to another shot or scene. These include such directions as FADE IN:, FADE TO:, CUT TO:, and DISSOLVE TO:. Transitions appear in all caps and are justified with the right margin (about space 75), except FADE IN:, which is flush with the left margin and should appear two lines below the act number. FADE OUT is used only at the end of an act (and is on the right margin).

TEASERS AND TAGS

Many one-hour episodic dramas begin with a teaser or end with a tag; some use both. A teaser is a short scene that airs at the beginning of the show, and a tag is a short scene that appears after the final act has been resolved. The tag almost always follows a commercial break and has the show's credits rolling alongside it. Both teasers and tags should run about two pages. Sometimes teasers and tags have little or nothing to do with that episode's story.

SLUG LINE

The slug line sets the scene and specifies the shot. It begins on the left margin (17 spaces from the left edge of the page) and is written in all caps, with a double-spaced line before and after it. Your first slug line should appear two lines below FADE IN:. Most slug lines begin with either EXT. (exterior shot) or INT. (interior shot). After you determine whether the shot is outside or inside, identify the specifics of the shot, such as a particular building or house, and then, if necessary, precisely where the shot takes place. With the slug line, organize the details by going from the general to the specific. End each slug line by indicating whether it's day or night. For example, your slug line will look like this:

```
INT. YMCA—MEN'S LOCKER ROOM—NIGHT
```

ACTION

The action descriptions are sentences or very short paragraphs that describe specifics about what happens, location, the time of year, and anything else important to the scene. The text within the action sentences begins on the left margin (17 spaces from the left edge of the page), is single-spaced (with regular capitalization), and should always be written in present tense. Do not justify the right margin (75). There should be one double-spaced line before and after the action text. If you have lots of description, break up the text to leave some white space—try not to allow a block of text to run more than five or six lines without a double-spaced break for the eyes (the more white space in a script, the better).

CHARACTER'S NAME

The speaking character's name (also called the character cue) should be in all caps and appear 43 spaces from the left edge of the page (about 30 spaces from the left margin). A double-spaced line should appear before the character's name, but there should be no double-space between the name and the dialogue, or between the name and the parenthetical (see below). Note: The first time you introduce a character into the script you must put that character's name in all caps (this occurs either in dialogue when one character refers to another or in the narrative description line, "JOE enters the room"). After the character has been introduced, use regular capitalization.

PARENTHETICAL COMMENT

Parenthetical comments, also known as parentheticals, help the speaker of the dialogue know what emotion you intend for the delivery. Parenthetical comments are typically short (often a word or two), are typed in regular text (not all caps), appear one line below the character's name (and thus one line above dialogue) at space 35, and are set in parentheses. A parenthetical should look like this:

```
          SCULLY
        (antagonistic)
     What in the hell's going on around here, Mulder?
```

DIALOGUE

Dialogue is typed in regular text (not all caps) and begins on the line below the speaking character's name (or one line below the parenthetical). The left margin for dialogue is at space 28 and the right margin is at space 60 (do not justify the right margin). Try to avoid large blocks of dialogue that run seven or more lines. If your character needs to say more than can fit in seven lines, add a blank line space between the text so it's more visually pleasing (e.g., a fourteen-line section of dialogue should be broken into two blocks of seven lines each).

In addition to the aforementioned regular elements of your one-hour episodic script, you will probably find yourself in situations where you might need some special formatting and cues. Here are some of the more common script elements you might need to inject in your one-hour episodic script.

CARRYING DIALOGUE FROM ONE PAGE TO THE NEXT

Do your best not to make a character flip to the next page in the middle of speaking. Sometimes, however, this cannot be avoided, and you must use what's called a continuation. To carry a character's dialogue onto the next page, use the indicator (MORE) on the bottom of the first page and (CONT'D) next to the speaker's name at the top of the next page:

```
                JOE
    I swear if I ever see you in this town again I'm going
                     (MORE)
_____NEW PAGE_____

                JOE (CONT'D)
    to kill you.
```

USING A NARRATIVE VOICE-OVER

If your script calls for a narrative voice-over, make sure you indicate it as such by typing "(V.O.)" next to the name of the character who's narrating. A scene with a voice narration should look like this:

```
          CAPTAIN SMITH (V.O.)
     Now how did she get into the apartment when the keys
     are inside?
```

HAVING A CHARACTER SPEAK OFF-CAMERA

When you have a character speaking off-camera, type "(O.C.)" next to the character's name. Let's say Steve is on camera in the kitchen while talking to Maggie who's off-camera on the back porch.

```
          STEVE
     Can you bring that old broom in here?


          MAGGIE (O.C.)
     What? You want me to put that filthy thing in our
     kitchen? You're crazy.


          STEVE
     I need it to sweep up all this flour I just spilled on
     the floor.


          MAGGIE (O.C.)
     Oh, you're pathetic.
```

OTHER DOS AND DON'TS

- Do number your pages and put a period after the number.
- Do keep dialogue short (keep to seven lines per block, then insert a double-space).
- Do spell out one- and two-digit numbers (one, ten, fifty), but use numbers for 100 and over.
- Do spell out personal titles except for Mr., Mrs. and Ms.
- Do spell out time indicators: eleven-thirty, not 11:30.
- Do spell out "okay," not OK or o.k.
- Don't use special effects directions, such as FX (visual).
- Don't use sound effects directions, such as SFX (sound).

- Don't use camera directions and camera angles.
- Don't number the first page.
- Don't number scenes (this is done in the final stages of story editing, before the script moves into preproduction).

What follows are formatting specifications for your one-hour episodic script as well as a sample one-hour episodic script title page and a sample first page of a one-hour episodic script.

TAB AND MARGIN SETTINGS
- Left margin: 17 spaces
- Dialogue left margin: 28 spaces
- Parenthetical directions: 35 spaces
- Character's name (above the dialogue): 43 spaces
- Dialogue right margin: 60 spaces
- Transitions: 66 spaces
- Page number followed by a period (in top right-hand corner, four lines from top of page): 72 spaces
- Right margin: 75 spaces

ALL CAPS
- Type of shot (INT. and EXT.)
- Setting or scene location (JOE'S ROOM)
- Time of day (DAY or NIGHT)
- The first time you introduce a character (JOHN walks in)
- The speaking character's name (PHIL), followed by dialogue
- Camera directions (PAN, CLOSE-UP, etc.)
- Important sound cues (Ted hears a GUNSHOT in the hallway.)
- Scene transitions (CUT TO:, DISSOLVE TO:, etc.)
- (MORE)

SINGLE SPACE
- within dialogue
- within action/scene descriptions (also called narrative)
- within camera directions, sound cues
- within stage directions
- between the character's name and dialogue
- between character's name and parenthetical
- between parenthetical and dialogue

DOUBLE SPACE
- between the scene location and action/scene descriptions
- between the action/scene descriptions and the speaking character's name
- between the speeches of the different characters
- between the paragraphs of lengthy dialogue or action descriptions
- between dialogue and a new speaking character's name
- between dialogue and stage or camera directions

TRIPLE SPACE
- before each new scene

Electronic One-Hour Episodic Drama Script Submissions

It is rare for an agent, producer, or story editor to request an episodic drama script via e-mail, but it might happen. If it does, make sure you get detailed guidelines as to how the script should be submitted and follow them meticulously.

> *Most agents/managers use readers to screen the material they receive. These readers are typically writers who are interning for the experience and are ultra-critical of format, etc. If your work isn't bulletproof as far as presentation goes, that's a big strike against you already. Your work may fail to sell for creative reasons or other reasons but it shouldn't fair because of simple things like grammar, punctuation and spelling and/or formatting.*
>
> *—Mark Sevi, screenwriter*

ONE-HOUR EPISODIC DRAMA SCRIPT

1.

Page number
followed by a
period (space 72 or
flush with right
margin—space 75).

ER
''October Outbreak''
Act One

Series title, episode title and
act number (underlined) are
centered near the top margin.

Transition is in all
caps.

FADE IN:

Slug line is in all
caps.

EXT. HOSPITAL—DAY

The outside of the hospital. It's October, and many leaves are
falling.

                                                CUT TO:

INT. E.R.- WAITING ROOM

Left margin at
space 17.

Start by showing a YOUNG MOTHER holding her ten-year-old crying
DAUGHTER on her lap. The girl is covered with a rash indicative
of scarlet fever. We then PAN ACROSS the crowded and busy room to
a couch showing four HISPANIC BOYS cuddled together. They, too,
are covered with the rash. DR. CARTER, clipboard in hand, walks
up to the boys.

First time a
character is
introduced, the
name is in all caps.

Action line is
single-spaced,
upper and
lowercase text.

                    DR. CARTER
          Hey guys, has your mother come back yet?

Dialogue left
margin is at space
28 (right margin is
60).

                    OLDEST BOY
          No. We haven't seen her.

Character cue is in all caps
(space 43).

                    DR. CARTER (V.O.)
             (to himself)
          Where in the hell is she?

Voice-over

Parentheticals are
on a separate line
(at space 35).

                    DR. CARTER (CONT'D)
          Um, okay, okay. So how's everybody doing?

Boys shrug their shoulders.

                    OLDEST BOY
          My little brother says he's really thirsty.

                    DR. CARTER
          Sure. We'll get something for him right away. How about
          the rest of you—you guys want something, too?

Dialogue is single-
spaced (do keep
blocks of dialogue
short).

Double-space
between changes
in dialogue and
action lines.

All the boys give a ''yes'' nod.

                    DR. CARTER
             (Waving his clipboard to ABBY)
          Somebody get these boys something to drink. ABBY, can
          you bring four cups of water for these guys?

1" margin on top
and bottom.

ONE-HOUR EPISODIC DRAMA SCRIPT, PAGE 2

Off camera.

2.

Page number
followed by a
period (space 72 or
flush with right
margin—space 75).

```
                    ABBY (O.C.)
        No problem, doctor. Right away.

                    DR. CARTER
                  (to boys)
        You guys hang tight for a minute and this nice lady will
        bring you some cold water.

                    OLDEST BOY
        All right.

        EXIT Dr. Carter.
```

Title Page

SUBMISSION TIPS

The title page includes the series' title, the episode's title, the author(s), and the author's contact information (this can be substituted with your agent's name and contact information if you have representation).

FORMATTING TIPS

- The one-hour episodic series name should be in all caps, centered, about one-third of the way down the page.
- Drop ten lines and put the episode title in quotes.
- Drop four lines and type "Story and Script" (don't type the quotation marks).
- Drop one line and type "by".
- Double-space again and type your name.
- In the lower right-hand corner, put your name, address, phone number, and e-mail, single-spaced, in regular text (not all caps).
- If you have an agent, put "Representation:," double-space, then put the agent's name, address, phone number, and e-mail instead of yours.
- In front of the title page, be sure to include a cover page with the title and author's name.
- Preferred cover page paper is a white, gray, cream, rust or pale blue cover of card stock, between 40 to 60 lb.
- The pages should be bound in brass brads, short enough so they don't cut through an envelope when mailed.
- Although your script should have three holes punched in it, only the first and third holes should have brads in them

OTHER DOS AND DON'TS

- Don't put any pictures or artwork on your title page.
- Don't use spiral or other machine-type bindings.
- Do use a back cover of the same card stock as the cover page.

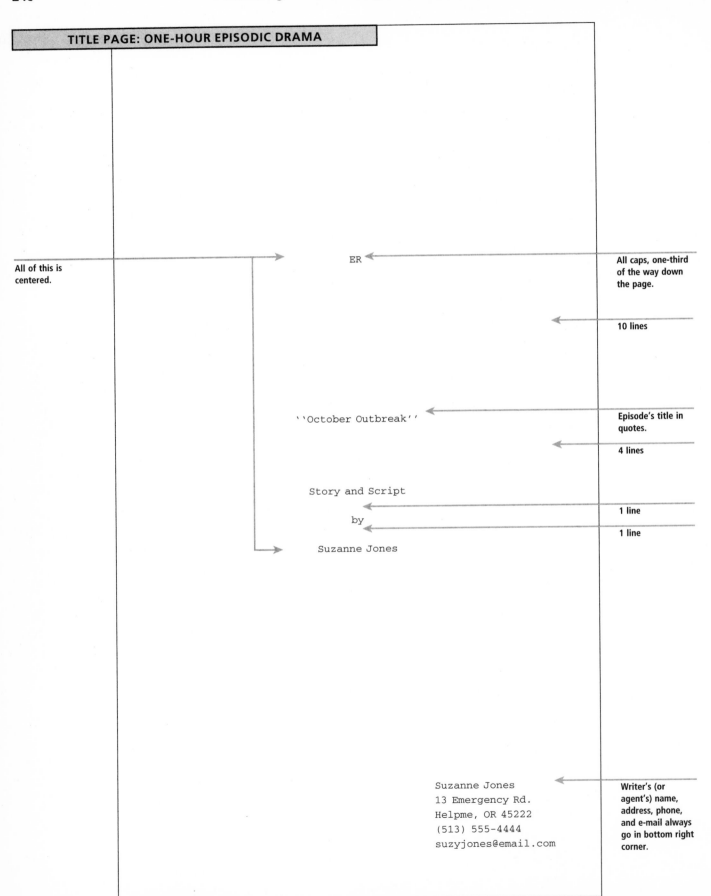

TITLE PAGE: ONE-HOUR EPISODIC DRAMA

All of this is
centered.

ER — All caps, one-third
of the way down
the page.

← 10 lines

``October Outbreak´´ — Episode's title in
quotes.

← 4 lines

Story and Script

by — 1 line

← 1 line

Suzanne Jones

Suzanne Jones
13 Emergency Rd.
Helpme, OR 45222
(513) 555-4444
suzyjones@email.com

Writer's (or
agent's) name,
address, phone,
and e-mail always
go in bottom right
corner.

Soaps

A finished soap script is the result of teamwork. Because soaps must be cranked out five days week, with multiple stories going at once to carry the drama from episode to episode (for seemingly perpetuity), a number of writers, producers, and executives are required to get the script in working order. The best way to keep up with such demand is the same way Henry Ford put together cars: division of labor. Soap scripts are an assembly line of sorts.

Here's how that assembly line works. The show's sponsor (usually a corporation, like Procter & Gamble) and the producers will meet with the show's head writer to create a yearlong, roughly sketched outline for the show. Then the head writer breaks that outline into specific weekly and daily outlines. Eventually, a short scene-by-scene synopsis (usually a paragraph or two per scene) is created for each episode; then the head writer sends the synopsis to various associate writers who write all the dialogue for a particular episode. So, most writers for soaps are associate writers who pen the dialogue for individual episodes.

The best way to become an associate writer is to send a spectacular spec script to the production company or to get an agent who represents the show's writers to also represent you (see page 217 for tips on locating the production company or an agent who represents the show's writers). One other option is to find out if the show has an apprentice program for writers (the show's sponsor usually offers this program) and, if so, enroll in it. To see if the show you wish to write for offers such a program, contact the production company.

STRUCTURE

Most soaps run for an hour, with a few that only run one-half hour. Either way, you can figure that the viewing time for a soap script is a little more than one minute per page. Therefore, a one-hour show script will run about seventy pages, and a half-hour show will be roughly thirty-five pages. Although commercial breaks will eat up some of this time, ignore them and write as if your show's either an hour or half-hour. Unlike one-hour episodic dramas and sitcoms, which have a set number of acts, soaps work in a different way because they're continually running. A soap episode is more a series of scenes than one story episode delineated into a beginning, a middle, and an end.

FORMAT

The script elements and formatting specifications for soaps is almost identical to those for motion pictures (see page 202). There are, however, a few differences you should be aware of. The primary difference is that all action directions are capitalized, appear in parentheses and get mixed in with the dialogue. Also, a soap script has practically no camera directions and relies heavily on dialogue.

One major problem with writing a spec script for a soap is that the formats vary so much from show to show. Many shows use the "standard" soap format demonstrated on page 243, but some opt for a format that looks more like a radio script:

```
JOHN: Would you please bring me some water?
MARY: I'm not your maid.
```

To determine what format the soap you want to write for uses, try to obtain back scripts from the production company. Finding the production company isn't too difficult: Tape the show, watch the credits, write down the name of the production company and get the phone number from one of the listed directories in Submitting Television Scripts, on page 216. You only need to talk to the secretary. Just say you want to write for the show and would like to obtain some back scripts. Offer to send an SASE with adequate postage. Making the call will pay off—it will be to your advantage that you're using the correct format for the show.

Electronic Soap Script Submissions

It is rare for an agent, producer, or story editor to request a soap script via e-mail, but it might happen. If it does, make sure you get detailed guidelines as to how the script should be submitted and follow them meticulously.

> *People don't equate screenwriting/television writing with great art. Novelists, poets, etc. are given more legitimacy as far as literary effort is concerned. Nevertheless, it really takes a "calling" to be a writer of any type, including for movie and television. If you don't just love it beyond all common sense, it's not for you.*
>
> *—Mark Sevi, screenwriter*

SOAP OPERA SCRIPT

1" margin on top and bottom.

Transition is in all caps.

FADE IN:

HAROLD DANFORTH'S DEN. HAROLD IS SEARCHNG THROUGH HIS DESK TRY-
ING TO FIND THE RECEIPT FOR THE NECKLACE HE BOUGHT FOR HIS MIS-
TRESS, ABIGAIL CHAMBERS. HIS WIFE, ELIZABETH DANFORTH, WALKS
INTO THE DEN.

Left margin is at space 17.

Page number followed by a period (space 72 or flush with right margin—space 75).

                    ELIZABETH
(OPENS THE DOOR) Well hello, darling. (SLOWLY CLOSES AND LOCKS
THE DOOR BEHIND HER)

Character cue is in all caps (space 43).

Action is in all caps, surrounded by parentheses (except at the beginning of a scene when no parentheses are required).

                    HAROLD
(NERVOUSLY CLOSES THE TOP DESK DRAWER AND LOOKS UP) Hi, dear.
How are you? (LOOKS BACK DOWN AND STARTS SORTING THROUGH SOME PA-
PERS ON HIS DESK) I'm just in here trying to find that letter
from the school board. Have you seen it? (KEEPS LOOKING DOWN,
SHUFFLING THE PAPERS)

                    ELIZABETH
(NOT RESPONDING, SLOWLY WALKS UP TO THE DESK AND JUST STANDS
THERE)

                    HAROLD
Dear? (KEEPS SHUFFLING THE PAPERS AND THEN LOOKS UP. HE SEES HER
RIGHT IN FRONT OF HIS FACE) Ah! (SCREAMS) Damn, you scared me.

                    ELIZABETH
I did, did I? Well what do you have to be scared about? It's only
me.

                    HAROLD
(FLUSTERED) You just surprised me, that's all. (LOOKS DOWN AND
SORTS MORE PAPERS) Where is that thing? I swear I saw it here
this morning.

Dialogue is single-spaced, upper and lowercase text (do keep blocks of dialogue short).

                    ELIZABETH
(CALMLY PULLS THE RECEIPT FROM HER LEFT SHIRT POCKET) Oh, could
this be what you're looking for, darling? (SHE LETS IT HANG IN
FRONT OF HIS FACE)

Double-spaced between changes in dialogue and action lines.

                    HAROLD
(LOOKS UP, SEES THE RECEIPT, AND GRABS IT OUT OF HER HAND) Damn
you. What the hell is this? (CRUMBLES UP THE RECEIPT)

                    ELIZABETH
(STARTS TO CRY) You know damn well what it is Harold. I suppose
you bought that necklace for me. But why would you buy me anything? Why, you haven't bought me anything for years.

                    HAROLD
(STANDS UP, WALKS AROUND THE DESK) Now dear. (TRIES TO HOLD ELIZ-
ABETH'S HAND)

                    ELIZABETH
(PUSHES HIS HAND AWAY) Don't ''now dear'' me, Harold! For God's
sake just admit you're having an affair. Please! I swear you're
nothing but a weak, selfish, lying man. (SLAPS HIM AND WALKS
AWAY. SLAMS THE DOOR ON HER WAY OUT)

                                        FADE OUT

Transition to leave scene.

Television Movies

A made for TV movie is similar in format to a regular motion picture, but much different when it comes to content. The primary difference is that almost all television movies are geared toward middle-aged (and older) female viewers. That might not sound too kind or fair, but it's the reality of television movies (especially when aired on Sunday and Monday nights during football season). With that in mind, remember that all television movie scripts have a high level of emotion, are more character driven than plot driven, and contain less action and violence than your average motion picture feature.

STRUCTURE

The television movie has seven acts, runs anywhere from 90 to 105 pages, and takes up about 90 to 95 minutes of viewing time. Almost all television movies are granted a two-hour block of time. Aside from the seven-act breaks (for commercials), a television movie has the same format as a regular motion picture screenplay (for formatting specifications, see page 202). Some writers prefer to break down their television movie script according to the seven-act breaks, with cliffhangers at the end of each act. Doing so can give you an edge because it shows the production company that you know how a television movie is structured and that you've tailored your script to work within that structure.

On the other hand, you might want to refrain from breaking down your script into seven acts for two reasons. First, all television movie production companies anticipate a spec submission to arrive in the regular motion picture feature format (you won't seem like an amateur if your script isn't divided into seven acts). Second, your television movie script might actually get sold as a feature movie (in which case you'll probably get a lot more money and the seven-act breaks won't matter). After you sell your script as a television movie, you can get together with the production company to put your script into the seven-act formula.

You might still be one of those people who wants to get the act-breaking out of the way from the get go. If that's true, here are the average page lengths for the average television movie, as outlined in David Trotter's *The Screenwriter's Bible* (Silman-James Press). Notice the first act is the longest (to draw the viewer into the story), and that the rest of the acts get progressively shorter (the viewer is already hooked so why not toss in more commercial breaks?):

    Act One: 18-23 pages
    Act Two: 12-15 pages
    Act Three: 12-15 pages
    Act Four: 9-12 pages
    Act Five: 9-12 pages
    Act Six: 9-12 pages
    Act Seven: 9-12 pages

With the end of each act comes a few commercials. As for your script, start each new act on a new page, drop ten lines, center and put the act number. Then drop three or four lines and begin the new scene. As mentioned earlier, every act except the last one should end with a cliffhanger or a moment of drama (this is done to hook viewers into sticking around for the next act, after the commercial break). The most dramatic act breaks should occur at the end of acts one and three, because these are considered the most crucial times when viewers might try to change channels. You don't want anybody changing channels when your script is on the air, and neither does the network.

FORMATTING SPECS

Follow the same formatting specs as you would for a motion picture screenplay (see chapter thirteen).

Electronic Television Movie Script Submissions

It is rare for an agent, producer or story editor to request a television movie script via e-mail, but it might happen. If it does, make sure you get detailed guidelines as to how the script should be submitted and follow them meticulously.

Writers often make mistakes by including a long synopsis or an improperly formatted script that is over 115 pages. And they worry too much about the color of the cover.
—Richard Krevolin, author of *Screenwriting From The Soul* and *How to Adapt Anything into a Screenplay*
(www.profk.com)

QUERY LETTER TO AGENT: TELEVISION MOVIE

Nice, simple letterhead

Sandra K. Warren
5535 Deer Tail Dr.
San Antonio, TX 78647
(210) 555-9999
sandyk@email.com

March 16, 2004

1 line

Jack Scagnetti Talent & Literary Agency
5330 Lankerskim Blvd.
N. Hollywood, CA 91601

1 line

Addresses letter to specific agent and spells name correctly.

Dear Mr. Scagnetti:

1 line

1" margin

I found the name of your agency in *Writer's Market* and I thought you might be interested in seeing my screenplay, ''Hidden Casualties: Battles On The Homefront.'' It's about the custody battle that ensues after Sergeant Sara Raye returns home injured from service in the Persian Gulf War. While Sergeant Raye was in Saudi Arabia, her ex-husband illegally manipulated the courts in another state and stole custody of her three children. Seventeen lawyers told her that there was nothing she could do; that she had lost her children and it would take years to get them back. Citing violation of rights as stipulated in the Soldiers and Sailors Civil Relief Act, she refused to give up. It wasn't until she went public with her story that the Army, in two unprecedented moves, stepped in to right the wrong.

Tells where she found agency and what her script is about. She tells a lot but shows this is a timely and unusual subject. She also quickly reveals conflict and tough battle to overcome problems, and the power of not giving up—things that are appealing in a good story.

Single-spaced text

Mentions the various audiences who will be interested in this story.

''Hidden Casualties'' is a story that will appeal to a wide range of audiences, from those interested in legal matters that bridge military and civilian life to those who served or had loved ones serving in the Persian Gulf, even to those who are serving elsewhere. Medical personnel, single parents and those concerned with women's issues and children's rights will also be interested.

1 line between paragraphs

This story is changing the way the military deals with single parents, and has been discussed in meetings with military lawyers throughout the country. It was profiled on CNN and on all major networks in southern Texas.

Reveals the real-life results of the action taken by the main character.

Tells enough about herself to show she's not a novice, and that tells me I should at least read what she's sent.

I'm a member of SCBWI (Society of Children's Book Writers and Illustrators) and have written multiple books, an educational video and an audiocassette in the educational field. My books include four story books, activity books, a ''how to'' book, reader's theater and a poetry collection.

I look forward to hearing from you. I've enclosed an SASE for your response.

Sincerely,

Signature

Sandra Warren

Encl.: SASE

Comments provided by Jack Scagnetti of the Jack Scagnetti Talent & Literary Agency.

CHAPTER FIFTEEN

THE AUDIO/VIDEO SCRIPT

Audio/Video Scripts for Corporate Clients

Audio-video scripts are used to inform, usually with a goal to instruct (educational videos for corporate clients) or sell (commercials). Video presentations are essential when businesses need to educate those in-house and those outside of the company. They are most often used to train new employees, to convince another company their product is worth investing in, to tell the history and mission of the business, and to explain procedural steps that go into a company's products. On the selling front, audio-video scripts are the backbone of television commercials, and advertising agencies would be lost without them.

FORMAT RATIONALE

Almost all audio-video scripts demand one thing: a clear script that complements the implementation of the ideas on camera. Common elements in audio-video presentations include animation, stock footage, music, illustrations, and narration. The scriptwriter directs the organization and flow of all these elements on the script's page, using an especially effective format—the two-column audio-video (A/V) format. Understanding and using the format is simple: The visual direction and description go on the left side of the page, and the dialogue and audio go on the right. While this certainly is only one way of conveying a message, it is the most effective and popular way to sell a product or communicate a message.

CORPORATE PROGRAMS

If you're producing a short format program to convey a business-to-business message or a business-to-consumer message, the two-column format is most appropriate because it helps clients who don't have a significant background in film or video. They can easily understand the connection between what is heard and what is seen. Also, the two-column format allows for making changes to the first drafts of your script, and ultimately makes it easier to produce.

COMMERCIALS

If you're producing a commercial, the two-column format is ideal for the same reasons explained in the preceding paragraph. Ad agencies and their customers pay thousands upon thousands of dollars for broadcast time, and many believe you have to stuff each spot with tons of information and images. A lot happens in most ten-, twenty-, or thirty-second commercials, and often most of the images are supported by a narration. It seems like some commercials have more scenes than full-length features. For these reasons, the two-column format allows everyone, even the graphic artists and editors, to know what is happening every second, if not every frame. Just be sure not to use too much video jargon; you want to make your script easy to understand for your clients.

FORMATTING SPECS

- Create a header at the top of the page. Include your company's information in the left hand top corner and the client and project information in the right hand corner. This information should be double-spaced, and your company's name should be in all caps.
- Separate the header of the script and the body with a line break.
- Video directions always go on the left side of the page, and audio on the right. The audio directions should always begin on the same line as the last line of the video directions.
- Music directions should be in all caps.
- Narration and dialogue should be in upper- and lower-case text and double-spaced.
- Video directions should be in all caps.
- Sound commentary and direction (other than narration) should be in all caps in parentheses.
- "FADE OUT" at the end of a script indicates that the script is finished.

OTHER DOS AND DON'TS

- Do read your script out loud to make sure the dialogue sounds natural.
- Do set up your A/V script in two columns.
- Don't submit your script via e-mail unless specifically requested.

I've found over the years that working with corporate clients requires a deep knowledge of their business goals and their market—you need to know what they are currently saying to their audience and, more importantly, how they are saying it. As far as the format for a corporate script is concerned, it seems that most clients prefer a script that clearly connects every word or phrase with a specific visual description. For those new to scriptwriting, the most important piece of advice I can offer is pretty simple—just because it sounds good on paper doesn't necessarily mean it will translate to film or video or will be understood when heard by the audience. So, read the script out loud and imagine how it will look if you had the same background and knowledge base as the target audience.

—Kurt Lex Angermeier, Creative Director, Panoptic Media

AUDIO/VIDEO SCRIPT

Include your company's information on the left.

ALL WORLD MEDIA

2222 Ninth St.

New York, NY 10000

(212) 555-1111

CLIENT: Baby Paper Products

PRODUCT: Happy Heinies

TITLE: ``Christmas Diapers''

LENGTH: 45 Seconds

Double-space information in header.
Include client and project information on right.

Separate the header of the script and the body with a line break.

VIDEO:

AUDIO:

OPEN WITH A FROWNING
BABY IN A SANTA HAT
AND CHRISTMAS OUTFIT.

MUSIC: (AWFUL SOUNDING VERSION
OF ``SILENT NIGHT'')

Music directions are in all caps.

NARRATOR: Do you want your

little loved one to have a

soggy Christmas?

Narration and dialogue is in upper- and lower-case text, double-spaced.

Video directions are in all caps.

SHOW SHOT OF INEXPENSIVE
SOGGY DIAPERS COMING APART
ON BABY'S BOTTOM.

(A BABY STARTS WHINING AND CRY-
ING UNCONTROLLABLY IN
BACKGROUND)

SHOT OF SNOWFLAKES FALLING
INTO A DIAPER

MUSIC: (``I'M DREAMING OF A
WHITE CHRISTMAS'')

NARRATOR: Or a happy white

Christmas?

SHOT OF SMILING BABY,
FOLLOWED BY SHOT OF A CLEAN,
WHITE, DRY STURDY DIAPER
ON BABY'S BOTTOM

(BABY GOO-GOOS HAPPILY.)

SHOT OF UGLY YELLOW DIAPER
JUXTAPOSED WITH CLEAN WHITE
DIAPER

Sound comments and direction (other than narration) go in parentheses and are in all caps.

NARRATOR: It's up to you, mom

and dad.

SHOT OF HAPPY BABY HOLDING
HAPPY HEINIES PACKAGE

NARRATOR: This holiday season,

make the right choice.

Indicates this script is finished.

FADE OUT.

Video always goes on the left side of the page, audio on the right. Notice the audio directions begin on the same line as the last line of the video directions.

CHAPTER SIXTEEN

THE PLAY SCRIPT

The Stage Play

STRUCTURE

Most plays contain one, two or three acts (some even have four or five acts), depending on what the playwright deems is the most appropriate length for what he or she is trying to accomplish. Using the following formatting specifics, plan on about one minute per page when performed out loud. Script lengths are generally 90 pages for a three-act play (30 pages per act), 100 to 105 pages for a two-act play (50 to 52 pages per act), and 20 to 50 pages for a one-act play.

Despite the number of acts and pages a play possesses, all plays should follow the basic "dramatic structure" and have three overarching movements—a beginning, a middle, and an end. Here's a rough sketch of what the overall dramatic structure of your play should look like, as outlined in Jeffrey Hatcher's *The Art & Craft of Playwriting* (Writer's Digest Books):

PART ONE (15-30 PERCENT OF THE PLAY)

Start of play.
Introduction of characters, place, time, setting or exposition.
Introduction of the primary inciting event.
Initial point of attack or primary conflict.
Introduction of the central dramatic question.

PART TWO (50-75 PERCENT OF THE PLAY)

Characters embark on journey/struggle/search for answers/goals.
Conflicts with other characters, events, circumstances.
Characters reassess situations, respond to obstacles and challenges, plan new tactics, succeed, fail, attack, retreat, surprise and are surprised, encounter major reversals (rising action).
A crisis is reached.
Characters embark on an action that will resolve the crisis and lead inexorably to the conclusion.

PART THREE (5-25 PERCENT OF THE PLAY)

The major characters or combatants engage in a final conflict (climax).
The character's goal is achieved or lost.

The central dramatic question is answered.
The actions suggest the themes or ideas of the play.
Following the climax is the resolution, in which a new order is established.
End of play.

The Title Page
SUBMISSION TIPS

The title page includes the name of the play, how many acts it contains, and your name and contact information (or the agent's name and contact information if you have representation). It also indicates if the play is based on a novel.

FORMATTING SPECS
- The title should be in all caps, centered, about one-third of the way down the page.
- Drop four lines and type (depending on what you write) either "A One-Act Play by," or "A Play in Two Acts by" or "A Play in Three Acts by."
- Drop four lines again and type your name (if your play is written with another person, use an ampersand between your names).
- If your play is based on a novel, drop six lines and type "Based on the novel *Novel's Title*," drop two more lines and type "by Author's Name."
- In the lower right-hand corner, put your name, address, phone number, and e-mail, single-spaced, in regular text (not all caps).
- If you have an agent, type "Representation:" skip a line and put the agent's name, address, phone number, and e-mail instead of yours.

OTHER DOS AND DON'TS
- Don't number the title page.
- Do include your agent's name and contact information if you have representation.
- Don't submit your play via e-mail unless specifically requested.

> These days it's tough for a new play to be produced in this country. Tough for experienced playwrights and more than intimidating for the struggling writer—the comer who keeps coming but never seems to arrive, or the novice without a church. But that's a challenge the talented, ambitious writer meets head-on. The tougher climate simply means our plays have to be better. So we'll make them better. We'll write the plays the audience stays for. We'll write the plays that compel.
>
> —Jeffrey Hatcher, *The Art & Craft of Playwriting*

TITLE PAGE: PLAY

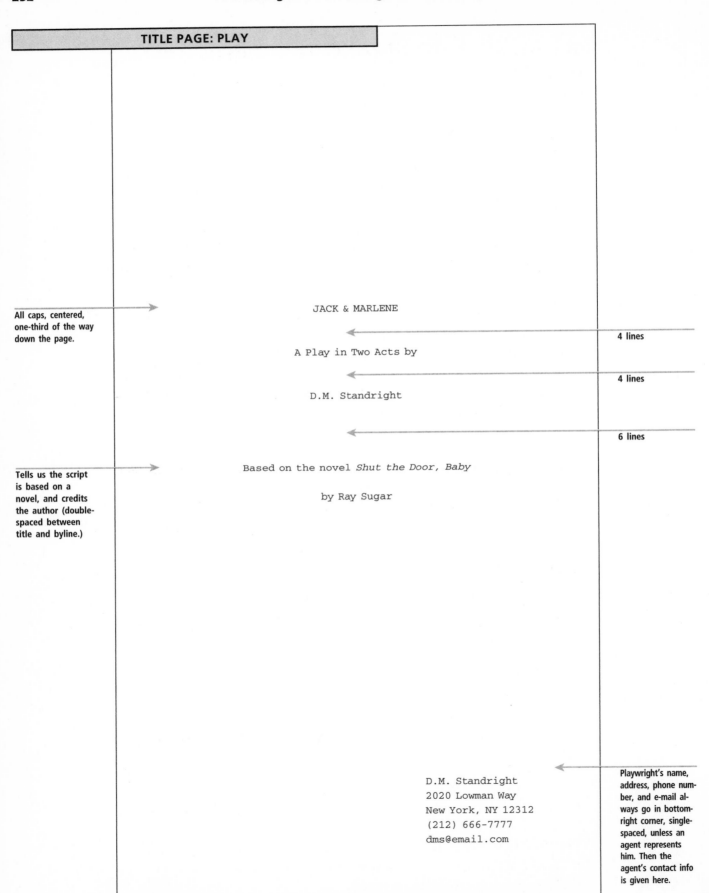

All caps, centered, one-third of the way down the page.

JACK & MARLENE

4 lines

A Play in Two Acts by

4 lines

D.M. Standright

6 lines

Tells us the script is based on a novel, and credits the author (double-spaced between title and byline.)

Based on the novel *Shut the Door, Baby*

by Ray Sugar

D.M. Standright
2020 Lowman Way
New York, NY 12312
(212) 666-7777
dms@email.com

Playwright's name, address, phone number, and e-mail always go in bottom-right corner, single-spaced, unless an agent represents him. Then the agent's contact info is given here.

Act and Scene Breakdown Page

SUBMISSION TIPS

The act and scene breakdown page lists the acts and scenes in the play and provides a quick outline of the play's contents.

FORMATTING SPECS

- Number the act and scene breakdown page (and the first three introductory pages detailed later) with a lowercase Roman numeral i, four lines from the top of the page, flush with the right margin.
- Drop four lines and type the play's title in all caps, underlined, and centered.
- Drop four more lines below the title, and on the left margin (about 1″) type "ACT ONE" in all caps, followed by a series of ellipses that move across the page to where you describe the day and date of the act. Do this for each subsequent act, triple-spacing between each line.
- If Act One is divided into two scenes, then the first line of the page breakdown reads ACT ONE: Scene One, followed by the series of ellipses.
- Scene Two appears two lines beneath the first line and looks the same.
- On the left margin, 1″ from the bottom of the page, include the approximate running time of the play. The words RUNNING TIME: should be in all caps and on the next line indicate the play's time length.

OTHER DOS AND DON'TS

- Don't forget to include the play's running time, written out (two hours and thirty minutes, as opposed to 2 hrs 30 min).
- Do include the number and time of intermissions in the running time.

Cast of Characters Page

SUBMISSION TIPS

The cast of characters page follows the act and scene breakdown and provides information about your characters.

FORMATTING SPECS

- The case of characters page should have the Roman numeral ii in the top right corner flush with the right margin.
- The words CAST OF CHARACTERS should be in all caps, centered, eight lines from the top of the page.
- Drop four lines and include each character's name (in all caps); follow each name with a series of ellipses and a brief description (in all caps) of that character.
- The character descriptions should include whatever you think is most important.

OTHER DOS AND DON'TS

- Don't forget to include secondary characters (those with few to no lines).
- Do keep character descriptions simple.

ACT AND SCENE BREAKDOWN PAGE: PLAY

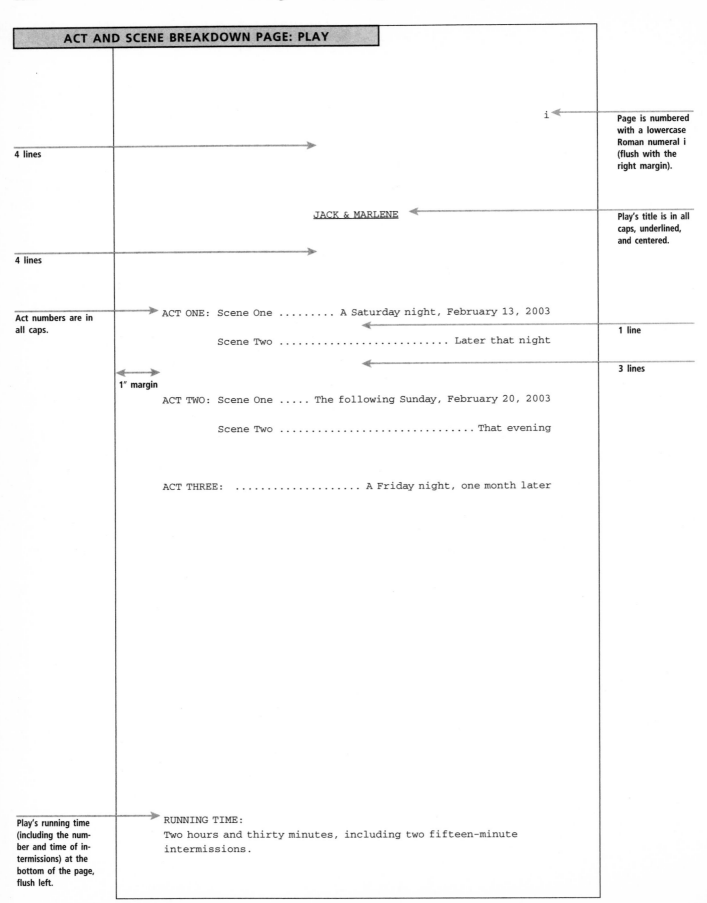

i

4 lines

Page is numbered with a lowercase Roman numeral i (flush with the right margin).

JACK & MARLENE

Play's title is in all caps, underlined, and centered.

4 lines

Act numbers are in all caps.

ACT ONE: Scene One .... A Saturday night, February 13, 2003

Scene Two .... Later that night

1 line

3 lines

1" margin

ACT TWO: Scene One ..... The following Sunday, February 20, 2003

Scene Two .... That evening

ACT THREE: .... A Friday night, one month later

Play's running time (including the number and time of intermissions) at the bottom of the page, flush left.

RUNNING TIME:
Two hours and thirty minutes, including two fifteen-minute intermissions.

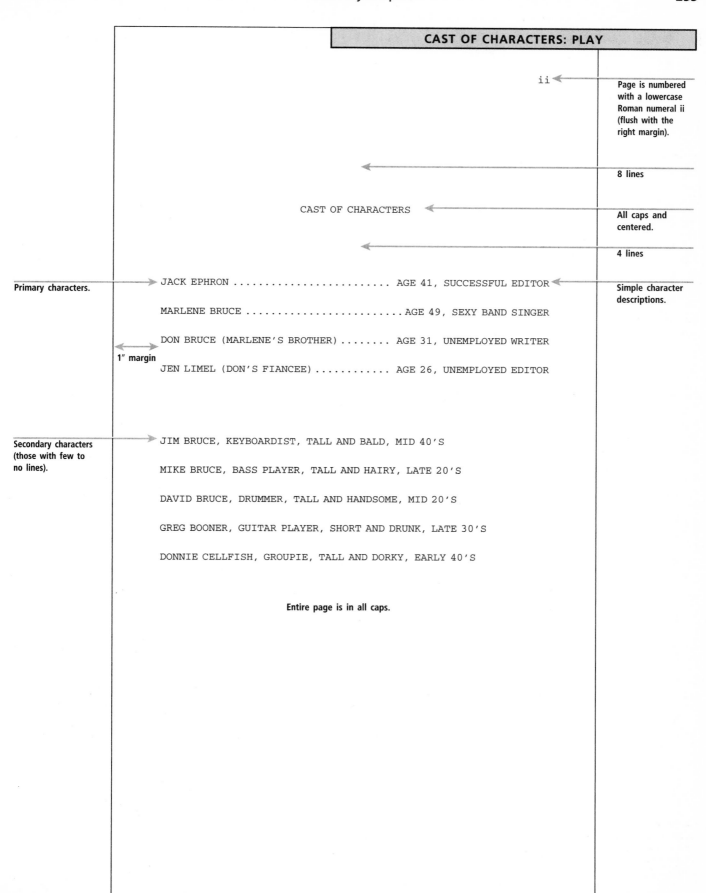

CAST OF CHARACTERS: PLAY

ii — Page is numbered with a lowercase Roman numeral ii (flush with the right margin).

← 8 lines

CAST OF CHARACTERS ← All caps and centered.

← 4 lines

Primary characters. → JACK EPHRON .... AGE 41, SUCCESSFUL EDITOR ← Simple character descriptions.

MARLENE BRUCE .... AGE 49, SEXY BAND SINGER

DON BRUCE (MARLENE'S BROTHER) .... AGE 31, UNEMPLOYED WRITER

1" margin

JEN LIMEL (DON'S FIANCEE) .... AGE 26, UNEMPLOYED EDITOR

Secondary characters (those with few to no lines). → JIM BRUCE, KEYBOARDIST, TALL AND BALD, MID 40'S

MIKE BRUCE, BASS PLAYER, TALL AND HAIRY, LATE 20'S

DAVID BRUCE, DRUMMER, TALL AND HANDSOME, MID 20'S

GREG BOONER, GUITAR PLAYER, SHORT AND DRUNK, LATE 30'S

DONNIE CELLFISH, GROUPIE, TALL AND DORKY, EARLY 40'S

Entire page is in all caps.

The Setting Page

SUBMISSION TIPS

The setting page details the setting of the play (you will also need to use a short setting description at the beginning of each scene) and is the last of your introductory pages (numbered page iii).

FORMATTING SPECS

- The word SETTING: appears in all caps, underlined, flush with the left margin, about eight lines from the top of the page.
- Tab 1½" from the left margin and begin the body of your description on the same line.
- Type the setting information in all caps or regular text, double-spaced (the sample on page 257 uses all caps).
- Some playwrights like to put the cast of characters and the setting on the same page, with the setting on the top of the page and the cast of characters below it. Whatever you decide, be consistent.

OTHER DOS AND DON'TS

- Do clearly detail everything about the setting of the play, including all furniture and props that should appear on the state, as well as the type of lighting.
- Don't leave out important details of the state in an effort to be brief; include every prop that should appear on the state and where it should appear.

> Realism is relatively new to theater. And those playwrights who require realistic sets stick to one or two. The rule of thumb: If the action requires a set, make it realistic. If the action doesn't, allow for a lot less.
>
> —Jeffrey Hatcher, *The Art & Craft of Playwriting*

SETTING PAGE: PLAY

iii

← 8 lines

Page is numbered with a lowercase Roman numeral iii (flush with the right margin).

All caps, flush with left margin (about eight lines from the top of the page).

Tab for the body of the description is set at 1½" from the left margin.

All caps (optional) and double-spaced text.

SETTING: BASEMENT OF JIM BRUCE'S HOUSE, THE BAND ROOM, STAGE

LEFT AND A SMALL SECTION, STAGE RIGHT, FRONT YARD.

RIGHT WALL OF BAND ROOM HAS A WASHER AND DRYER, A

FEW OLD COUCHES WITH A FEW DOGS SITTING ON THEM,

AND A SINK. LOTS OF BEER AND WHISKEY BOTTLES ARE ON

THE WASHER AND DRYER. A LIGHTED CIGARETTE IS EMIT-

TING SMOKE FROM AN ASHTRAY. THREE TALL BURNING CAN-

DLES ARE ALSO ON THE WASHER AND DRYER.

← 2 lines

UPSTAGE RIGHT WALL OF BAND ROOM, STAIRS LEADING TO

THE FIRST FLOOR.

← 2 lines

CENTER WALL OF BAND ROOM, BAND STAGE. DRUM SET, TWO

SETS OF KEYBOARDS, BASS AMP, GUITAR AMP, TWO MICRO-

PHONE STANDS, MONITORS. IN BACK, SOUNDBOARD AND

DESK WITH COMPUTER ON IT. CANDLES BURNING ON TOP OF

SOUNDBOARD AND ON TOP OF DESK AROUND COMPUTER.

Clearly specified everything about the setting of the play.

LEFT WALL BAND ROOM, ONE SMALL COUCH WITH A BROWN

DOG LYING ON IT. A P.A. SPEAKER IS ON ONE END OF THE

COUCH AND AN END TABLE IS ON THE OTHER. THE END TA-

BLE HAS LOTS OF LIGHTED CANDLES ON IT.

The Script Pages

After the introductory pages comes the play script itself. The script pages include the following information, which should be formatted as specified.

DIALOGUE

Following the scene description, double-space and begin the dialogue. Formatting the dialogue is simple. The speaking character's name appears in all caps, centered. Double-space and begin the text of the dialogue. The dialogue should be in regular text (not all caps) and single-spaced.

PARENTHETICALS

Parentheticals include description, expression or direction that helps the actor or director know what you intend. There are two types of parentheticals in playwrighting:

1. A parenthetical that appears within the dialogue lines. When the direction indicates an action or emotion to occur while the character is speaking, the parenthetical is put in lines of dialogue. If the parenthetical is used to signal the character's mood or delivery, it is placed between the character's name and the first word of dialogue. All the text is lowercase.

2. A parenthetical that falls between or outside of spoken lines. When there are more detailed directions (often physical directions), the parenthetical will be set apart from the dialogue by a triple-space, and the text will have the same indented margins as the dialogue (beginning five spaces in from the left margin). The text is both upper and lowercase, and is single-spaced within the parenthetical. Triple-space to go back to dialogue.

THE ACT ENDING

To end an act simply type *"Curtain Falls"* (italicize or underline it), centered, at the bottom of the page.

FORMATTING SPECS

- Use 1″ margins.
- The first page is numbered with the Arabic numeral 1.
- On this first page, center the play's title in all caps, eight lines from the top.
- Double-space after the title and put the words "Act One" (don't type the quotations), in upper and lowercase, centered, and underlined.
- Double-space again and put the scene number in upper and lowercase (Scene One).
- Skip four lines and begin the scene description/introduction, which should just be a few double-spaced lines that describe and set up the scene.
- Character cues should be placed centered above the line of dialogue.
- The dialogue should be single-spaced and double-spaced when a new character starts to speak.
- When a character's name is used in a parenthetical it should appear in all caps.
- When a character enters a room both the character's name and the work ENTERS should appear in all caps.

OTHER DOS AND DON'TS

- Do number all your script pages and put a period after the number.
- Do use all caps for the scene description/introduction.
- Don't submit your script via e-mail unless specifically requested by the publisher.

1.

JACK & MARLENE

<u>Act One</u>

Scene One

A PURPLE LIGHT SHINES ON WASHER AND DRYER. THE BAND BEGINS PLAY-
ING IN THE PITCH DARK, CENTER STAGE. JACK, DON AND JEN ENTER FROM
THE STEPS. A BRIGHT FLOOD OF RED LIGHTS SHINES DOWN ON MARLENE.
SHE STARTS TO SING.

MARLENE

(looks up from her microphone, notices JACK in the room. She
stops singing and screams) Ahhhh! Oh my God. You must be Jack.

(the music stops)

JIM

So Marlene, are you ready to put a bag over your head yet?

JACK

(laughing nervously, looks at MARLENE) So I guess I shouldn't
ask you to marry me yet. I'll wait a few hours. (everybody
laughs, JACK takes a sip of beer and looks at MARLENE) I'm just
teasing of course. It is good to finally meet you.

MARLENE

It's good to meet you, too.

JACK

Thanks. Well, you can go back to singing now. We'll just watch.

(JACK walks over to the washer and dryer and starts talking with
DON and JEN. The band starts up again. MARLENE begins to sing.
JACK stops talking and stares at MARLENE, transfixed by her
voice, her lips on the microphone and her radiating beauty.)

JACK

(glowing with delight, yells over the music to DON and JEN) Wow.
I am blown away. My God, you guys didn't tell me she was so sexy,
so lively.
(They watch the band play the rest of the song. The music stops,
DON, JEN and JACK clap.)

JACK

(impressed, looking in the general direction of the band) That
was great. Really. (focuses in on MARLENE, smiles) A real treat.

MARLENE

(blushing) Well thank you.

(MARLENE moves from behind the microphone, stares at JACK and
then walks up the steps. Stage goes black.)

<u>Curtain Falls</u>

Annotations (margin notes):

- Page number with Arabic numeral 1.
- Play's title, centered and in all caps.
- 1 line
- Act number goes in upper and lower-case, centered, and underlined.
- Scene number is in upper and lowercase (not underlined).
- 1 line
- 1 line
- Briefly describes the setting for this scene.
- Character cue is in all caps, centered.
- Double-space between the character's name and dialogue.
- 1" margin
- Dialogue is single-spaced (double-spaced when a new person starts to speak).
- Character's name in a parenthetical appears in all caps.
- Parenthetical within the dialogue lines—signals the character's mood or delivery.
- Parenthetical falls outside of spoken lines—more detailed directions (often physical).
- Lets us know the act is finished.

Once Your Play Is Finished

When your play is finished you need to begin marketing it, which might take longer than writing it. Before you begin marketing it, however, have your script bound (two brads and a cover are fine) and copyrighted with the Copyright Office of the Library of Congress, or registered with the Writers Guild of America (7000 West Third Street, Los Angeles, California 90048-4329, [800] 548-4532, www.wga.org). Write either agency and ask for information and an application.

Your first goal will be to at least get a reading of your play. You might be lucky and get a small production. Community theaters or smaller regional houses are good places to start. Volunteer at a local theater. You will get a sense of how a theater operates, the various elements that go into presenting a play, and what can and cannot be done physically as well as dramatically. Personal contacts cannot be overemphasized. Get to know the literary manager or artistic director of local theaters, which is the best way to get your script considered for production. Find out about any playwrights groups in your area through local theaters or the drama departments of nearby colleges and universities. Use your creativity to connect with people who might be able to push your work.

Contests can be a good way to get noticed. Many playwrighting contests offer as a prize at least a staged reading and often a full production. Once you've had a reading or workshop production, set your sights on a small production. Use this as a learning experience.

Seeing your play on stage can help you view it more objectively and give you the chance to correct any flaws or inconsistencies. Incorporate into your revisions any comments and ideas from the actors, director or even audience members. Use a small production as a marketing tool—keep track of all the press reviews and any interviews you give.

After you've been produced on a small scale, you can take your play in several directions. You can aim for a larger commercial production; you can try to get it published; or you can seek an artistic grant. (Choosing one direction does not rule out pursuing others at the same time.) Once you have successfully pursued at least one of those avenues, look for an agent. *The Dramatists Sourcebook*, published annually by Theatre Communications Group (520 Eighth Avenue, 24th Floor, New York City, New York 10018, [212] 609-5900, www.tcg.org), lists opportunities in all these areas. The Dramatists Guild of America (1501 Broadway, Suite 701, New York City, New York 10036, [212] 398-9366, www.dramaguild.com) has three helpful publications: a bimonthly newsletter with articles, news and up-to-date information and opportunities; a quarterly journal; and an annual directory that lists theaters, agents, workshops, grants, and contests.

To submit your play to larger theaters you'll need to put together a submission package. This will include a one-page query letter briefly describing the play to the literary manager (also called a dramaturg). Mention any reviews and give the number of cast members and sets. You should also send a two- to three-page synopsis, a ten-page sample of the most interesting section of your play, your resume, and your press kit. Be sure not to send your complete manuscript to anyone until it is requested. For more on querying and submitting, see page 204 in Submitting Your Screenplay to an Agent or Production Company.

part 5

VERSE

CHAPTER SEVENTEEN

POETRY

Cover Letter

SUBMISSION TIPS

Until recent years, most editors didn't expect or want cover letters along with a poetry submission; however, now many editors do specify that they want cover letters.

The best approach is to read a publication's listing in *Poet's Market* and/or to request a copy of its submission guidelines (see Request for Guidelines Letter on page 22).

FORMATTING SPECS

- The cover letter should be no longer than one page, and not a tightly packed page.
- Introduce the work you are submitting (i.e. enclosed are three poems . . .).
- Provide a brief biography that includes listing some of your published work if you have any and your background, including occupation, hobbies, interests or other life events that have bearing on your work.
- Note why you think the poetry you're submitting would be appropriate for the publication (giving you a chance to show your familiarity with the publication).
- Mention if the work you are submitting has been previously published or if you are making simultaneous submissions. Check to make sure simultaneous submissions are accepted by the publication before sending them.

OTHER DOS AND DON'TS

- Don't ever request guidelines in the cover letter of your submission. It's too late at this point.
- Don't ask for criticism. You may get it, but it's not the editor's job to coach you.

Electronic Cover Letter

SUBMISSION TIPS

Before you send a cover letter and poems to a publication via e-mail, make sure they accept electronic submissions by contacting the publication directly or checking out their writer's guidelines. Never send poems via e-mail unless you have permission from the editor or if their submission guidelines state it is acceptable.

FORMATTING SPECS

- Include the same information in your cover letter as you would in a paper cover letter—name, address, phone, fax, etc. It's not necessary to include your e-mail address in the body of the e-mail, since the editor can easily click "Reply" to respond.
- Use the subject line to introduce the theme or concept of your poems, unless the publisher's guidelines indicate what you should type there.
- Follow the same format you would with a paper cover letter, including the date, salutation, and block paragraph format.

OTHER DOS AND DON'TS

- Don't use all caps or exclamation points in the subject line.
- Don't insert clip art graphics or other images in your cover letter. Keep it simple.
- Do use formal communication like you would in a paper cover letter.

Since *Poetry Midwest* is freely available online, there is no excuse for not reading an issue to sample the type of work the journal tends to feature. Poets should do their research before submitting to any journal; otherwise, they may be wasting not only their time, but the editor's time, too. Online journals are deluged with submissions, and following posted guidelines will let the editor know you want your submission seriously considered.

—**Matthew W. Schmeer, Editor/Publisher,** *Poetry Midwest*

COVER LETTER: POETRY

Susan Sturmundrang
43 Clovernook Place
Whittier, CA 90054
(310) 555-6700
Fax: (310) 555-6283
E-mail: ssturm@email.com

Complete contact information (you don't need to include the e-mail address if you're submitting via e-mail).

January 5, 2004

1 line

Addresses a specific editor.

Ben Byron
Poetry Review
444 Canal St.
St. Louis, MO 55435

1 line

Dear Mr. Byron:

1 line

Introduces the work being submitted.

Enclosed are five of my poems on a theme of alienation and root-lessness in modern culture, which I believe would fit well with your review's focus on modern cultural issues.

1 line

Introduces the poet, including publication credits and relevant information.

My poetry has been published in a number of literary and gen-eral-interest magazines, including *The Atlantic Monthly* and *The New Yorker*. I teach English Literature at the University of Cali-fornia-Riverside and have spent most of my life wandering the country in search of a place to call home.

1 line between paragraphs.

Notifies editor of simultaneous submissions.

I understand from your guidelines that simultaneous submissions are acceptable, and I wanted to let you know that I have submit-ted the enclosed poems to two other publications for which I also believe they are appropriate.

Single-spaced text

Thanks very much for your time and consideration. I look forward to hearing from you.

Best wishes,

Signature

Susan Sturmundrang

Notes enclosure; the SASE isn't necessary if you're sending your poems via e-mail.

Encl.: SASE

POETRY COVER LETTER: MISTAKES TO AVOID

Include all of your contact information here—name, address, phone, and e-mail.

Don't send your submission to "Poetry Editor" unless the publisher's guidelines specifically request you do so.

Find out how many poems a publication wants you to send by reading their submission guidelines.

Be polite—thank the editor for his or her time and indicate that you look forward to hearing back.

Don't forget to include a SASE unless you're sending your submission via e-mail or the publisher's guidelines stipulate that submissions aren't returned.

Andrew Angst
(784) 555-8585

Poetry Editor
Poetry Review
444 Canal St.
St. Louis, MO 55435

Dear Sir or Madam,

I am sending you a collection of my poems—there are 56 of them in all. They cover all sorts of issues, from global politics to deep personal feelings of love and loss.

I hope you'll publish at least one or two of my poems in your magazine. I've been writing poems since I was a child and would give anything to have them published.

If you don't want to publish them please return them to me.

Sincerely,

Andrew Angst

Most publications have a specific focus, and you should note why you think your poems would be appropriate.

Provide some background information on yourself.

Don't ask for your poems to be returned to you—your should be sending neatly typed copies, not your originals.

Poem Submission

SUBMISSION TIPS

In poetry above all other forms, substance supersedes format. Your submissions should be neat and correspond to the rules of the genre. You don't get any points for fancy fonts or colored paper. In fact, your submission is likely to be viewed less favorably if you garnish it in such ways.

The best approach is to read a publication's listing in *Poet's Market* and/or to request a copy of its submission guidelines (see Request for Guidelines Letter on page 22).

Generally, submit three to five poems at a time, though some editors prefer seven or more poems if they feature a poet. Again, the publication's guidelines will help here.

FORMATTING SPECS

- Use standard white bond, laser, or ink-jet paper.
- Submit each poem on a separate page, except for haiku.
- Center a title in all caps above the poem. If there is a subtitle, use upper and lower case and underline it. Skip one line and center below the title.
- Put your name, address, phone number, e-mail, and fax number in the upper left corner.
- Fold the poems together into thirds for insertion into the envelope. Fold the cover letter separately and place it on top of the poems.
- If your poem continues over to a second sheet, start the second page with a new stanza whenever possible or applicable.
- Editor preferences vary on whether submissions should be double- or single-spaced. Check the publication's guidelines. Unless otherwise directed, single-space.
- If the line of poetry extends beyond the margin, indent the second line. If you are double-spacing the entire poem, single-space the continuation of a line.
- Put in an extra space (or two, when double-spacing) before the beginning of a stanza.
- Margins will vary, depending on the poem, but generally run at least 2″-2½″ on the sides, with the poem roughly centered top to bottom on the page.
- If you don't use a cover letter, find out if the publication wants biographical information and include such information on a separate sheet under the centered, capitalized heading "BIOGRAPHICAL INFORMATION" or "ABOUT THE POET."
- If your poem runs more than one page, use a header (generally, the title or your last name) in the top left corner and a page number in the top right corner on the second and subsequent pages.
- Paper clip pages of the same poem together, but submit one-page poems loose-leaf, folded.

OTHER DOS AND DON'TS

- Do enclose a SASE, which makes it easier for the editor to respond.
- Don't handwrite your poems.
- Don't use onion skin, colored, or erasable paper.

- Don't put copyright symbols or information on your poem. It's copyrighted regardless of this, and the only thing you're likely to accomplish is to insult the editor's intelligence or intentions.
- Do address your submission and cover letter, if any, by name to the poetry editor or other editor who routinely reviews poetry submission.
- Don't submit previously published work or make simultaneous submissions unless you know the publication accepts them and you note it in a cover letter.

Electronic Poem Submission
SUBMISSION TIPS
E-mail submissions are only acceptable when you have permission from the publication or if their submission guidelines indicate it is acceptable. Don't forget to include your cover letter in the body of your e-mail.

FORMATTING SPECS
- Before you send the poems, find out how the editor prefers to receive files. He may want the poems attached as separate files or included in the body of the e-mail.
- Follow the same formatting specs as above for a paper manuscript submission.
- If the editor doesn't specify a particular file format for an attached file, save it as a text file. Most word processing programs can read basic text files.

OTHER DOS AND DON'TS
- Don't use all caps in your subject line.
- Do ask for specific file format guidelines to make sure the editor can open your files.
- Don't justify text or align the right margin.
- Don't put any copyright information on your poem. It's copyrighted when you write it, and the editor is aware of this.

> Note, too, the number of poems the editor recommends including in the e-mail submission. If no quantity is given specifically for e-mails, go with the number of poems an editor recommends submitting in general.
>
> —*Poet's Market*

POETRY SUBMISSION

Author contact
information goes in
upper left corner

Walt Whitman
1819 Poetry Lane
West Hills, NY 10000
(123)555-4321
waltwhit@email.com

MIRACLES

Center title in all
caps.

4 lines

Margins should be
2″ - 2½″ on both
sides.

Why, who makes much of a miracle?
As to me I know of nothing else but miracles,
Whether I walk the streets of Manhattan,
Or dart my sight over the roofs of houses to-
          ward the sky,

Single space unless
otherwise directed
by publisher's
guidelines.

Or wade with naked feet along the beach just in
          the edge of the water,
Or stand under the trees in the woods,
Or talk by day with anyone I love, or sleep in
          the bed at night with anyone I love,
Or sit at the table at dinner with the rest,
Or look at strangers opposite me riding in the

Indent a line if it
runs over.

          car,
Or watch honeybees busy around the hive of a sum-
          mer forenoon,
Or animals feeding in the fields,
Or birds, or the wonderfulness of insects in
          the air,
Or the wonderfulness of the sundown, or of
          stars shining so quiet and bright,
Or the exquisite delicate thin curve of the new
          moon in spring;
These with the rest, on and all, are to me
          miracles,
The whole referring, yet each distinct and in
          its place.

To me every hour of the light and dark is a
          miracle,
Every cubic inch of space is a miracle,
Every square yard of the surface of the earth is
          spread with the same,
Every foot of the interior swarms with the
          same.
To me the sea is a continual miracle,
The fishes that swim-the rocks-the motion of
          the waves-the ships with men in them,
What stranger miracles are there?

CHAPTER EIGHTEEN

GREETING CARDS

What to Submit

The extremely short form of greeting card verse, concepts, and gags doesn't leave much room for formatting worries. They can be submitted on anything from $3'' \times 5''$ card to standard sheets of paper or electronically. The preferences of various markets vary, so contact the company and receive a copy of its submission guidelines. Each publisher is different, so above all else, follow the guidelines they indicate.

Writersmarket.com is a good source for contacts at a variety of specialty and niche players. The larger companies, such as Hallmark and American Greetings are reluctant to issue open invitations for submissions, though you can call for submission information.

Greeting card submissions each need to be given an I.D. number. It is up to each individual how they want to I.D. their submissions. They can be given sequential numbers based on the year or by anything that makes it easy for the publisher to identify the submissions and for the writer to reference them.

FORMATTING SPECS

- Include a brief cover letter detailing how many card ideas you've submitted and why you think they're appropriate for the line.
- In the cover letter, mention if you are making simultaneous submissions.
- Submit two to four greeting card ideas per page or card.
- Margins are irrelevant for most submissions, but for versions with longer blocks of copy, follow the guidelines for poetry, with margins of at least 2″ on the side and the verse roughly centered vertically on the page.
- Single-space when a line of verse needs to run on to a new line of the page. Double-space between lines of verse.
- If you have illustration ideas, detail them in parentheses before the verse.
- Enclose an SASE for editors to respond, but make your submissions disposable. It's cheaper and easier to print them over again from your computer than it is to keep recycling paper versions.
- Include each idea's I.D. number before the verse.
- Include your name, address, phone number, and e-mail in the upper left corner. Also include your name again before each sumission.
- Pay attention to where your lines break and break them where you see fit.
- If it is not obvious, indicate on what page of the card a line will be placed.

OTHER DOS AND DON'TS

- Do address your submission and cover letter to the appropriate contact person.
- Do get submission guidelines in writing (using a letter similar to the Request for Guidelines Letter on page 22) whenever they're available before you submit. Preferences vary widely.
- Don't request guidelines in a cover letter along with submissions. Get the guidelines first.
- Don't make simultaneous submissions unless they're okay with the company.
- Do research the company and the line before you make your submission. When possible, visit the company's Web site and check out samples of its line in stores.
- Don't bother with putting a copyright on your submissions. They're copyrighted regardless, and the only thing you will accomplish is insulting the reader.
- Don't suggest an illustration unless it is necessary.
- Don't submit more than ten to fifteen ideas in a submission.

ELECTRONIC SUBMISSIONS

Because of their brevity, greeting card verse and gags are ideal for electronic submissions. Check submission guidelines or listings in writersmarket.com for details on whether a company accepts submissions via e-mail.

If you do submit electronically, your best bet will likely be a format similar to the print version modeled here. Essentially, your cover letter will be the e-mail, with the submission either following the letter text in the body of the e-mail message or as an attachment. If you are making several submissions, group them consecutively after the letter message or in a single attachment rather than creating the hassle of multiple attachments of very small files. Make sure you find out what file format an editor prefers to receive files.

Writers should always create a sentiment true to life experience, but not so specific that it limits its audience. For example, a card is much more sendable if you keep physical descriptions of a person's face or surroundings out of the sentiment. Also, think about who might be sending the card. If you believe the sentiment could come from more than one person (perhaps a couple), try not to limit the sentiment by using "I" in the copy.

Noelle Sanderson, director of editorial, *Paramount Cards, Inc.*

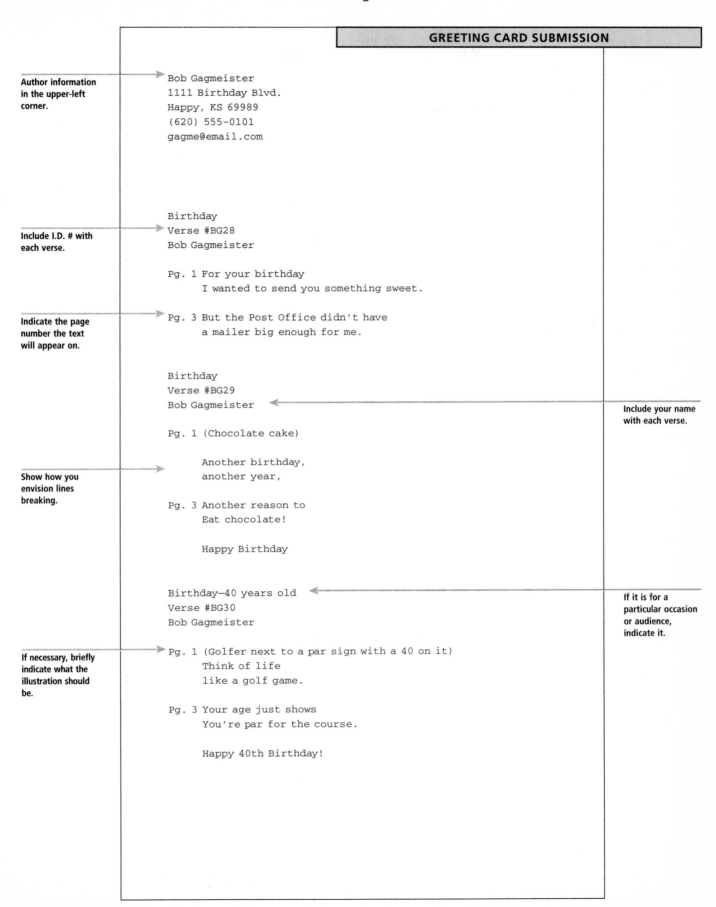

GREETING CARD SUBMISSION

Author information in the upper-left corner.

Bob Gagmeister
1111 Birthday Blvd.
Happy, KS 69989
(620) 555-0101
gagme@email.com

Include I.D. # with each verse.

Birthday
Verse #BG28
Bob Gagmeister

Pg. 1 For your birthday
        I wanted to send you something sweet.

Indicate the page number the text will appear on.

Pg. 3 But the Post Office didn't have
        a mailer big enough for me.

Birthday
Verse #BG29
Bob Gagmeister

Include your name with each verse.

Pg. 1 (Chocolate cake)

Show how you envision lines breaking.

        Another birthday,
        another year,

Pg. 3 Another reason to
        Eat chocolate!

        Happy Birthday

Birthday—40 years old
Verse #BG30
Bob Gagmeister

If it is for a particular occasion or audience, indicate it.

If necessary, briefly indicate what the illustration should be.

Pg. 1 (Golfer next to a par sign with a 40 on it)
        Think of life
        like a golf game.

Pg. 3 Your age just shows
        You're par for the course.

        Happy 40th Birthday!

Appendix

Record Keeping and Forms

Some freelancers keep detailed forms tracking submissions of queries and manuscripts to publications and other markets. But the time required and paperwork generated by such efforts yields questionable value.

In the interests of saving time and forests, sensible use of your computer and other everyday records can eliminate need for tedious sets of specialized logs. With computer memory as cheap as it is today, there's no reason not to keep everything you do on your computer hard drive in perpetuity. The trick is simply organizing your hard drive in a way that will permit you to go back and grab the information when you need it.

The key is to keep the information you generate and back it up regularly. Even if you don't back up regularly and your hard drive crashes, the records you lose won't likely be as valuable as the time you would have wasted filling out logs. And you can usually retrieve most of the data from a stricken hard drive, anyway, with some professional help.

Following is an outline of the types of records you actually need and the most painless ways to keep them.

SUBMISSION TRACKING CHECKLIST

Your calendar/appointment book and computer should provide all the record keeping you need when it comes to queries and manuscript submissions. Here's all you need to do to track submissions:

- Keep a special folder or folders for queries, with file names descriptive enough that you'll be able to understand what they represent. When you need to keep up with how long it's been since you made a query, use the View menu of Windows to display your queries by date. A side benefit of saving your queries is having a ready supply of templates to use in creating new ones.
- Use a similar strategy for manuscript submissions by keeping a file of cover letters. If it's important to you to have a record of when a query or manuscript was accepted or rejected, the rights sold or the fee, make a notation on the query or cover letter file when you receive word.
- For an easy, paper free way to keep track of your submissions, writersmarket.com offers a Submission Tracker when you subscribe to their interactive Web site. The searchable database allows you to find the markets you want to submit to, and the Submission Tracker keeps a record of what you sent, when you sent it, and whether or not you received a reply. It will even remind you when you need to follow-up.

CONTACT TRACKING

It's a good idea to track contacts, either in the marketing or preparation of articles and books—but it's a bad idea to create mounds of paper to do this. The computer is the perfect place to keep such lists, which are constantly changing. Here are some tips on using your computer to track contacts:

- Keep files that make sense for you, such as a folder with magazine editors, book editors or editors in a particular specialized market where you work.
- Likewise, keep files of contacts for each project or a master file of all your contacts. Database programs were designed to keep this kind of information, but you may find it easier to store your contact list as a word processing file and use the find function to retrieve the names or other information you need.

INCOME AND EXPENSE TRACKING TIPS

You can track a variety of expenses several different ways. Regardless of whether you're reimbursed by a publisher for expenses, you'll need to track them for tax purposes. The IRS expects some kind of regular record-keeping system for both income and expenses, which can be through one of the many personal or professional accounting packages out there or a paper ledger system. You'll also need an auto mileage log if you use your car in your work, and you may need to log business and personal time on your computer or mobile phone to deduct equipment costs.

Here are a few tips to make tracking as pain-free as possible:

- For phone expenses, either arrange with your long-distance carrier for account codes (which is possible for all business and some home lines) or assign each publication/client to a particular carrier (for instance, your main line for your biggest market, 10-10-321 for another client, etc.).
- Keep a daily calendar or appointment book that shows what projects you're working on and who you called. You can check this against long-distance bills.
- Keep your appointment book along with your tax records each year to substantiate the business nature of long-distance calls and business use of your home office.
- If you use a personal computer for both business and personal use, keep a daily log of how many personal and business hours you spend on it. These numbers can be tallied at year-end for deduction purposes.
- If you use a mobile phone, get detailed billing, which will make the job of determining business and personal use much easier.
- Keep a separate checking account for business, and keep detailed records in your check register, recording the payer for checks you deposit and details of the expense for the checks. This can serve as a record-keeping system—or at least allow you to construct one at year-end—if you don't want a more elaborate system.

FORMS, FORMS, FORMS

There are still a few paper forms that you will need from time to time. They include permission forms for using copyrighted material, model contracts and agreements, and release forms for photographic subjects. (Note: You don't need the latter for photojournalism-type shots in public places, but you do need these for models or when using a photograph in a home or on private property.)

Note, too, that while it always helps to have a contract or a form, many articles are written without them. You can generally write articles safely without a formal contract, and the risk is relatively slight. If you're worried, however, it doesn't hurt to send the editor a letter of agreement spelling out terms you've agreed to verbally or a model contract that you use.

Keep in mind that in the absence of a verbal or written agreement on rights, the default is First North American Rights or one-time use. Publishers or clients cannot make a work-for-hire agreement or buy unrestricted use without an explicit written agreement.

Publishers have their own model contracts in many cases. Keep in mind that these are negotiable, and if you see terms you don't like, you can change them at any time.

What follows are a permission form, a sample release form, and a letter of agreement that can make your life easier.

PERMISSION TO USE COPYRIGHTED MATERIAL

I hereby grant permission to _____
to quote or otherwise reprint the following:

_____
_____
_____

From: (Publication's name)_____
By: (Author's name)_____

This material will be published in a _____
by the title _____
to be published by _____,
Address: _____
    _____
    _____

This request shall apply to all future editions and adaptations
of _____.

I am the copyright holder or authorized by the copyright holder
to grant this permission.

Signed:

Print name: _____
Title: _____
Date: _____

SAMPLE RELEASE FORM

Date: _____

I, _____ ,

hereby consent that my picture, portrait and/or name and reproductions thereof may be used by _____ as (s)he may desire in connection with professional activities and may be used, exhibited or published through any or all media, including for advertising or commercial purposes. This release is irrevocable.

I am (am not) over 18 years old.

Name _____

Address _____

City _____ State ____ ZIP _____

Signature _____

Consent of Parent or Guardian

I, _____ ,

certify that I am parent/guardian of _____ ,

and hereby consent that his/her name, picture, portrait or representation may be used by _____ in connection with his/her professional activities and may be exhibited, reproduced, published or used through any medium in connection with those professional activities, including for advertising or commercial purposes. This release is irrevocable.

Name _____

Address _____

City _____ State ____ ZIP _____

Signature _____

LETTER OF AGREEMENT

Jack Neff
555 W. Fourth St.
Cincinnati, OH 45200
(513) 555-9000
writer@email.com

October 12, 2004

Richard Goodwell
Greenfield Digest
101 Warsaw Parkway
Rochester, NY 10322

Dear Mr. Goodwell:

This letter is to confirm the assignment we discussed earlier to-day for me to write an article tentatively titled ''Brownfield to Greenfield—The Challenges Ahead'' on the following terms:

1) The article will be approximately 1,500 words, including one sidebar.
2) The article is due Nov. 15, 2004.
3) Payment of $750 is due upon acceptance.
4) *Greenfield Digest* will review and either accept or seek revisions of the article within thirty days of receipt.
5) A revised version will be due within ten days of notice, with final decision on acceptance within fourteen days of receipt of revised article.
6) *Greenfield Digest* buys First North American Rights. Electronic and reprint rights are negotiable.
7) Should *Greenfield Digest* cancel the assignment before completion, a kill fee of $325 will immediately become due.
8) *Greenfield Digest* will pay reasonable telephone, database research and incidental fees, due upon receipt of an invoice and documentation of expenses.

Thanks for the assignment and for your time. If you have any questions or concerns, please feel free to call. Enclosed is an SASE in which you can return a signed copy of this letter. You may keep the original for your records.

Sincerely,

Jack Neff

I understand and agree to the terms stated above.

_____   _____

Richard Goodwell, Editor,   Date
Greenfield Digest

INDEX